DAUGHTERS, DADS, AND THE

PATH THROUGH GRIEF

About the Cover

*P*ictured on the cover are daughters and dads (and family) who appear within the book. At different stages in their lives and relationships in the photos, they — in the authors' words — ". . . embrace the whole of the Italian American father-daughter relationship as we talk about love and loss and what comes after . . . our fathers shaped our lives, and shape us still, even in their physical absence."

1. Author Donna H. DiCello, Psy.D., with her father, Leopoldo Giuseppe DiCello.

2. Author Lorraine Mangione, Ph.D., with close family, from left to right: Jim Schumacher; Charles Canton; Jacque Waters; Anthony Mangione; Lorraine Mangione; Johnny Miele; Joseph Mangione (author's father, in front); JoAnn Mangione; Alessandria Schumacher; Ciro Mangione; Angie Testa; Joseph Mangione.

3. Interviewee (and noted author and poet) Daniela Gioseffi, with her father, Donato Gioseffi. Her poem, "American Sonnets for My Father" appears in Part VI.

DAUGHTERS,
DADS, AND THE
PATH THROUGH GRIEF

Tales from Italian America

DONNA H. DiCELLO, PSY.D.
LORRAINE MANGIONE, PH.D.

Impact Publishers®
ATASCADERO, CALIFORNIA

ATTENTION ORGANIZATIONS AND CORPORATIONS:
This book is available at quantity discounts on bulk purchases for educational, business, or sales promotional use. For further information, please contact Impact Publishers, P.O. Box 6016, Atascadero, California 93423-6016. Phone: 805-466-5917, e-mail: info@impactpublishers.com

Library of Congress Cataloging-in-Publication Data

Mangione, Lorraine.
    Daughters, dads, and the path through grief : tales from Italian America / Lorraine Mangione, Ph.D. and Donna DiCello, Psy.D.
        pages cm
    Includes bibliographical references and index.
    ISBN 978-1-886230-95-8 (alk. paper)
    1. Fathers and daughters. 2. Parents--Death. 3. Grief. 4. Italian Americans. I. Title.
    HQ755.85.M257 2013
    306.874—dc23
                                                                    2013031974

Publisher's Note: This publication is designed to provide accurate and authoritative information in regard to the subject matter covered. It is sold with the understanding that the publisher is not engaged in rendering psychological, medical, legal, or other professional services. If expert assistance or counseling is needed, the services of a competent professional should be sought.

Impact strives to make our books readable, grammatically correct, and free of gender bias. Thus, we alternate feminine and masculine pronouns rather than use the cumbersome "he or she" combination, or the popular — if incorrect — "they."

Impact Publishers and colophon are registered trademarks of Impact Publishers, Inc.

Cover concept developed by Tyler Varsell, Goshen, Connecticut
Cover design by Gayle Force Design, Cayucos, California
Book design and composition by UB Communications, Parsippany, New Jersey
Printed in the United States of America on acid-free, recycled paper
Published by **Impact Publishers®**
POST OFFICE BOX 6016
ATASCADERO, CALIFORNIA 93423-6016
www.impactpublishers.com

MIX
Paper from
responsible sources
FSC
www.fsc.org   FSC® C011935

Dedications

To my mother, Joyce Fazzolari Mangione,
for my father said he could not have been who he was without her being who she was,
and he was right.

To his beloved mother, Pietra Lilly Cardinale Mangione,
my kinetic grandmother, my original muse, the first storyteller,
for all our walks down 13th Avenue.

and

To my father, Joseph Salvatore Mangione,
who said to me, "You always listened, Lorraine. You are one of the few who listen." We were
deep in conversation about reheating ziti in a pan without oil and other basics of life.
I'm still listening.

Lorraine Mangione

To my father, Leopoldo Giuseppe DiCello,
who was proud to have daughters and who, for a thousand reasons, I miss every day.
The roses still bloom, Poppy.

To my mother, Regina B. DiCello,
who had the presence of mind to marry my father, always knowing a good thing when
she saw it.

and

To my "first cousin, once removed," Michaela Angela DiCello Stella, who lived widely and
richly for 106 years. Even in death she is my inspiration, and I am proud to say I share
some of her genes.

Donna H. DiCello

Many Italian American writers "share the same goal: to find a life on earth for the dead who have given life to us."

— Tamburri, Giordano, & Gardaphe (2000)

Table of Contents

Preface

*E*very relationship tells a story. The two of us writing this book, clinical psychologists who have lost their dads, have had relationships with our fathers that have spanned years of living, growing, and changing; our relationships have encompassed conflict and controversy, sustenance and support, learning and teaching. The underlying connection is strong and flexible enough to have embraced a huge spectrum of feelings and experiences throughout the decades. We write this book with a foundation in those relationships, and we hope to speak to daughters whose lives have similarly intertwined with their dads' and who now live with the loss of them.

This book is about daughters and their fathers and the bond that exists between them. It focuses on the intensity and richness of that connection, not in some idealized or abstract way but through real-life experiences and real-life relationships.

This book is also about grief — bearing it, feeling it, expressing it, and understanding it. It is about what happens to the father-daughter bond when the father dies: how it undergoes transmutation and transformation and how a daughter is left to make sense of the complexity of the relationship and face how deep and wide this loss can be, whether the relationship has been a positive or a troubled one. We have lived through the sadness, the rage, the questioning, the missing, the disbelief, and the foundering, realizing both the gifts and pains of memory after such a monumental loss as the death of a parent.

We know something of the levels of change that occur after losing a parent and how our sense of self is forever altered, even in midlife, when we might have thought that sense was fairly stable and complete. As a result, this book is our attempt to speak to others dealing with grief, particularly those who have lost their father.

We could not talk about our relationships with our fathers without discussing our heritage, which has served as the rich context for many of the gifts our fathers have given us — food, family connection, mysticism and spirituality, the sacramental aspects of living life with passion. Therefore, this book is also about what it means to be an Italian American daughter who has lost her father.

We tell a textured story of the father-daughter relationship across the daughter's lifespan, of the loss of the father and the daughter's subsequent grieving and reworking, and of their shared Italian American culture. Woven together, these three themes provide the framework of this book; we then expand this framework with the stories that women we interviewed recounted about the fathers they have loved and lost. We also tell pieces of our own stories that were so influential in writing this work.

The path through grief is long. It is a path of growing, being, relating, loving, losing, and finding someone in a different way. It is the path of our lives and the relationships that continue.

The Psychology We Carry with Us

Psychology is the kind of life's work and discipline you bring your whole self to, and it includes, on some level, your family and development. We briefly describe our journeys to psychology and how we see ourselves as psychologists.

Understanding the Worlds of Words and Relationships (Donna)

I believe that my foray into psychology came from a deep desire to understand human relationships and interconnections — both the puzzling relationships I saw in my own family and the relational connections I experienced with others.

From the time I learned to read at four years old I read every book available to me, and in literature I found a way to understand how people thought about and related to each other. When I was in the second grade Louisa May Alcott's *Little Women* served as my first exploration of how families functioned and the importance of sibling relationships. I loved reading about the March sisters, how different each one was and how they disagreed but still remained loving with one another. I also wondered how Mrs. March seamlessly managed to keep her family going, and at this tender age I questioned the absence of Mr. March throughout the story! I loved words, I loved stories, and I loved figuring out the *why* of things.

When a number of years ago my best friend from high school resurrected notes we had written to each other in school, it was clear that even then I was interested in the how and why of relationships. I saw in those innocent pages of adolescent yearnings the psychologist in me yet unformed.

I decided at the age of twelve that I wanted to become a psychologist, a choice no doubt also born of my father's encouragement to question. I recall sending off inquiries (long before the age of email!) to a government-sponsored organization offering information on what being a psychologist was all about.

When the thick envelopes arrived in reply I would steal away to the third floor of our house (my secret refuge) and pore over the pamphlets for hours, trying to determine whether industrial psychology would be my calling (it would not) and whether the amount of schooling required for a doctorate would be manageable (I loved school, and my father was clear that an undergraduate degree, at the very least, was in my future).

I read all of those pamphlets at least twice and was bitten by the psychology bug. I thought it was a great way to make a living. Psychology encompassed my family's emphasis on "doing good" in the world and seemed to be the natural place where I could embed my intellectual curiosity.

Buddhism came later and was a spiritual "coming home." It taught me about living a meaningful and purposeful life, with its focus on awareness, compassion, and the alleviation of suffering. It has come to inform how I approach the world and how I try to live in it. Therefore, my approach to psychology, in my teaching, clinical work, and, in this case, writing about grief and the father-daughter relationship, is relational, inquisitive, and multilayered. My perspective draws on not only my interpersonal approach to human discourse but also what Buddhism has to offer.

The Search for Meaning (Lorraine)

The call to psychology came early in life for me also, and I have wondered if I was led to psychology partly because my childhood avocation of priest (evidenced by my celebrating the Eucharist in my room) was not open to women. I joined, in a way, the "secular priesthood" of psychology but never lost my sense of spirituality and transformation of the Mass.

Old friends remind me that I announced, around tenth grade and before psychology became a household word, that I was going to be a psychologist. My interest was based on having read a book that promised to tell what Freud *really meant* as well as Viktor Frankl's *Man's Search for Meaning*, a moving treatise on his experiences in World War II concentration camps and his development of existential psychology.

The suffering during World War II of Jews and others in concentration camps was real and alive for me, as my dad fought in the army of liberation and came home with pictures of the horror. His experience with people in a concentration camp in Austria clearly had shaken him, and only once or twice in my childhood did he talk about it and show the pictures that usually lay buried in a suitcase in the basement.

The idea that suffering needed a witness was formed early in my psyche. The best antidotes to suffering — family, friends, relationships, conversations, amicable arguments, and attentiveness to each other — were as well. Mine was a "talky" family, as are many Italian families, and no subject was taboo, not politics, religion, sex, people, relationships, joys, disagreements, or sorrows. We sat at table, during and between courses and over cups of demitasse, and talked *a lot*.

We also listened, as my parents were great models for listening, an essential skill for psychologists. We solved major life problems, or just talked about them enough that they dissipated, sitting around that table. We had the capacity to step back and look at issues with an inch or two of separation from our reactions and emotions and consider the conflicts or losses in another light.

In psychology we call that "taking a metastance" or "listening with the third ear." This capacity to step back and listen on a deeper level is critical to understanding and helping others. By whatever name, my family engaged in this process in the dining room many years ago. I bring all of this to my teaching, research, and clinical work: the primacy of relationships, existential questions that frame our lives, knowledge of the pains of humanity but also resilience and growth, and an abiding sense of the spiritual.

Carrying Our Psychology Forward

Throughout *Daughters, Dads, and the Path through Grief* — as you read our stories and those of our fathers, the stories of the women who have lost their fathers, and our explanations of the theories and ideas that frame this book — you will encounter the themes we have begun to describe; our beliefs, values, and assumptions in psychology; and how we see sadness and resilience as Italian American women navigate grief and find new ways to continue their relationships with their dads.

Acknowledgments

*A*s with many undertakings in Italian American culture, this book took a village to bring it to fruition, and there are many to whom we need to say *Molto grazie!*

First, we would like to thank Anthony Tamburri, dean of the Calandra Institute at City University of New York; Spencer Di Scala, president of the Dante Alighieri Society of Massachusetts; Aileen Riotto Sirey, past president of the national chapter of the National Organization of Italian American Women (NOIAW); Alphonse D'Angelo, the Italian teacher from Lorraine's high school who should have made her take Italian!; Anthony Riccio, who writes about the Italian experience throughout New England; Dominick Carielli, director of the Center for Italian American Studies at Brooklyn College; Marielena Tecce from Antioch University New England and the North End of Boston; the Italian American Psychology Assembly (IAPA); the *Italian Americana Journal*; Michael Palma, editor and poet; the West Albany Italian Club; Nello Picone of the Southington, Connecticut Unico Club; and Joyce Szewczynski of Springfield College in Massachusetts. All offered their heartfelt support and were instrumental in our finding the special women who tell their stories here.

We also are indebted to Melissa Alberti Froehner, our publisher at Impact Publishers, Inc., who believed in our project, who answered each of our questions with patience and good humor (in the Italian way!), and who was simply a delight to work with. We also thank our copyeditor at Impact, Kelly Burch.

A special thanks goes to Karen Dunn, *assistante eccezionale*, who from the beginning kept all of our material together in ways we could not and whose sharp eye and editorial feedback made this a better book. Through transcription she became as connected to the women whose stories are told here as we did.

I (Donna) would also like to extend my thanks to the generations of Italian American women writers, past and present, who have blazed this path for us; the office of the dean at the College of Arts and Sciences at the University of Hartford, who provided a research grant to help make this project possible;

Dusty Miller, whose counsel was invaluable; Laura Streckfuss and Heather Bernstein, two of my wonderful students, who gave their time transcribing and providing feedback; Jennie Bernstein, my former research assistant extraordinaire, who has two of the best editorial eyes I have ever come across; my friend of forty-four years, Kate Bonvicini, sister Italian and über-supporter of this project and a million other things; my sister, Darlene Dunn, who inherited our father's sense of humor and keeps him alive for me in that way; and my niece Elizabeth Dunn and nephew Andrew Dunn, who a hundred times a day make Grampy proud; you are the lights of my life!

Finally, I would like to thank my extraordinary spouse, Janice Kozen, an honorary Italian and my port in the storm, who read through multiple drafts and was not afraid to tell me, "This word doesn't belong here."

I (Lorraine) am grateful for my Italian American sensibility and education, and I offer thanks to those Italians who ventured across the sea to the New World; the writers, historians, poets, and scholars who constructed a foundation of what it means to be Italian in America; the Italian American Psychology Assembly, which helped me see the possibility of contributing to this meaning-making; Anthony Riccio, oral historian, who carries such a deep Italian understanding; and the Calandra Institute, for its marvelous learning opportunities.

I am also grateful for the many hands involved in creating this book: Kathi Borden, chair of the Department of Clinical Psychology at Antioch University New England, who creatively helped with time and assistants; Megan Lyons, research assistant, who did everything with grace and intelligence, especially thinking through Part VI; Liz Allyn, administrative assistant, who goes above and beyond; Paul Lippmann, who consulted with me about everything; Franklin Shontz, my University of Kansas mentor who taught me how to honor people in research; Roz Forti, for reading the manuscript and for being Italian; JoAnn Basgall and Thea Litsios, for their discerning eyes; Kristine Bertini, former student and author who understood this process; Luli Emmons, Dusty Miller, Beth Bishop, Sara Weinberger, and Vicky Korson, almost Italians who encouraged this leap; Kathi Dunn, who astutely read an earlier version; Ted Ellenhorn, who asked about Catholicism at just the right moment; Marti Straus, for publishing advice; students Alyssa Lanza, Laura Halvorsen, and Maureen O'Reilly, who helped organize interviews; and Traeci Stevens, an excellent transcriber.

I hold close the people connected to my father and to me, whose voices I hear as I write: my sister JoAnn, who just last week had a "sad day, crying about Daddy"; my brother Ciro, who was my father's best nurse ever; my brother Joseph, who figured out that food equals love; Cathy McKay, who just left us and may be debating politics with my dad right now; my dad's best friend from James Monroe High School in the Bronx, Alan Moss, and his wife Sally, who still tell stories I haven't heard; Bharvi Parikh, Tommy McKay, Debbie Guglielmo, Martha Cook, Liz McKay, Pat Bradbury, and Susan Keady, honorary sons and daughters; Trina, Paula, Mary, Linda, and both Michaels, who loved their "Uncle Joey"; Krista, Johnny, and Anthony, who loved their Papa; Aunt Mary and Aunt Lee, very much alive, who are the touchstones of a world that is fading; my grandparents Ciro Mangione and Pietra Lilly Cardinale, my aunts and uncles, and my Sicilian sister Lisa McCann, who remain near; Lisa's aunts and uncles, true Italian American inspirations; Ronnie and Rosa Krom, Laurie and Russ Plourd, and Nancy and Mark Ricciardelli, old friends who carry something of my father; Eileen Fisher, my dad's waitress/friend who made mussels white in a wok (blasphemous in his kitchen!) when he was recuperating and narrowly avoided a food crisis; Mike Roberts and the guys from the restaurant; Sal and Roberta from the Visiting Nurses Association of Southington, Connecticut; and finally, mostly, my mother — how I wanted to speak with her and ask more about her relationship with her father, Rocco James Fazzolari, and hear her voice on all of this!

I am blessed by the faith and love from my family, including my husband, Jim Schumacher, an Italian in disguise who passed the tests my father put before him and who loved my dad. I always thought I would have a little dark baby, but my blond-haired, blue-eyed daughter *is* my Italian child. Alessandria shares the language, family, food, history, and culture — all of it — in her own way. When she would say to me, "Mama, you have a book to write," I knew I had to get to work.

And finally, we would both like to thank the women whose stories are told in these pages — you opened up your hearts, your homes, and your family histories to us, and for that we are eternally grateful and feel enormously privileged. *Molto grazie, con affetto.*

Introduction

Shifting the Sun

When your father dies, say the Irish,
you lose your umbrella against bad weather.
May his sun be your light, say the Armenians.

When your father dies, say the Welsh,
you sink a foot deeper into the earth.
May you inherit his light, say the Armenians.

When your father dies, say the Canadians,
you run out of excuses.
May you inherit his sun, say the Armenians.

When your father dies, say the French,
you become your own father.
May you stand up in his light, say the Armenians.

When your father dies, say the Indians,
he comes back as the thunder.
May you inherit his light, say the Armenians.

When your father dies, say the Russians,
he takes your childhood with him.
May you inherit his light, say the Armenians.

When your father dies, say the English,
you join his club you vowed you wouldn't.
May you inherit his sun, say the Armenians.

When your father dies, say the Armenians,
your sun shifts forever.
And you walk in his light.

© Diana Der-Hovanessian

From "Selected Poems"
Sheep Meadow Press: Rhinebeck, NY, 1994.
Reprinted by permission of the author.

Yes, your sun shifts forever when you lose your father — for whoever your father has been to you, your place in the world changes. The ground also shifts, and you become changed somehow, sometimes forever. As this poem suggests in a myriad of eloquently metaphorical ways, the impact of his death reaches far into our emotional and spiritual lives, touching the core of who we are and who we become.

When my (Lorraine's) father died, we lost the table, for the table had always been his element. My Italian American father's life revolved around the table, and I was to speak of it in his eulogy, the table as the center, my father as the center. The table stood as the heart of life from his birth through his childhood on the Lower East Side of Manhattan, during World War II, and into our family and later the restaurant. We lost the center, we lost gravity, we lost something to hold us together as individuals and as a family. I lost that deep sense of ever being completely held or fed or heard again, around that table, ever.

For his senior honors English class, my (Donna's) nephew, Andrew, wrote "Loss of a Lion," a heartfelt essay about my father's death when my nephew was thirteen years old. His perceptiveness regarding what we had lost stunned me. He wrote, "*As a 13-year-old who had never dreaded or tried to avoid a family function because of this man's presence, it was as though a light had flickered and died, only to be replaced by a dark void.*" Yes, this is what we lost — the light in a room, a day made shiny by his presence, a Pied Piper of a man who called others to him with his generous heart.

Our experiences are reflected in the poem above, but beyond that, we also wondered what the loss of a father specifically means for a *daughter*. Though we begin here with loss, this book examines the father-daughter relationship over time — from its early years to beyond death — and in that way reveals this relationship as multifaceted, rich, and complex. As you will read in this book, this bond lays the foundation for how a girl grows up and who she is to become as a woman, and it certainly helps shape her capacity for love, for work, and for negotiating the adult world. Fathers and daughters are often discussed in psychology solely with regard to negative or hurtful interactions, but we believe in considering the bitter with the sweet — and within these pages you will find many stories that balance the two.

We anchor our thinking about this relationship in Italian American culture. There has been little attention given to grief in psychology among Italian

Americans (they are even omitted from the wonderful poem at the beginning of this introduction!) and even less to the father-daughter connection within this culture. In the stories in this book you will find not only how revered these daughters were by their fathers but also how their heritage influenced both their connection to their dads and their ultimate separation from them through death. It is their heritage that enabled them to have continued bonds with their fathers, even after his passing.

Father and Daughter over Time

"Father and daughter" conjures up a whole range of images and associations, some immediately conscious and vivid, others that emerge slowly and take shape over time. The images resonate with various life stages. For some people "father and daughter" brings to mind the girl and her dad at play, reading a book, out swimming, somehow lost in that world of childhood and unselfconsciousness, when being with Daddy was as easy and natural as breathing and playing.

Others may instantly imagine the teen years or young adulthood and the seemingly inevitable conflict and struggle for control interspersed in the calmer ebb and flow of daily life between a growing daughter and her dad. At this stage, you may sometimes have needed to turn your back on your dad to become the woman you were meant to be, or you may have sensed that your feelings and thoughts fell lifeless to the floor instead of reaching your father's ears and heart.

The relationship built in the teen years and young adulthood streams into adulthood, when a woman and her dad may share life as something approaching friends, speaking of work and family and the world of politics and society, coming together and moving apart as they negotiate their intersecting worlds, and perhaps knowing when and where it is better to speak and not to speak.

Sometimes the relationship circle grew larger with a spouse, partner, children, nieces, and nephews, and all the milestones and transitions that families bring. Or maybe the relationship itself changed to include tenderness toward a dad who had begun to falter, who no longer quite remembered everything you told him, or who finally wanted to tell you some of what *he* was feeling.

This book is a testament to and celebration of the bonds between the fathers and daughters whose stories are told here. Throughout these pages, we embrace the whole of the Italian American father-daughter relationship as we talk about love and loss and what comes after. It is about how our fathers shaped our lives, and shape us still, even in their physical absence — it is about how we live as *fatherless daughters*.

Welcome to *Daughters, Dads, and the Path Through Grief*

Every journey begins with preparation, whether it's a trip around the world or a trip into someone's heart and soul. We gather our tools, our necessities, our papers, and our provisions for the long road ahead. Yet, we know that we cannot prepare for everything that will happen along the way, and that is part of the value of a journey, coming upon the unexpected and the serendipitous.

We hope to discover new and interesting little places, new bends in the road, as we travel the sometimes ragged, sometimes gentle terrain of our lives with our fathers. At this point you have started and you will continue to make the necessary preparations for reading this book and embarking on your journey through your life with your father.

There are three important themes that intersect and provide the scaffolding for this work: the father-daughter relationship, grief and its many varieties, and Italian American culture. The core of this book is the stories of the women we interviewed, who spoke, with all their hearts and souls, about their relationships with their fathers and what it has meant to lose their fathers.

We see these themes come to life as the women talk about the richness and complexity of their lives with their fathers over time; about the years of living, talking, eating, arguing, laughing, and just being with their fathers; about the pain of the loss of their fathers; and about working out ways to live without him in their lives.

Our Way of Understanding People

Who we are as psychologists is fundamental to this book. Psychology is a multifaceted discipline of many theories and worldviews. Our worldviews serve as the lens through which we view our stories and the stories of the women who were involved in the project and, ultimately, the father-daughter relationship, loss and grieving, and the Italian American culture.

We bring a tradition of introspection, of respecting human psychological processes and knowing they are not part of a prescribed time table, of privileging the deep connections to others that are so often ignored or not reinforced in our culture, of working with clients who have lost parents and other significant people, of taking a step backward and reflecting on what is happening in order to make sense of it all, and of understanding that the rational and conscious levels are not all there is.

We come from various theoretical traditions in psychology, which include object relations and relational perspectives within psychodynamic theory, attachment theory, existentialism, meaning-making, mindfulness, group processes and dynamics, the role of culture, the centrality of narratives to our lives, and human development across the lifespan.

Explanations of the psychological perspectives we take and the theoretical traditions we uphold in relation to grief are highlighted in gray boxes that are interspersed throughout the book.

In writing this book, we have integrated our concepts and values as psychologists working within these theoretical frames. We value the primacy of relationship and our deep mutuality and interdependence on each other, and we see the importance of culture and how culture shapes us and we shape culture. Embedded in our view is the significance of the big moments of life — which certainly include death and its aftermath — the existential issues of our "aloneness" in the world, and our desire to make meaning in the stories we construct about our lives.

Change and Hope

We are who we are only because of a lifetime of growth. Some of the seeds for our development are with us at birth, the "nature" part, our genetics. Other seeds can be found in our environment, the "nurture" part, what happens around us. We both are and are not the same person at forty-five or sixty-five as we were at twenty-five. We see both the continuity and the evolution, knowing we have changed, sometimes dramatically, sometimes not so dramatically, on the surface and deeply within ourselves.

As psychologists we profoundly believe in hope and the possibility of change, things that can be in short supply when a loved one is ill or has died. To paraphrase Nancy McWilliams, a psychologist within the psychoanalytic tradition, we know from working with people in psychotherapy that often we are the only ones who have any hope at that time, and clients need the psychotherapist to carry that hope for them as they struggle through the challenges that brought them to us (1999). We also agree with C. Rick Snyder, a researcher who speaks of hope as something active, realistic, and even purposeful (1994, 2000). Once found and cultivated, hope can carry a person far.

We trust that this book will carry hope for those who need it, for the loss of a parent can cause great sorrow and despair. Our faith stems from understanding the resources that all human beings have, including the women whose lives and losses are described in this book and those of you reading this book who may be on your own journey through loss. Fundamentally, those resources are the individual's capacity for nurturing relationships and forging new connections, for creativity and meaning-making.

Our belief in those capacities and our experience of our own sorrowful journeys through loss underlie our hope for all the daughters who have lost their fathers. We can move forward; we can find the path toward something solid and sustaining, although it may not be the path that we first imagined or that others around us are taking.

The values and concepts threading throughout the book — relationship, attachment, culture, loss, meaning, hope, and development — are reflected in the tales of our storytellers, whose narratives about their fathers and their loss of those fathers will take us on journeys through sorrow and the dark days of loss and into the possibilities of renewal and reconnection.

Who Are the Women in This Book?

The women who contributed their words, feelings, thoughts, and reflections are a marvelous group of Italian American women who represent a wide sweep of ages, lifestyles, careers, and family structures. The book paints a broad stroke of who the Italian American woman is today.

We interviewed fifty-one women from age thirty-three to age eighty-six who grew up and now live primarily in the Northeast. The women have various family structures (married, single, partnered, divorced, widowed, with or without children), a range of religious practices and beliefs, and diverse sexual orientations. Some grew up in Italian communities and others in mainstream America.

Their educations range from completing eighth grade to having earned a doctoral degree. Some work in the political arena, while others are business owners, artists, stay-at-home mothers, retail clerks, poets, professors, writers, secretaries, teacher's aides, nurses, documentary filmmakers, administrators, administrative assistants, attorneys, teachers, or publishers. Their families come mainly from southern Italy and Sicily, with a few from Tuscany and Liguria.

We found these women through many means: newspaper advertisements; listservs and flyers at Italian clubs and societies, churches, bakeries, and community centers; word of mouth; and direct contact. The response to our outreach was huge! We had to turn away many more women than we interviewed.

Our major criteria for choosing women were that their fathers be of Italian descent and that their relationship with their father be generally sound. We did not interview women who experienced abandonment or abuse from their fathers, for we felt that their experiences represented a different realm and could be the subject of a study in its own right. We let the women themselves decide if they met our criterion regarding abandonment or abuse.

As psychologists who are both clinicians and researchers, we wanted to be mindful of the possible hurtful effects of interviewing women with deeply troubled situations. This is a specific sample, therefore, and also a self-selected one in that the women *chose* to be interviewed, rather than a random sample that might represent the world at large more accurately. Within the domain of women we interviewed, we strove for as much variety in backgrounds and experiences as we could find.

We hope that as you read the words of these remarkably eloquent and expressive women, you will refer to their brief biographies to help contextualize what you are reading. While they may not speak for *all* Italian American daughters, they certainly speak profoundly about themselves and their experiences. We hope these stories continue what other texts — such as Carol Bonomo Albright and Christine Palamidessi Moore's *American Woman, Italian*

Style: Italian Americana's Best Writings on Women and Elizabeth Messina's (1994) work on life-span development — have done to broaden the landscape of what Italian American women have to say about their lives, culture, and relationships.

For those women who wished to remain anonymous, we have used only their initials and have not included their biographies.

The Narratives: Talking about Dads and Daughters

Learning from stories is a strong, meaningful tradition within psychology. The women whose oral histories we have compiled in *Daughters, Dads, and the Path through Grief* have used their stories to interpret their relationships with their fathers. These daughters' rich, textured narratives are both healing and empowering. We've organized the book by the stages of life; so excerpts of each woman's story, rather than the story in its entirety, appear throughout.

Stories are also critically important in Italian American culture. Mary Jo Bona, a professor of Italian American studies, describes a multitude of Italian Americans and their experiences and creations, including their storytelling traditions. She comments, "The stories produced by Italian Americans are acts of survival" (2010, p. 3), and she explains why she views it this way: "Through narrative, Italian American storytellers have constructed another space to revise hierarchical discourse, to give voice to those without power to shape perception or invent alternative worlds" (p. 3). Stories help us understand ourselves and our worlds in our own ways.

We approached each interview with an open mind and a set of questions that addressed the lifelong relationship between the daughters and their fathers. We asked about a variety of times and experiences, and we left room for the women to elaborate and bring up points about which we had not thought to ask. We are grateful to the women for their openness, availability, and honesty in speaking about their relationships with their fathers from childhood through adulthood (complete with conflicts and closeness) and what his death has meant — none of which is easy!

The women invited us into their homes or studios or even their bakeries, or we met at a quiet restaurant or town library.

Locations included a house overlooking Lorraine's junior high school and a house overlooking the New York City skyline, both significant settings for Italians, who settled in the small towns and the big cities of America. Biscotti or tea breads (often homemade!) or an amazing Italian lunch of artichokes and olives sometimes accompanied the interview.

Each interview was a privilege, and we sincerely hope that we have captured some of the specialness of each person's stories in the pages to come. It was hard to not include everything — we've tried to provide a range of examples that we felt would speak to many women.

We hope you the reader will feel the same profound connection to these stories that we felt during our hours of sitting with the women, tearing up with and laughing with them, feeling flashes of recognition of our own dads, and hearing the multilayered and multimeaning stories unfold.

Finding Yourself and Your Dad through "Pause and Reflect"

If the women's stories are the core of the book, the roadmap for each reader's experience is provided by the reflections and activities offered in each part, exercises that we designed to bring readers to a more interactive, here-and-now experience of the journey through their relationships with their fathers.

In reading the tales and musings to come, we hope you will sit and visit with the wealth of different voices and images. Yet we also hope you will move beyond these stories to make this book more truly about you and what is going on in your life and with your own process. The "Pause and Reflect" suggestions at the end of each part will help you do this.

These simple exercises are based on the stories told by the daughters and the portion of the life course discussed in the part of the book in which they appear. There are many types of exercises, such as writing, self-reflection, dream work, and interviewing other family members. They are a way to summarize and integrate what you have read in the hope that your own relationship with your father will come more sharply into focus.

You might want to get a companion notebook to accompany you on this journey through your life with your father, a book for jotting down thoughts and feelings, doing the exercises that involve writing, and recording important issues, memories, and experiences that you have in connection with your grief. You can take this slowly — you do not need to suddenly start reading and writing every day for a certain amount of time. You can do all of this or just a small part of it in your own time and at your own pace.

Overview of the Book

The six parts of *Daughters, Dads, and the Path through Grief* follow the life course. Part I, *Defying Stereotypes: Who Are Our Fathers?*, introduces the many dads who live in this book, including some who may surprise you. Part II, *Learning, Doing, and Being: Early Ties with Our Fathers*, demonstrates our connectedness with our fathers in childhood. Part III, *Stepping into Adulthood: Connection and Disconnection*, examines how our conflicts and disagreements with our fathers existed within a strong relationship and ponders the life-changing situations in which our fathers saw us as adult women for the first time.

Part IV, *Holding On, Letting Go: Our Fathers through Illness and Death*, describes our experiences of the beginnings of our fathers' illnesses and the immediacy of our fathers' deaths. Part V, *Aftershock: Missing Our Fathers through Time and Space*, reveals how we coped with the early feelings of shock, disbelief, and unrelenting sadness after the loss; how our belief systems affected us; and how we experienced life without our dads. In Part VI, *Living with Our Fathers in Our Hearts*, we describe how our fathers' deaths have changed us and changed our world, what the loss has given us, and how we continue to keep our fathers alive.

We begin each part with an introduction to the psychological implications and possibilities of that period of life, written either from a psychological perspective or from that of Italian American culture. Gray boxes with more psychological ideas and commentary expand on this perspective in some chapters. You will also hear from us, as daughters, as we share our experiences of our fathers.

The heart of the book, however, is the voices of the Italian American daughters as they reflect on their lives with their fathers and on their fathers' deaths. At the end of each part we encourage you to join in as a participant through the "Pause and Reflect" suggestions, which help you review your relationship with your father, or sit with and process your grief at his loss.

This journey, for each of us, has been complex, steadfast, and enlightening. We invite all daughters who love their fathers (or who feel confusion or ambivalence), all fathers who cherish their daughters (or who at times don't quite understand what is happening between their daughters and themselves), and all who wish to sit with and contemplate this vast and rich relationship to join us by finding your own place in these stories as you read and consider your own life's paths.

We invite you to weep and struggle with us, to join us on these journeys through grief and mourning, to consider culture and ethnicity and how they have shaped you and your dad and your ideas about relationship and grief. We believe doing so will ultimately kindle within you a greater joy and a greater hope about the deep bonds between fathers and daughters.

We invite you to read this book with your whole heart and soul, or as much of that as you can manage, depending on where you are in the grieving process. Some of you may be ready to plunge in, while others may be more tentative. It is important to do this at your own pace and with whatever you need for your own preparation.

We also invite you to read it in the order that seems most accessible to you at the moment. Although we are great believers in the importance of the lifecycle, we also realize that you may need to go right to the part on death and its immediate aftermath or on how this works out years later, depending on where you are and how you are processing your grief.

What we do ask of everyone is that you bring yourself, and your dad, in whatever way you can right now, to the reading of this book. Our wish is that you will travel your own journey through sorrow and the dark days of loss and into the possibilities of renewal and reconnection.

As you read the daughters' stories, it is important for you to see their fathers in their full context, to see who they were as *people*, not just who they were in their role as a parent. Therefore, as we introduce them to you in Part I, you will see how they broke stereotypes, how they defied great odds, and how they lived their lives with integrity and determination and passed this on to their daughters.

PART ONE

DEFYING STEREOTYPES: WHO ARE OUR FATHERS?

*O*nce the idea for this book had germinated, we began to focus more sharply on our own relationships with our fathers. We both started delving into history, journals, memorabilia, documents, and photographs and thinking in a more concentrated way about our relationships with our fathers.

We felt we needed firm grounding in our relationships with our dads to know what and how to ask the women about themselves and their dads. Since our relationships with our fathers are central to writing this book, it seemed important to introduce them here as well.

Coming to Terms with Complexity: My Dad Leo (Donna)

Leopoldo ("Leo") Giuseppe DiCello was the youngest of seven, born (at thirteen pounds!) to parents who had emigrated from Catanzaro, Calabria before the turn of the century, leaving behind their olive groves and vineyards for a less agrarian life in America.

Leo was the favored son, born at home the day after his oldest brother, Antonio, was killed in World War I in France, a convergence of events that impacted him psychologically for the rest of his life. He was also the jokester, the intelligent one, the one who was unbearably connected to his mother after his father passed away when he was thirteen years old. This connection later caused him to sacrifice his own aspirations to become a dentist, when homesickness propelled him to leave the university that had given him a full athletic scholarship.

He married my mother in 1951, having been smitten with her from the day he saw her walking down his street in her pink angora sweater, her blonde hair draped across her forehead à la Veronica Lake. He asked his sister with desire in his voice, "Who's *that*?" For the entirety of his adult life, he toiled in a factory without complaint, always saving for a family vacation, a new car, a college fund, a move to a better town.

He loved people, a quality that often led to my mother's utter frustration. Early in their marriage my parents owned a dry cleaning business, so after a day at the factory my father would go to the store, hop in their truck, and deliver the clothes to his customers. Hours would go by until finally my mother, ready to close the store, would have to call each customer on the list to locate my dad — he had the habit of stopping for a cup of coffee and a chat at each house!

He was sentimentally inclined but had rough edges; a family man; a lover of the "Rat Pack," a good laugh, and Old Spice cologne; a man who knew someone wherever he went; a devoted father who always told my sister and me that "education is everything"; a man who did not complain once during his weekly chemotherapy treatments at the end of his life.

He is the man I see in a favorite photograph above my writing desk — holding me tightly on a sled in the cold crispness of the winter when I was five years old, smiling, looking like a movie star with sunglasses on and his dark Italian hair gleaming, steering our course and keeping me safe. I am bundled in my red parka (I remember that it was red, my favorite color at five), the hood tied tightly around my chubby cheeks, my bangs cut straight across, framing a face that I know must have been cold given the amount of snow surrounding us. I am not looking at the camera, but I am all smiles.

We are at the tipping point, that moment right before we sail down the hill. My mother must be taking the photograph. I imagine her laughing, holding the old Brownie camera, her gloved hands trying to find the right button to click. "Hold tight, Daddy — we're going to go too fast!" We look happy, my Poppy and I.

Writing this book has made me more aware of how complex a man he was — in his stubbornness, in his unrealized ambitions, in his soft heart — and has sharpened my awareness about the things I could never understand about him and did not like and my realization of how deep our connection actually went. We had many adventures together — movies, hours at the beach, graduations, trips to the Italian market, discussions of regrets and times past. This book is our latest big adventure, and in it I must now carry *him* along.

Pursue Your Dreams and Eat Cannoli (Lorraine)

Joseph Salvatore Mangione, known as Joey by his family even as an adult, was also born into a world framed with death. He was named after his brother who had died as a baby a few years earlier and whose death was a mystery, as many were in those days.

My father was born fifth of six in the years preceding the Depression on the Lower East Side in Manhattan. His family later moved to the Bronx, and he grew up in all the rough and tumble of life in those neighborhoods of Italians, Jews, Poles, and Irish and in a large extended family of Sicilians from the small towns of Bivona and Alessandria Della Rocca.

He loved the streets and the freedom and the play, the stickball and kick-the-can and the candy store, the illicit winemaking and being told to hush about it. He saw Babe Ruth play and followed Joe DiMaggio. Yet he was always looking for ways to earn a few cents and contribute to the family. He was an entrepreneur from age five, when he sold newspapers. Later he worked as a Shabbas boy, turning on the lights for his Jewish neighbors. That sense of industry balanced by a love of living and the pleasure of friends and family characterized him his whole life as he ventured into new places and businesses.

His dad, Papá to us, worked throughout the Depression, and his house, with his mother, Mamá, presiding, always had pastry on Sundays, cannoli and sfogliatelle, even during hard times, so all the family came to their home. There they are, the enduring two sides of my father — working industriously and having pastry on Sunday with family!

His life was changed by the bombing of Pearl Harbor. He enlisted in the Army to fight in World War II rather than go to college at the technology institute that had accepted him. When he returned from the war, having won and lost a good deal of money gambling on the homeward-bound British ship, he was ready to go, move, do something with his life.

He entered into a series of businesses, first with his older brother Lenny then later on his own. He did the unthinkable — married a woman who was only half-Italian and moved to what Papá called "the end of the Earth," which aptly characterized central Connecticut from a New Yorker's point of view. Family visited with huge bags of crusty semolina bread, provolone with that wickedly sharp bite, dry sausage, and olives, fearing that there was no food at all where we lived. They were just about right!

My father was a draftsman, an architect, a salesman, a building contractor, and the builder and then owner/cook of a fantastic little restaurant, *Macaroni Mangione*, in his later years. At age fifty he turned his life's zeal for cooking into his business — wow, he is my role model for that alone!

He was always brimming over with new ideas and possibilities and was smarter than almost anyone I knew, except my mother, and he was so articulate and well-read that we just had to spend most of our years together arguing, taking point and counterpoint. Talk about stubborn! Yet we relished that intensity, even if it was maddening and divisive at times.

My friends and I came of age in the 1970s, and when they held consciousness-raising groups about being held back as women by society and family, I had little to add because both my parents always assumed I would and could do whatever I wanted. My father was so proud of my educational accomplishments and my ability to argue.

The true passion and love of his life was my mother, a woman of grace and style who was the original psychologist in our house and who had the temperament and intellect of a diplomat. She was tall, with Ukrainian eyes and cheekbones from her mother and a sense of anarchy from her father, who was from Calabria.

The last years of my dad's life were again framed in death, as my mother died, several years younger than he was, in an unclear, unexpected, and unsettled way, seven years before he died. Never did he imagine that, plan for it, or think about it, and it overwhelmed him.

Strengthened by his indomitable optimistic spirit, which eventually shone through in the hard years that followed, he embraced two lifelines: his cooking, for himself, any of his four children, or friends; and the arrival of my daughter, Alessandria Joyce, named after Papá's hometown in Sicily and my mother, who always filled him with joy.

CHAPTER ONE

MEETING THE DADS

*W*e have introduced you to our fathers. Now you will meet many other fathers. Throughout this book you may come to know your father in a new and fuller way as you reflect on these stories with your own memories and musings.

"Well, my father was my father." As Anna D. quietly yet confidently spoke those words in response to my (Lorraine's) request to tell me something about her father in one of our early interviews, I settled in, reassured that we were asking the right questions and finding the right people to answer them. "My father was my father" spoke to me of both the closeness and the strength of her relationship and of the significance of being a father. This was what we were hoping to hear about — Italian American fathers and daughters, and what they meant to each other.

Anna D., who came from southern Italy when she was fifteen and who met with me in her elegant and bustling bakery where her father helped out every day, elaborated on this initial description, but the feeling, tone, and weight of her first words stayed with me throughout the months of talking with women about their fathers. First and most fundamentally, our fathers were our fathers.

When we moved into who the fathers were, we saw a vast array of types of men and types of dads, which was both a delight and a surprise to us.

There were reticent dads who deferred to others and more garrulous dads who were often in the middle of everything, strict dads who laid down the law and dads who could be talked into anything, affectionate dads and distant dads. There were Italian food dads who passed on their love of cooking and dads who never even wanted pasta. There were dads who favored boys and those who favored girls, handsome blonde-haired, blue-eyed dads and handsome dark-haired, dark-eyed dads (but always handsome!).

School experience varied tremendously, from completing fifth grade to obtaining a master's degree through night school. They had jobs that included business owner, accountant, tradesman, artist, farmer, engineer, pharmacist, chef, laborer, salesman, and social worker.

We met dads who lived in an Italian American neighborhood of friends and family (sometimes with their own mom and dad right upstairs) and those who lived in mainstream America, dads born in Italy and dads born in the United States, dads who fought in World War II or Korea and those with no military background, dads who had experienced discrimination as Italians in America and those who had not, and dads whose Italian identity was foremost and those who felt it was crucial to become American.

We love the diversity and the range of dads, the inability to pigeonhole or typecast (as Italians have often been) our fathers.

The fathers were born between 1893 and 1931. Over half of them were born in America from parents born in Italy, a few were born in America from parents born here too, and a few were born in Italy. Many came from the major southern regions of Italy, including Calabria, Campania, Basilicata, Apulia, Abruzzo, and Sicily, and a few came from Lombardy, Tuscany, and Liguria in the north.

Their deaths took place between 1954 and 2010, and their ages when they died ranged from fifty-one to one hundred. Most of them were married once, a few were divorced, and a few were widowed and married again.

In some ways they can be seen as typical men of their time, European immigrants to this country in the first half of the twentieth century, but, as one of the women we interviewed pointed out, no one really thinks her father is typical! We see ways these Italian American dads share so much with each other and ways each man is truly unique. We hope you will see that too as you meet some of the fathers.

The dads you will meet in these pages are not the television and movie stereotypes of Italian American men. Stereotypes are powerful and seductive. They often portray an idealized or a vilified image that may have some basis in reality but is overgeneralized and ultimately can be used to oppress and demean people. Social psychology tells us how insidious and pervasive stereotypes can be, and many writers from Italian American studies have chronicled the use of stereotyping of and prejudice against Italian

Americans, as Ciongoli and Parini did in *Beyond the Godfather*. We agree with Richard Gambino, professor emeritus at Queens College and a pioneer in the study of Italian Americans and their experience, who comments, "Much of the Italian American experience is trapped in inauthentic myths" (1975, p. 269).

Given how Italians were and continue to be stereotyped in the mass media and other, more subtle venues, the remembrances of Italian American fathers are an important contribution from the women in our project. Let us introduce you to several of these men as individuals.

Many of the women saw her father as special, often because of his devotion to his family and work or because of personal characteristics such as great intelligence, humility, a remarkable way with people, his strength of character or personality, or his sense of compassion and kindness.

To introduce the dads, in this chapter we highlight several of the descriptions that were the most complete and vivid. These descriptions sometimes encompassed great contradiction or a source of questioning for the daughter. The contradictions illustrate the multiple layers of these relationships and the complexity of the fathers, who extend beyond stereotype.

"An Exceptional Person"

C.Z., a professor of dance, describes her father as

> an exceptional person I would say. He was very well loved and respected in his community. He just passed away, and [at] ninety-four years old, he had lost so many of his friends and his community; they all passed. Yet hundreds of people turned out for his funeral services. We heard so many really interesting stories; many were new to us about him. I think I used to imagine that he was sort of an old soul because he's very quiet, a very humble person. He didn't speak a lot. He had a terrific sense of humor, but, again, he didn't ever dominate a social setting. When people would meet him, even for a short period of time, they would always say, "Oh your father's so cute; he's so sweet." It was sort of an aura that he had. He was very calm and very grounded. That's how I would describe him. He was a good dad.

"Not Typical"

Giovanna B.L.M., a noted Sicilian-born writer and instructor on culture and food, fills her home with art, books, Italian artifacts, and musical instruments and captures her father with that phrase:

> I suppose everybody says that their father was not typical; so, he was not typical. Not typical in the sense that, as an infant, he would take me out, which was simply not done in Sicily. You didn't take your children out; you didn't take babies out or push them in a baby carriage, because that was not macho. My father did, and he took great pleasure in family and children and developing children, so in that way he was not typical.
>
> He was a very charming man, a very handsome man. He loved to entertain, so I think my lifelong interests [stem from him] . . . I was his assistant. He was a very, very good cook . . . I remember once, here in the United States, we were at a wedding . . . For some reason my father, whenever the whole thing was over, invited everybody from the whole table to come to the house for a dish of pasta. We got home at something like one in the morning, and he made pasta for everybody.
>
> He was expansive and generous but ahead of his time in other, very important respects. One of them was the education of children. He always said, "Educate a man and you will have educated one person; educate a woman and you will have educated a family." I went to the best high school — I went to the Bronx High School of Science when I was only here three years.

"Everybody Loved Him"

Christine P., a highly regarded writer and artist originally from Pittsburgh who has lived most of her adult life in Boston, gave a vivid picture of her father:

> He was very charismatic. Everybody loved him. A tall blonde Italian guy. Very close relationship with his mother. Had two sisters, two daughters, always wished he had a son or more boys in the family . . .
>
> He liked to play games. He was very athletic so he played lots of sports, played cards, and was a volunteer fireman. Played golf, hung out

with the guys, and remained friends all his life with his childhood friends.

Stayed where he was born . . . He spoke Italian; he didn't learn English until after he went to school. A lot of his friends were also Italian, Toscani, and they remained friends all their life from that neighborhood. Anytime I'd go anywhere with my father, we'd be in Florida, we'd be in North Carolina, we'd be even in Italy, and somebody would say, "Aldo!" People knew him everywhere.

He was very down to earth, not an intellectual, though he read a lot and did a lot of crossword puzzles. He always beat us at games. He never was easy on us: ping-pong, tennis. I remember he'd say, "Get the lead out of your feet." He would run me all over that tennis court.

When I was in Catholic school, he studied the catechism with me. That was really nice. You had to memorize all those things. I don't know why he got that job, but he took that job on. He wasn't at all religious.

His father was a communist who died young in a coalmine crash. He was an organizer of workers. I think my father had a strange relationship with his father, because he never talks about it . . .

He had his nights of playing cards with his friends; he visited his mother every single day. He had his beer-drinking nights. He had his TV shows. He had his chair; he [was] patriarchal. He kind of managed to get it the way he wanted.

Despite intense conflicts between her and her dad later in life, Christine P. commented:

When I go back and visit western Pennsylvania, people still talk about my dad. He was a very vibrant person who impacted a lot of people's lives. I think with his kindness mostly, his kindness, his genuineness. He didn't pretend to be anything other than what he was.

"A Feeling for the Stones in the Road"

A childhood accident left a great mark on Daniela's father. She is a respected poet and writer, and we met in her handsome book-lined writing studio in Brooklyn Heights (their picture appears on this book's cover):

I think because he had been lame, or differently abled, as a boy he became very compassionate. As a child at the age of two, he fell off a table where he was born, in Puglia. There were no doctors in this one-goat village, so the hip became distorted . . . he always limped. You may remember seeing older people limping along with a great big shoe — that was my father. His father was a shoe craftsman, an artisan of leather in the village, so he would always build the homemade shoe for my father with the heel so he could walk better . . .

I think this made him, rather than bitter, as some people become when they are differently abled, he became very compassionate . . . We used to say that he had a feeling for the stones in the road. Indeed, everyone felt like he was their chief emotional confidant when it came to feelings.

Upon arrival in America, after watching his sister's burial at sea

he spent thirty days and nights in Ellis Island Hospital with smallpox and diphtheria. My grandmother Lucia sat for thirty days and nights beside his bed to watch over him, and her first English word was "water," and she would beg extra water. In order to get extra water for my father, she would carry water for all the patients in the ward. She washed the fever out of him, with just the folk wisdom of a lot of water. She kept putting water into him, and that's how he survived his ordeal of passage to the New World.

She speaks of her father being inspired by a Jewish immigrant scientist, Professor Steinmetz at General Electric in Schenectady, New York (where her father sold newspapers and shined shoes), who would buy his papers and gave him an extra nickel because he also had a disability. Her father

was very inspired to attend Union College to become a revered scientist like Professor Steinmetz. While he worked his way through school, he also fed the entire family with his newspaper route and tending the parking lot at night.

He told me this story where he would work at General Electric at night, and in order to get a few winks of sleep, he'd climb up on top of a crane and sleep on the platform of the crane — he had to tie himself to it — because there were rats in the factory at night . . .

I don't know how he managed to be among the first Italian American immigrants to achieve Phi Beta Kappa in Union College's Alpha Chapter while working so hard and never sleeping nights, but he did. I think of him as an almost miraculous human being. I had a great sense of worship for him . . . His brothers and sisters worshipped him as well. They called him Dan, and my grandfather, when he graduated from college, called him Master Donato.

He got a job for thirty dollars a week during the Great Depression and fed the whole family of seven brothers and sisters and his parents . . . that was a fortune.

He invented products with his company, for which he did not necessarily get credit:

He was always having his brain picked, because he had this humility from being this small, lame guy. But he also had great pride in his Italian background . . .

I look at this little, skinny, lame immigrant who couldn't speak a word of English, who came here with practically nothing but the clothes on his back, came from a shoemaker father and a mother who never worked outside of the home, and I wonder at what he managed to achieve with his hard labor and tenacity. He worked so incredibly hard with this tenacity — he really was an exceptional person.

"Extremely Involved in Politics"

Rosa, a long-time and much beloved U.S. congresswoman from the state of Connecticut, described her father rising to political eminence in Connecticut from very humble beginnings and without formal education:

He came from Italy at age thirteen. His mother died in Italy when he was age two, of tuberculosis. As a matter of fact, this is always poignant, at some point when he was two years old they took him away from his mother because they were afraid of infection. He never saw her again.

His dad came to America first, and I don't know on what subsequent trip he came as well. His father remarried. When they came, they settled in Wooster Square [the Italian American neighborhood in New Haven], lived with family there.

When he came here he was put into the seventh grade in the U.S. He left school . . . [the same year] because he couldn't read or write the English language. They made fun of him. This particular story is interesting: They asked him to define the word "janitor." He didn't know what "janitor" meant, so he drew on his Italian, which was *genitori*, and obviously it was not the definition of "janitor." It was "parents" or "parentage." Teachers, classmates laughed; he left school, never went back for a formal education.

He spent eight or nine years in the Army, before Pearl Harbor. In the United States Army he taught himself the clarinet and wound up being the first clarinetist in the United States Army band.

He was probably one of the most — well, in two respects, both with music and with books — he had probably one of the finest libraries and was one of the best-read individuals you have ever met. He educated himself through reading, and I have all of his books . . . classics, politics, history . . . everything. He could quote Émile Zola.

In terms of music . . . my parents took me to the opera at the Met at age nine. I saw the opera *Aida*. He used to sit down with me and listen to the symphonies, and he'd say to me, "Do you hear the French horn?" I heard nothing, you know; what did I hear? All of that was self-taught.

Politics became his passion, which also eventually became Rosa's career path, a passion that focused on the common working person, as Rosa goes on to say:

What I do as a [congressional] representative with regard to workers is not something I learned in the twenty-one years I've been in this institution. My father would say to me, "Why can't businesses focus on the people, the people who make these businesses strong for them? They create the profits, etc. in the good times; where are they in the bad times? What they do is they let these people go." Extremely involved in politics, felt politics was a way of moving forward.

Very strong ethnic identity — Italian culture, history — he knew it to a fare-thee-well, was very proud of it, and defended it. He helped with newly arrived immigrants, translated for them.

Both my father and mother served in politics in New Haven. My dad served on the city council but served a shorter period of time, because it was a nonpaying job, and he was trying to send me to college, graduate school, and so forth. He took a job, gave up the seat on the council. Politics, bareknuckled politics in the city of New Haven.

He would always say to me, "You've done a lot of book learning, but until you learn what people's lives are about, you're never going to succeed in politics. You've got to understand." I regret that he never saw me elected to the House.

She shared many of these thoughts when a sculpture titled "The Family Table" was dedicated in Wooster Square for the DeLauro family's contributions in New Haven.

"An Enigma"

B., a renowned visual artist and writer whose work resonates with themes of family, culture, and identity, began by saying that her father was "an enigma," a theme that flowed throughout her interview. She explained:

> There were so many parts of his life as he lived it that still raise questions for me . . . At the time of my birth my father was working at the Library of Congress . . . When my father voluntarily went into the service, he did not have to enter the service because he was a government employee, but he had three brothers that were in the service, and I guess he decided to enlist.
>
> They kept his job open and wanted him to go back to the library, but my mother in the meantime had moved back to Boston . . . That was a pivotal moment in my father's life, that decision not to go back to the library. When I visited the Library of Congress, and when I saw that environment, I thought, "Oh! This was a perfect place for my father. Perfect."
>
> The rest of his life seemed so disjointed and out of tune with his innate character. I would say his innate character was very spiritual and philosophical. He had spent three years in Maryknoll Seminary intending to become a foreign missionary, and we were connected

with Maryknoll through his whole life, through his friends and through literature that always came to the house . . . My father's life still has a lot of mystery attached to it. One of the mysteries is why he left the seminary . . .

For the rest of his life my father would always read St. Thomas Aquinas in Latin. He would read Cicero and Latin writings in Latin. He could speak Latin the way I'm speaking in English. Even when he was working two jobs, which was most of his life, he would be sitting at the kitchen table at two in the morning with a bowl of cornflakes and he would have one of these tomes, often St. Thomas Aquinas.

Even in discussions, especially with my brother . . . and myself, discussions about religion, philosophy that had to do with this pattern of thought, a Jesuit pattern of thought, he was a logician par excellence, so it was impossible to argue with him as he would always catch you on the faulty logic. He had spent eight years with the Jesuits at B.C. High at Boston College, which was pretty unusual for a young boy at his age; in fact, in his yearbook, he's one of the very few Italian names. Everyone else was Irish.

It's just mysterious to me that someone of my father's mental capability and the amount of education that he had, compared to anybody else that we knew, he had the highest amount of education. The fact that I had two parents who had graduated from college was so extraordinary at that time. I was born in '42 and they graduated in the late thirties. I mean, hardly anyone, second-generation kids of immigrant parents, got to university at that time. It was always a mystery to me. I felt, why was my father not at something like the Library of Congress, not teaching?

Then I think he got into this family bind, which when I did the research for Ellis Island [an art exhibit], I began to understand more the dilemma of second-generation children of immigrants, where there was that "Go out. Don't learn Italian. Go out into the world. Do well. But never forget the family."

When I did that research, two and two started to make perhaps four, that my father felt incredible responsibility to his brothers and sisters who had not graduated from college. Most of them didn't even graduate from high school; he was trying to create a situation where they had more economic and personal independence.

B. describes her father as "a man of constant surprises" as she tells this story of his relationship to Chinese culture:

I remember taking my father to Chinatown in San Francisco. Did we eat at any of the major Chinese restaurants? Absolutely not. He found the most [authentic] Chinese restaurant on the second floor in Chinatown, where we were the only people who were not Chinese, right? And did I know that he spoke Chinese? He was actually saying things in Chinese to people and he picked up a Chinese newspaper.

When I was doing my work for the Ellis Island show, I find, both on his Army documents and at the seminary, that he studied Chinese for three years! What can I say?

B. summed up her father's life:

He did it. He lived his life, really sharing the fullest of all his gifts. His intellect and his spirituality — this is probably what I neglected to say when you asked my father's influence. There was that intellectual freedom but also a deep spirituality. My father was a humble person and deeply, deeply spiritual. I think that that was a great sustenance to him . . .

He never regretted, he never talked about regretting not going back to the library. He never talked about regretting not being a teacher, which he had been at some point. He never regretted starting the dry cleaning shop for his brothers. There were never any regrets. He lived a very, very full life. Hidden, in a lot of ways . . . It was a life of deep integrity.

"Entrepreneurial Spirit"

Linda G. is a lawyer living outside of Boston, on whose wall hangs a lovely framed poster from their family's town in Puglia. She says her father

was high energy, highly motivated. The family was, in my experience compared to some other Italian families I know, very interested in rapid assimilation. For example, they did not live in the Italian section of town, and very little Italian was spoken at home. Invariably some would be . . . They really were very interested in becoming educated and becoming American . . .

He was very intelligent and very high energy, very mechanically inclined. He was a pilot. He learned to fly as a teenager. Flying was his true love all his life . . . When he joined the Army in World War II, he went into the Air Corps. That just increased his knowledge of flying, his capabilities, his licensure.

He married my mother as the war was winding down. He was a little bit afraid of his mother. Didn't tell his mother he was getting married, certainly didn't tell his mother he was marrying someone not Italian. That was a point of contention for sure . . .

They had a very interesting young marriage, which I think really tells something about my dad and his sense of adventure. He and my mom went to work on the Algonquin Pipeline, which was a major construction project, bringing natural gas through Texas . . . up through the Midwest, into New England, and then Canada. My mom was a book-keeper so she worked in the office and he worked on the construction end. They actually lived in a house trailer that they pulled with their big car.

They had a lot of adventures living in Texas, Oklahoma, meeting people from different walks of life. So that was pretty interesting. I think it was a little lonely too. They were pretty much by themselves. They did that for several years. I was born four years after they were married, and they were in Nebraska when I was born. [They had] their entrepreneurial spirit and that was kind of neat. Then my dad started his own construction company. And the pattern continued.

I really think that even though there were times in his life where he found it to be a struggle, you know as a child of the Depression, I think he really was of that generation that really felt they could do anything. I mean so much changed during the period of time when he was a boy until he died. I used to talk to my grandmother about that. Like the development of the light bulb, the radio, TV, airplanes and jets, not to mention walking on the moon.

He had interests and he pursued them. He was responsible, earned a good living. I think he did the right thing, even though sometimes [he] would have probably rather not. I shouldn't say that, but you know, temptation was always there.

"Self-Made Man"

Helen, highly esteemed as a foremother of Italian American women writers, spoke from her book-filled apartment overlooking the Hudson River. Her father shared a similar entrepreneurial spirit at a time in history when immigrants faced untold obstacles:

He was a self-made man, in the old-fashioned way. He had to leave school very early. He was the oldest child of his family. His father was an immigrant from Italy and never had a position, really. I think he was a janitor. I'm not even sure.

My father had to set goals for himself, which he did! He left high school and went to work, to support his family, really. He started as a helper at a wholesale fruit company, and he began to love that business. When he was only nineteen, he incorporated his own business! That was the Syracuse Fruit Company, and he became known as the Banana King of Central New York. It's one of those old-fashioned stories that they did in those days. It's hard to believe. I could always think of my father as a successful man and somebody that was very inspiring.

Helen's homage to her father took the form of the written word, when as a teenager she penned an endearing, humorous poem for him for his fifty-first birthday:

To My Dad

'Tis over fifty years ago that good old Pop was born,
'Twas quite a gay occasion too for was on Christmas morn.
Now no special star shone for Pop that night,
Still folks here tell of a much better sight.
For the heavens shook with a great Hosanna
When appeared in the sky a mighty banana.

All flecked with brown and with golden hue,

It brought peace to Pop and a good business too!

Yes, 'tis two score and ten since Pop's first birth date,

When for lack of a manger he was laid in a crate.

That crate wasn't the least bit frilly or floozy,

But written on the sides was sun-kissed and juicy.

All plump and all red was this tiny bambino,

Like an Ashtabula tomato was cute little Nino.

Now when Pop came from pink clouds to live on the earth,

There was in old Syracuse of wise men a dearth,

So none came on a camel with incense to give,

Just Fred in a Chevy to teach Pop to live.

And though Pop's none the wiser he's balder at least,

Who wouldn't be, too, with Jocko [Helen's brother] the beast?

So now on this eve of the fifty-first year,

We are all gathered here to give a big cheer.

To Pop and his moneybags may they long increase,

And may the gold of bananas never cease.

Here's to a sport, never all wet like Venice,

He's Antonio my father, the Merchant of Lettuce!

© Helen Barolini

Reprinted by permission of the author.

"Could Do Just about Anything"

In her home, C.N. keeps her parents' dining room table and exquisite fruit plates set up just as her parents had. A stunning picture of her father as a young man presided over the room, as she commented that her dad

> . . . was very much a fun person. He had a very good sense of humor and a real independence . . . [He was a] self-made man, very hardworking, very strong. He obviously was a Depression era child. When he was fourteen, he stopped going to school during the day and became an apprentice to a tool and die maker to help support the family . . . in Newark, New Jersey.

He went to high school in the evening, after working full time during the day. He was one of nine children, the second oldest male, so he definitely always saw himself as the guy who took care of the younger brothers and sisters.

He was a very, very capable guy. I realized as an adult how spoiled I was growing up with someone who could fix and do just about anything. Anything. Anytime there was something broken or needed to be repaired it was always, well, my dad could do it. He could just take care of things. He very much saw himself in that role, sort of a protector.

He started his own business when he was in his late twenties, early thirties . . . It started out as just a small tool and die shop, and he built it into, as technology evolved, an injection molding shop. Plastic injection molding.

He was very fun loving; conservative, politically; very family oriented. Definitely a product of his times but also strongly identified as an Italian, and he was very proud of that.

It was interesting because when I was a child, he and my mother both spoke Italian to each other and to their parents. So, when I was young, I wanted to learn to speak Italian. They refused to teach me because they felt they had been discriminated against growing up. They had run into prejudice. They said that my brother and I were Americans, and we should speak English. They didn't want us to be exposed to that kind of prejudice.

I thought it was interesting because later, when my father was more elderly, he traveled to Italy a number of times for business . . . he was using his Italian more when he traveled. At that point, I think he regretted that he hadn't [taught us Italian]. I was interested in learning Italian again, and he was proud that I was doing that.

Yet tragedy struck their family when C.N. was fourteen. Her brother died in a swimming accident at age nineteen:

Neither of my parents were ever the same. They had been extremely proud of him. He had done very well in school and gotten a scholarship to Yale. They could not have been more proud of him. I think my father had always thought that he was building his business to hand on to him.

After he died, it just really took a lot out of him . . . He was actually kind of bitter in his later years, because he felt that he could never understand why that happened. He eventually gave up his business, sold his business, and went to work for someone else. They were absolutely devastated. It was a horrible time for our family of course, as it is for any family that experiences that sort of thing.

My relationship with my father was a little complicated because, as much as I loved him and enjoyed spending time with him, his relationship with my mother had a lot of negatives. He didn't treat her particularly well, which was difficult to deal with. When this happened, it put the two of them at odds with each other. There was a lot of fighting and arguing. They were both very depressed for a couple of years. As I said, I don't think that either one ever really got over it.

"Interesting and Complex"

Patricia R., a professor of sociology and an avid traveler to Italy, sees her father as

> a very interesting and complex man, very smart, but not formally educated, full of life, frustrated that he didn't speak English well, would always be embarrassed in those situations and so he never stayed in school. But he taught himself to read the *Wall Street Journal* and to figure out stocks. He never made a lot of money, but somehow he managed to invest whatever he made.

By "complex" she meant

> he was full of contradictions. He was warm and lively and pleasant, and he also had a temper. He was always articulate with words, gestures, and curses. He could cook. He worked really hard. He loved his family. We lived in an area of Pittsburgh, which was a neighborhood of immigrant and African American heritages, and everybody came to our house. Everybody was always welcome. We had a big garden.
>
> Another interesting thing, he fixed everything. There was no task he couldn't undertake . . . and that included the old dog and cat. He would operate on them; they came in with a big cut, he'd cut them open and

operate on them and fix them. My brother became a surgeon. I always say to my brother, "Obviously Dad was the first surgeon in the family."

He adored the opera and Italian music, and so I go to the opera . . . He loved sports. And my brother loved sports. When I grew older after I moved away, I would go back and visit and we would sit on Saturday afternoons, there in the summertime, and he would have sports on the TV and we would have the opera on the radio at the same time. That's the way we passed the afternoon. And when he watched sports, he didn't watch them in a quiet way.

She spoke of how, despite some differences, they remained close because of shared values:

The acceptance of everybody who was different, he had those values because he brought everybody into our house, and in a racially mixed neighborhood. Another value, take care of people you meet. He sometimes couldn't take care of himself. Of course he had this great love of Italy because everything was better in Italy. I had to agree with him after I went there.

Her dad

was famous in Pittsburgh in the area where he lived. Always had pictures in the paper because he was in all the Senior Olympics. They called him the unofficial mayor of Pittsburgh . . . He was known. He was known for his garlic, for his tomatoes.

"A Rough Wisdom"

Marianna D.T., a noted author and professor of English who has written a number of essays and books about her Italian American heritage, paints a picture of her father that is sometimes awash in contradictions:

My dad was a very exuberant person, not wildly so, but lively. He was a good, responsible man, despite some decisions he made in his life. Politically he was a puzzle to me, because he identified as a Republican but was also part of the working class — I never quite understood how those went together!

He was a loyal husband, a devoted father, evident by the amount of time I spent with him. I had a close relationship with him. I think that my father had a "rough" wisdom; it wasn't a profound wisdom. Some of the things I remember him saying when I was growing up spoke to that. When my first child died I remember him saying to me, "It should have been me, not the baby"; that's how he was. Salt of the earth. He was that type of person, too, very stoic, very pragmatic.

We have met several dads, and we have seen the complexity and sometimes the contradictions that can exist in a person. We have heard daughters describe their dads with warmth and admiration but also at times with confusion or sadness. True connection can hold intricacy and even ambivalence and does not turn people into one-dimensional, idealized characters.

CHAPTER TWO

KNOWING THE DADS

*A*s we came to know the fathers, a few compelling themes stood out, and we will explore them in this chapter.

These themes were feeling that *family was truly the center of their lives,* including for some fathers their parents and brothers and sisters, so individual potential and accomplishment were secondary to the needs of the family; taking seriously the *mantle of fatherhood,* a role in our culture that has been denigrated and is perhaps now resurrecting; being *generous, hospitable, and helpful* toward all, both family and community members; having a *strong bond* with their daughters — these dads and daughters really meant a great deal to each other, whether it could be vocalized or not; believing in *hard work and using one's intelligence* and talents to succeed in this world, usually from humble beginnings, although it sometimes made them absent dads (who nevertheless took pride in their daughters for doing well); and placing *immense value on education* for themselves and their children, even for their daughters, in most cases, at a time when higher education for women was not a norm in our society.

We encountered two additional, minor themes that are also significant and contribute to our understanding of some of the fathers. These were *unmet potential* and the dad's *relationship to World War II.*

Family Comes First

Family here refers to the whole extended family, including our parents' parents, who may have lived nearby; our aunts, uncles, and cousins; and our parents' grandchildren and great-grandchildren. Many of the dads held caretaking or authority roles within their families of origin. It was not unusual for the dads to start a business for the family, as B.'s father did with dry cleaning; or discipline their brothers or help a family member get a job, as Daniela's father did.

Having a special relationship with his mother seemed a given for several dads, which involved visiting her, helping her out, and feeling a great loss when she died.

R.M., a professor whose ties to Italy are still strong, describes her dad's relationship to his family:

> Funny thing, my dad was the leader of the whole extended family. Every succeeding immigrant that came over, of course my dad had found them jobs and got them into a complete network in the community . . . with jobs and services. My mother, my aunt, my sister, and I put up apartment after apartment.
>
> I remember growing up, collecting clothes and furniture and combining and setting up apartments. Many succeeding immigrants being blown away [by the new apartment] . . . But dad was seen as a leader. He was extremely outgoing and vivacious in nature. He really was. And he told a lot of jokes.

When asked why he became such a leader, she said:

> He had the nature and the character. And he was well respected by the community, whether it's the little mom and pop shops on the street or whether . . . He was highly skilled. He was a very good raconteur. He told stories and he joked and he knew all the dialects around Italy. He was very funny about that . . . I grew up speaking Italian.

One can almost see and hear her father orchestrating the foundations of the next family from Italy.

The Mantle of Fatherhood

We heard of steadfastness and consistency in so many dads. These fathers were always there, present, good providers, urging their children to better themselves as they sought to do the same. We were surprised at the number of dads with strong faith in God, sometimes seen as more typically the mother's realm, and how they passed this on to their daughters. We heard about the differences in raising boys and girls and how the different roles of each gender played out in their families.

Pat M.'s father was born in southern Italy, and she wants to share his memory, Italian culture, and sense of faith and God with her grandkids. She described her father:

> He had a lot of faith, respect, love, and he was very honest. He wasn't mean; he was a very gentle person. He was very strict. We really had to be good at all times. We knew this not only by his actions, well mostly by his actions, but we wanted to please him. We were not afraid of him. How could I say it? [He never] punished us at all; we were never really punished. We just did what he wanted, and we knew we had to do it for some reason. I can't understand why, but my younger sister wasn't like that. She got away with a lot more.
>
> Every day he would say, "Because of God I am here, and hopefully I will be here next year with His grace." A very strong sense of faith. He always encouraged us to have the right friends and [know] where to go.
>
> One thing, this is really funny, when I would be going out [he would say], "Wipe those lips." He did not like us to wear red lipstick, and he would always say, "One bad apple spoils the bunch."

R.L., one of our younger participants, showed a very moving slide show of family pictures and history at the beginning of our interview. Her father was a gentle and shy man who had occasional temper outbursts, and she wonders in retrospect if he could have been somewhat depressed. She speaks of his great sense of compassion:

> He was very, very sensitive. You know how when you are a kid you scratch your knees? He'd wash it out . . . I remember him putting a Band-Aid on and I remember him telling me, "Somewhere a black father is putting this Band-Aid on his child and his child feels bad because you know how Band-Aids are 'flesh colored.'" Now they make them, as soon as they started making the see-through kind, I was like, "Oh! they finally caught on."
>
> He would say profound things about children and the passage of time, because he really loved children and the raising of children, which feels very Italian, and he would say, "You always remember the first time you pick up your child, but you never remember the last time."

A sense of authority characterized these men as fathers, although some wore that authority lightly and others let you know who the boss was. Stories about strictness, overprotectiveness, and even jealousy interwove with tales of laissez-faire dads who deferred to the mother in childrearing. You will hear more of this in Part III as the daughters describe becoming young women.

Fathers continued to be fathers even to their adult daughters, and incredibly helpful fathers were in abundance. P.B., whose house in the woods in Connecticut was filled with remarkable pictures of family and other people important to her, describes her dad helping out in a business venture:

> He was always, his purpose in life was to make sure that his kids had the best, to enable us to do the best that we could. Like, if we needed him to help out. I remember when I first got into the catering business, my husband and I did a party for this real estate company. I had my mother in an apron passing hors d'oeuvres, and my dad was helping me in the kitchen and bartending.

Joyce, from the West Albany Italian community, has a home bursting with pictures and mementos and could recite the many Italian aphorisms that her father used to say. When asked what changed in her life when she married, Joyce commented:

> Nothing changed. Everything, me not being in the house just meant that he came here. He was here every day. Matter of fact, that weeping willow tree he planted when we first moved in. He planted two but one died . . . It's funny because we had that bad ice storm two years ago and it took a lot off of that tree. I was heartbroken.
>
> But no, my father was here every day. If I wasn't here because I was working, I would always know he was here because either there was cookie crumbs on the countertop, or there was a plant or a bush planted, or my yard was raked. I could always tell my father was here.

Generosity, Hospitality, and Community

Giving to others, both formally through clubs or town government and informally to family and friends, seems to describe these men. Whether they did it with fun and a bit of ostentation (like Verna's dad as Christopher

Columbus in the town parade) or quiet humility (like Andrianna's dad inviting a homeless person for Thanksgiving), many of the dads were givers.

Several of the men had suffered in their lives, including from poverty, the early death of their parents, childhood illness, separation from family because of immigration, and severe discrimination. Some of their daughters saw depression and sadness in them, which turned into compassion, kindness, and acceptance in at least a portion of the dads.

Madeline Z. lives next to Lorraine's junior high school in her Connecticut home, which is filled with paintings, pictures, and a lovely piano. She brought out her wedding album and spoke of her father's sadness at seeing her wed since she was the youngest. She describes a "hardworking man" who gave away much of what he had:

He worked hard all the time . . . When he bought the house when my mother came to this country, he bought a house with a lot of land, and he planted vegetables, planted trees. My mother did all the canning.

[He was] kindhearted, very generous, always generous with fruits and stuff in the garden; he just gave them away to his friends. He made his wine. He had men over, playing cards and drinking all his wine. He was a very generous man, too generous. He was kindhearted.

She felt sometimes he gave

too much. He gave too much . . . If you wanted his shirt he'd give it to you. He was that type of a man. He was a good man. Well liked, they liked him at the Italian club.

Andrianna comes from the Troy, New York Italian community and is still an athlete in her late seventies. She welcomed me (Lorraine) like a family member, with a hug, tea and plates of homemade cookies, and a complete tour of her house — including all the wonderful family pictures in gold frames. She tells a similar story about her dad and how he treated people:

Saturday nights, there was this man named Joe that delivered bread to the house. This gentleman would come in, and he'd say, "Hey, Joe, sit down."

He'd go, "No, that's okay, Mr. Renna."

"Come on, Joe." He'd get a bottle of wine out, give him a glass of wine. Now this guy, my dad didn't even know him. This is the type of thing that you don't forget. *Always making someone feel important.* Here's a man just delivering bread, but he made him feel like he was so important.

He did this with my father-in-law, who was a very shy man, when he came to the house. This is what he did with everyone. Here's a man who worked seven days a week, but when you come in that house, he made you feel like you were the number one person.

Civic-minded fathers were not in short supply with this group. LuLu spoke in her whimsical and welcoming apartment in East Harlem, filled with props from her many performances (including her dad's fedora), her childhood dollhouse, and her colorful and skillfully made art pieces. Over homemade cookies and cappuccino she recounted how her father was very active in his community of East Harlem, having run one of the first settlement houses for Italian immigrants; he was so revered there that a street is named after him: Pete Pascale Place. With a great deal of emotion in her voice, she described her father as

a radical Italian; he used to say to me, "Making money is not important. It matters what you believe in." I would say that he devoted his life to the people of East Harlem; he was beloved by the Black and Hispanic communities here. He was on many community boards, and they looked to him as being the most fair and open-minded person. He united so many people.

Barbara D., a former town mayor, had a father who

was a very gentle, smart, patient guy. He respected people; he had patience with them. He also had a lot of interests. He was a pharmacist by trade but was also an artist who liked to paint. He was also a great believer in community service and politics. He served on the Board of Recreation and also served as the mayor of Hamden. He loved to give back to the community.

A Special — Sometimes Complicated — Bond

Many women expressed a special bond with their dads, which is, in fact, a thread throughout this book. Phrases like "the favorite" or "Daddy's girl" from childhood and "special closeness" or "understood each other" later in life described this relationship.

Many of the women shared "special moments" with their dads growing up or as adults: going to Mass and then out to Friendly's with just him, taking bus rides to nowhere and sitting up on the window seat, working on building a television with him, playing in his place of business, or loving opera together. These were moments when a father's character and his capacity as a father shone through.

Weekends with dad might include him cooking a full spaghetti dinner in the park for the whole family. Those were valuable times and traditions that, for some, continued into adulthood. Golfing and dancing together only grew better as the daughters grew up. In the coming chapters we will hear detailed examples of these special times.

A few women described their weddings as very special. It was important to their dads that they have a wonderful wedding with plenty of family and friends, and he worked hard to provide it.

Despite the extraordinary bond, some of the fathers were private and reticent when it came to emotional issues, and a few women expressed a sense of "superficiality." Some wished they and their dads had been more open, especially in saying "I love you" or talking about difficult issues.

C.Z. describes this:

> I regret living far away frankly, because a lot of things I missed. I would say it was always sweet. My father was just a sweet man, and you could always count on getting, like, a love fix, a positive connection with him, if it was short or long. And we called him Poppy. Everybody wanted to kiss him all the time because he was so cute.
>
> Toward the end of his life he had a stroke, and there were many years where he was failing. He had dementia. There was always this aura of sweetness. You wanted to hug him . . . It was always sweet and maybe superficial . . . It was physical, like a hug or a kiss or "I love you" and "I love you." I remember at the end he forgot who I was for a while. I'd come into a room and he didn't recognize me. I had to remind him. Then he could barely talk and he was really out of it; he'd always manage to say, "I love you." He could still say it, still spit it out. It was always that level of deep connection.
>
> In our family we tell each other we love each other a lot. We kiss; we hug. As far as having any conversations with my father, I really wish I had

more. I can't really recall any long conversations with my dad. That's because of who we were as father and daughter. Maybe if I'd been around more and matured in his company, that might have deepened and developed, and it really didn't.

A nurse and teacher whose father was born in Sicily, Jackie comes from a family that was immersed in creating art. She speaks of a close relationship with her father:

> . . . but I don't think discussions ever got way, way down into the feeling level. It was pretty superficial . . . Oh, there was a lot of hugging and kissing in the family, and he always contacted me if he was concerned about something or he was worried about me or I was worried about him. It was pretty mutual. I think I was a very attentive daughter . . .
>
> I'll just tell you about one very hard thing that happened in my life. I have a son who died in 1999, and my father could not support me. My son was twenty-nine, and I think one of the things was, my father adored him. That was part of it, but that was tough, that was the hardest thing. I still made my trips to New Jersey, and nothing changed, but I wanted and needed their sympathy and empathy. How I understood it was they were hurting so much that they couldn't . . . That was the tough time. But I wouldn't say it really affected my relationship, though, with them. I was just in it . . .
>
> How do I understand it? Only because I thought he was hurting so much himself, but I think it's also the piece that his generation didn't emote . . . Talking about feelings. There was no talking about feelings. I mean we might talk about anger, like if they were angry with somebody, but they wouldn't talk about, there wasn't any processing . . . That was in 1999 and my father died exactly a year after that. His nurses used to tell me that he talked about it all the time to them, but he couldn't talk about it to me. So that's how I did understand it, that it was just too painful.

Louise, an energetic woman working in management, has deep family ties in the Albany and Troy Italian societies and helped connect us with participants. She describes her early marriage and how her father's feelings were unstated at first but later changed:

It's interesting because I got married at eighteen the first time, and I did not know that neither of my parents, even though they kept telling me I was too young to get married, cared for him. As it turned out four years later, they were right. I depended on my father a lot because it was a scary relationship.

It wasn't for very long, like, I had gone out with him for quite a while before we got married . . . but he lost his job and started drinking, and so it got scary. I would consult with my father all the time about how unhappy I was and that kind of thing.

For some women, talking about deep feelings and possible conflicts was the norm. In Andrianna's house her father was able to bring up something very emotional:

My sister got married at nineteen. Now don't forget we're identical twins. Her husband-to-be was in the service. That night she came in to tell my dad they were going to get married, and he looked at her and he said, "Josie, okay." He says, "Please, now as a dad, I just want you to be honest with me. Is there a problem?" Meaning, is she pregnant? They didn't use that word.

My sister started to cry. She said, "Dad, how could you say that?"

He said, "Honey, I don't mean it nasty, because I'll be by you all the way, but I just want to make sure." Because she was going to Kentucky with the husband-to-be. It was all done fast because her husband-to-be wanted to get married sooner [rather] than waiting for him to get out of the service. That was a big thing right there.

Lisa speaks to her young son in Italian and uses Italian in her work, as well. Her communication and relationship with her parents, however, experienced a change over the years — from closeness with her mother to closeness with her father — because of *what* she could talk about with each of them and how each saw the world:

Because I have a twin sister . . . I was my mother's pet child and my sister was my father's . . . and then it switched . . . A little later in my teens, I just realized more and more how close and similar I was with my father. Being at that age, I was having the usual issues girls have with their mothers, and we had some differences in our personalities that were similar, but in terms of the way we dealt with people, my father and I were similar in how we looked at people and how we appreciated connecting with people.

When I had boyfriends that went wrong, when I talked to my mother, it would be, "Ah! Forget it." That kind of thing. But my father, he would talk about it at a level that I understood because we connected. We were similar. I realized that in my teens, and it became more and more obvious to me, and he just, he understood me. He knew he understood me. He knew that. There were times he would talk to me and he would say . . . that we were similar.

Carol A., a much respected writer, teacher, and editor of the journal *Italian Americana* who works to promote knowledge of Italian culture and identity, stated that her father was the parent who told her about the facts of life — not quite typical in a traditional Italian family!

Hard Work and Initiative

The men you are coming to know worked hard to support their families and to help the next generation, taking great pride in their work and their ability to take care of their families and help their children do better. We consistently heard combinations of these characteristics: very intelligent, could do anything, worked hard, multitalented, entrepreneurial, always trying to do more, high energy, mechanically inclined, could fix anything, great mind.

While a sense of duty seems to be part of it, we also heard of these dads' strong desire to do better, to do the right thing, to push themselves and accomplish, and to make the world and their community better places. Some women felt their dads worked too hard and were missed at home, which may be part of the reason those special moments described above were so special.

C.Z. describes the closeness yet yearning for more that she felt with her father:

I'm the middle child. And I didn't feel ignored. I didn't feel neglected because I was the only [girl] and he was my first "boyfriend," and it was all this really wonderful developmental relationship with my dad.

That was the really good part about my dad. The bad part was that he was gone a lot because he was so involved in his business. He also was a real stalwart community member. He participated in the local town politics. He was the third selectman in the town. He was on building committees, zoning committees. So not only would he have this really busy work life with twelve-, fourteen-hour days, then he would often go out at night to town meetings.

He was an absentee dad a lot, and that was a shame because I feel like I didn't get to know him as well as I wanted to. I know we all felt that way. He was so busy all the time. That put a lot of stress on my mom.

Work started early in life for many of these men, whether in the fields or in factories. G.D.F. talked about her father starting to work as a boy in Brooklyn, taking on the role of the "Sabbath boy" for the Jews in the neighborhood, lighting their stoves when they could not because of the holy day. A quiet woman who respected her father's strong work ethic, she said her father would have loved the condo on a lake with great views she had just moved into and wished she could have shown him.

Carol A.'s father started several small businesses and invested his money, believing in

this dream of America. His older brother became secretary to a stockbroker. I always thought of the older brother as more American; that's what I associated with being American so early on. Before the [stock market] crash even, my father was investing money from his small business. I think at the time it was a trucking business, investing in the stock market. He was successful in his various small businesses, as so many people at that time were, plus he made these very good investments.

He also believed in this dream of America, that his son could grow up, if he had the ability, to be the president of the United States. He truly believed in America; he liked history.

Carol A. also notes her father's experience of depression when he retired, which she attributes to the predominance of the provider role in his life. During that period it was difficult for an Italian American man to be the sole provider for his family, and he took a lot of satisfaction from that role.

After talking about her father's strong work ethic, Louise offered this anecdote:

When we first moved in over here, my father was going to go on a job with Lou [her husband]. It was a Saturday morning. We're upstairs, still in bed. I remember saying to Lou, "I think somebody's outside in the back."

He's like, "No, can't be."

"I'm telling you, I think somebody's outside." It was eight o'clock; we were still in bed. So he gets up.

"I don't see anybody." Well, we come downstairs . . . and my father is sitting in the chair, because we had the patio set up, waiting to go on the job . . . My father was so used to that, when you work, you work early. It was hysterical. He didn't want to wake us up. So he was sitting out there just enjoying the yard.

Anna D. always sensed the pride that her father felt in their accomplishments:

He was very proud of our success. Coming from Italy, not having anything, I started working, I met my husband, we got married, and as soon as I got married in 1977, we bought a house. My husband and I bought this building. We bought two cars. My son was born. It was a big year . . . That made him very, very proud.

The sense of overcoming great odds was embedded in many of the stories. Maria T., a respected and award-winning poet, described her father as one such example and went on with admiration in her voice:

Oh, what an extraordinary man. My father really raised himself up by his bootstraps. He was the youngest of a large family. All of his brothers and sisters were born in Italy; he was born here. He never knew his father; he died when my father was an infant.

His mother, very heroically, tried to keep his lumberyard business in the Bronx going on her own. My father had five brothers and a sister, a very large family, and this widow trying to support them. I didn't learn this until years later. She ended up dying of a face cancer, which probably was related to being in a lumberyard.

My poor father, here he was orphaned when he was eight or nine. He and the next youngest brother were shipped off to an orphanage upstate, but not for adoption. It was a home for boys, run by nuns, upstate in Sparkill, New York. It sounded like a life of deprivation up there. They were pretty rough on the kids. It was during the Depression, stories of having to walk miles to school.

My father always had this very positive attitude towards life, which was just wonderful. He was just a happy-go-lucky kind of guy; what would have crushed a lot of people or made them very bitter, he wasn't like that at all.

He ended up being the only person in his family to get a college education and then go on to get a master's and then all but get a doctorate. He was a teacher his whole life. He was also incredibly creative. For years he taught industrial arts, but in the later years of his career he taught special ed.

He was the kind of person who could take junk, castoffs; for example, a printing shop would be going out of business and he went there and he'd collect the plates that they used to print newspapers back then and make metal sculptures. He was just amazing. He was extraordinary because of what he made of his life.

Maria G., a musician and music teacher, also fondly recounted how her father had to weather obstacles, working hard to become educated and thus inspiring her, too:

My father was educated by the Jesuits, an all-boys school, mostly for the wealthy. My father was a day student. He did very, very well. He was very intelligent and was a top student. In fact, one year he was supposed to get a gold medal for being the number one student at an evening ceremony. They were poor, and his father said to him, "How can we go there? We don't have the right clothes for this kind of an occasion."

Nobody went, not even my father. The next morning he went to the priest to see about getting his award, and the priest said, "The award ceremony was last night. You didn't show up; you don't get the award." My father was crushed. But it didn't stop him. He studied Latin on his own; that's how he got his degree. He was trying to better himself. He also learned to play piano, the organ, and in fact eventually became the organist in the local church!

Education, Education, Education

While a few dads saw girls as not needing a formal education beyond high school, most stressed education. B. described her father as

> a hard taskmaster. He always expected me to do very well in everything that I was involved in. I was the oldest child and he saw me as setting an example for the others and, in quotes, "bringing honor and glory to the family."
>
> This was enormously important to him. So when I would come home with a report card with fifteen nineties out of sixteen, he would say, "So . . . what did Jeanette get?" I said, "Well, she got sixteen, but I just can't sing. I just didn't get a ninety in music!" It was very funny. On the other hand, he was very interested in who I was and very supportive.

Marianna D.T.'s father was ambivalently supportive of her academic achievement, which she writes about in her lead essay in the book *Crossing Ocean Parkway: Readings by an Italian American Daughter* describing her high school experience:

> Although my scores are superb, the guidance counselor has recommended the secretarial track; when I protested, the conference with my parents was arranged . . . My father also prefers the secretarial track, but he wavers, half proud of my aberrantly high scores, half worried. I press the attack, saying that if I were Jewish I would have been placed, without question, in the academic track . . . I am allowed to insist on the change into the academic track.

Madeline Z.'s father was tremendously proud of her for finishing high school when many in the extended family didn't:

> [He was] very proud that I graduated, because I was the last one to graduate. My brother had graduated already. And he had gone to college, didn't finish college. He was proud of his kids. They all finished school. Because his brother's girls didn't finish school. Of course they were girls. They didn't like school.

She was a girl, yet Madeleine noted,

> he wanted me to finish school. No quitting. If I ever wanted to quit, no way. He wanted his kids to finish high school, because he never finished school.

Education was a given in Diana F.'s family. President of the Washington, D.C., chapter of the National Organization of Italian American Women, Diana describes her father's position, the love of all things Italian, in this way:

> I was the baby girl, and the only girl. For example, there were some relatives in the family who couldn't understand why I was going to college, and I remember my mother getting very upset. My father told my mother, "Why are you getting upset? You're not going to change their mind. She's my daughter, she's going to college, and that's that. You think I'm going to listen to them?"

Unmet Potential?

Several women wondered or agonized about their fathers not fulfilling their own potential, whether due to immigrant status, inability to get an education, discrimination, or the needs of the family coming first. Some women commented that their dads felt fulfilled while they had concerns about him leaving dreams behind. Life offers many choices, and it seems the fathers made the choice that fit themselves and their families at the time.

Anne P., a professor of psychology, brought her eulogy to the interview and spoke of connections between her father, her children, Italy, and being Italian:

> I was thinking earlier that he didn't use the GI Bill or do what he needed to sort of occupationally better himself. But I think if you were to ask him, he would probably say that he thought overall he had a very good life. He had a fifty-three-year marriage with someone that he absolutely adored right up till she died. He had three children who stayed close to him and who he really loved. So I think probably some of that is from my sort of — or I picked it up because I wasn't raised that way, sort of — upper middle class, let's move up here.

CarolP (this abbreviation is preferred by the interviewee) is an engineer who lives in the same house in the Italian section in which she grew up. She shared the quintessential mid-twentieth-century picture of her father as a young sailor and said she felt her father didn't understand all that he had done:

> He would always say things like, "Oh you're so smart; you went to college." And it kind of bummed me out because I always thought, you know, "*You're* so smart. It's not about the education; it's about the person inside." That's what I've learned.
>
> I've got friends who didn't even graduate high school that I'm in awe of, and I could never make him understand how intelligent he was because intelligence to him meant you had a degree or multiple degrees. That was always a sticking point . . . He'd say things to my brothers, like, you need to be more like your sister. She's got a degree; she does this and that.

Laura M., a professor of psychology whose father had died very recently and suddenly, said that her father was a farmer. Somehow Laura always felt that wasn't exactly what he wanted to do in life; but it was the family business, so he went into it. She wonders about baseball, which he excelled at, being more of his passion and how that might have played out if he could have followed it.

B.'s father started several dry cleaning shops, and she expresses her sadness at how hard her father had to work:

> I remember going in there with my mother when I was little . . . my father was working . . . with one of those undershirts that has narrow straps . . . and he was very, very tanned and sweating. I remember looking into his eyes and feeling so sad that my father was working so hard. It felt wrong. It felt really wrong. That was something that was in my life a huge amount . . . just feeling like my father's life didn't fit. It wasn't right.

Military and Choices

Many of the men served in World War II or the Korean War, and many seem to belong among those television journalist Tom Brokaw described as the Greatest Generation, the men who fought in World War II and came home ready to take on the world. Typically they did not talk about the war, and some daughters definitely had questions they would have liked to discuss with their fathers.

In listening to the daughters, we came away with the feeling that serving in the military, particularly during World War II, was a major rite of passage toward becoming a full-fledged American. The fathers' experiences of World War II represented a life-changing and principled stance.

We heard about B.'s father enlisting although he did not have to, given his job at the Library of Congress, and how that affected the rest of his life.

No less impacted by their military service were the fathers who fought for Italy, such as Giovanna B.L.M.'s father who fought in

> the so-called campaign in Africa. He was a young man, and as an idealistic young man, he really believed that the Italians would bring civilization to people who didn't understand what a camera was, who didn't eat with utensils, who were very primitive; so he felt that the compact would lift or increase the culture of the indigenous people. Well by the time he came back in the late thirties, he got married. By the time World War II came, he realized they were not bringing civilization to Africa — quite the contrary. And the regime at the time, he was simply not going to fight for the Fascists.

Giovanni's father emigrated, and after the war he went back for his wife and children.

Anne P.'s father's service left her questioning:

> I never could reconcile the father that I knew with his being [in the war]. I don't know how he survived, because he was such a gentle, kind person. I don't know how he put on a uniform and picked up a rifle and killed people . . . He was in action . . . He was in the European Theater.
>
> I remember as a young kid once asking him, "Did you kill people?" I don't think he ever answered, or he didn't want to answer . . . He was awarded the Bronze Star. He was in a number of battles . . . in what they called the Second Wave, in England, Belgium, France, Germany.
>
> One of the questions I wish I'd asked him is how did you get through it? What did you do to survive? I think he probably would have said that he just did what he had to do because he was someone who did what he had to do.

He was engaged to my mom. She actually wanted to get married before the war and he said, "No, because if I come back maimed or disabled, I don't want you to be stuck with me." I mean you could say if they were really madly in love they would have gotten married anyway, but I think that was sort of another way of his taking care of her and putting her first.

We are struck by how these men's potentially perilous choices affected their lives and their families and how these decisions echoed over the years.

Beginning with stories of our own fathers, Part I fleshes out a picture of the Italian American man — his contradictions, his qualities that defy stereotype, who he was, and what his struggles were. As children, we often fail to recognize that our parents were people *before* they were our parents, with their own dreams, challenges, and hopes. The portraits included here set the stage for the relationships we discuss in this book. Just as the men were complex and multidimensional, so too were their relationships with their daughters.

PAUSE AND REFLECT

Throughout Part I, you have met a number of dads — dads who fought hard for their families and for their country, dads who were able to realize their own potential, and dads who made different choices. Perhaps some of these men reminded you of your father or their stories resonated with you in a significant way. We now suggest that you spend some time with your dad in your mind and think about who he was, not just as your father but as a man with his own thoughts, dreams, and aspirations.

✦ *Let yourself sit for a moment and think about your dad, what he was like as a person, how he or his ancestors came to this country, how the period when he was a boy and a young man affected him, and what the challenges of his life were as he grew up.*

✦ *Is there an older relative you can ask about your dad and his history, how he was seen, what was important to him, how he and your mother were as young adults together?*

✦ *Character matters and character endures. What was your dad's character? And how did that affect the kind of father he was to you?*

PART TWO

LEARNING, DOING, BEING: EARLY TIES WITH OUR DADS

*O*ur earliest years with our families — our parents and brothers and sisters — form the basis for so much of what transpires in our adult relationships with our families, colleagues, friends, and intimate partners. The attachments we form in the early days shape our later attachments as well as our general approach to, and outlook on, the world.

Do we become confident and sure in our relationships or are they characterized by anxiety and insecurity? Do we feel needy and wanting, as if we can never get enough, or do we feel self-sufficient and able to enter into a relationship as a whole person? Do we feel able to take on what life has to offer with poise and a sense of the capacity to master it, or do we tremble in our indecision and sense of inadequacy? Our relational, competent selves are forged in those early relationships, particularly with our parents.

These early templates can also inform how we deal with our grief as adults, raising these questions: Do we feel the secure base within ourselves that allows us to bear our grief and experience our memories fully? How do we keep the relationship alive once we have lost our loved one?

That early childhood matrix of parent and child has been described as a holding environment, in which the parent and child are attuned to one another and safety and protection are the backdrop to play and exploration. With a strong hand to hold, literally or metaphorically, the child can go anywhere. From this secure base, the child can explore the world in its entirety. The return to mother or father with the expectation of love and help — at age two, or six, or sixteen, or far into adulthood — has to be experienced in early childhood in order to open the door for later returns.

Cooking, Walking, Talking: Acts of Father and Daughter (Lorraine)

In cooking there is love, and in cooking there is history. My father sat by his mother and watched her cook, absorbed her cooking. He was not "taught" by her in any way that we use that word, but as a risotto absorbs wine or broth, he absorbed the cooking of his mother. Nor did he help her, according to my father and my Aunt Mary. Mamá was at one with the act and art of cooking, and helpers did not really have a place.

I imagine he absorbed many things from those times: her love, her caring, her intense feelings for great food, her carefulness, her patience, her creativity, the wielding of a knife to peel an orange, the breaking of spaghetti for soup, the cupping of a hand to measure salt, the flipping of a cutlet at the right moment, the stuffing of an artichoke — and the aromas.

In our family, too, the aromas were there from the beginning, the very early smells, some wonderful and inviting and warm, others not so enticing, more acrid, more pungent. Sauce cooking for hours, letting the tomatoes mellow and sweeten, had all of us standing around the kitchen wondering when it would be done, waiting for a taste when my father stirred the sauce. The sharper smells of garlic and bitter olives, the very ones that today I love, were too much for me as a child.

When my father sautéed garlic for long thin pasta with garlic and oil or esoteric greens that no one else in my American neighborhood ever ate, he was happy; the world was as it should be — rich, spicy, textured. But for me, better the fruity, earthy, sweet redness of tomato sauce. Why could we not just have sauce every day? Was there a problem with that?

Sauce with bread, sauce with macaroni, ricotta in the sauce, dropped eggs in sauce, a pork sauce, marinara sauce, even sauce with pigskin if you could avoid the pigskin — they were the fundamentals of eating! And both my mother and father made spectacular sauce. When sauce is cooking now, as then, the house fills up, my heart fills up, and all the stars have aligned.

Cooking. He was always cooking, or wanting to cook, or making a mess in the kitchen. He could not do anything simple. Scrambled eggs became eggs with a bit of cheese, and how about some oregano, and really, they are great with peppers and onions. So we didn't let him near a peanut butter and jelly sandwich! Cooking, inventing, trying out, cooking again — it was his way, and it became the way of the family, all of us absorbing.

Into this world I was born a few days before his twenty-ninth birthday, his first dark-haired baby. What greater blessing for such an Italian father — a dark-haired, dark-eyed baby girl looking at him with his black hair and black mustache. Something was forged, something Italian, something that held us together for a lifetime and longer.

When I was little, maybe three or five, and over many years, he would take my hand, and we would walk around the house. We would "survey the estate" hand in hand, and he always sang, "Let's take an old-fashioned walk." Which is what we did: we walked, we talked, we looked at bushes, trees, grass, birds, dogs, whatever was in bloom, whoever wandered through, a flower that was fading, a tree just starting to bud.

The lilac tree in the side yard was my favorite; I was always hoping it would be in bloom, only later in life realizing how quickly the bloom comes and goes. The thin red maple tree in the front, which he gave my mother for an anniversary, turned out to be the wrong tree (she had long admired Japanese maples), but we loved it anyway and watched it grow. We kids gathered the sticky seedpods and "cooked" them. The giant angel trumpets in the backyard, in the corner by the house where no one bothered them, grew bountifully like some fantastical species, and I believed the angels came to play on them.

He would sing, "I'm just bursting with talk," and he was; we both were. We would talk and talk about the sky and trees; the house and what needed to be repaired; dreams and plans for the house and yard, which would grow and change over the years of my childhood; things right before our eyes that we saw and touched; the earth and its seasons; the way all of life came forth in the spring, grew abundantly all summer, sometimes withering in the heat, and came to a rest in the fall. We watched all of it and talked about all of it.

Testing the Waters: Learning How to Swim (Donna)

Some of my earliest and best memories with my father took place at Seaside Park, the longest stretch of beach in the city where I grew up. It was the backdrop for many of my family photographs — me, at two, with a curly mop of hair, in a sunsuit, sitting in the sand trying to get my sneakers back on; my mother's hourglass figure in her striped bathing suit, laughing with her arm in the air, most likely shooing my father away from taking yet another photo; my cousins and me standing in a line, grinning from ear to ear, our eyes squinting from the sun, with melting Italian ices in our hands.

I loved the beach more than anything, and even as a small child fantasized that I actually had salt water, not blood, in my veins and that someday I would teach myself to breathe under water, just like a dolphin.

It was to Seaside Park that my mother, my sister, and I headed most hot summer mornings, our lunch packed and our sunscreen on. If my sister and I were lucky, we had change in our pockets for Fudgsicles or soft-serve ice cream cones later in the afternoon.

The afternoons that my father joined us after work were the best for me. After working all day in an excruciatingly hot, noisy factory, he would walk to the beach and find us at our usual spot, by that time eating our ice cream or hunting for shells. I remember how happy he would be to peel off the clothes that smelled of copper and acid, revealing his bathing suit underneath, his back as brown as a berry from those many afternoons with us.

He would dive into the waves, and I would count one . . . two . . . three . . . four . . . until I saw his black head of hair resurface, usually popping up quite a distance from where it had entered. He would take my hands and pull me through the water in circles, sometimes dipping me, laughing along with my squeals of delight that always followed. I loved our ocean ritual.

One day during the summer I was four, he realized that I should learn how to swim. This did not sit well with my mother, who, I think, was sure I would drown off the coast of Long Island Sound at such a tender age. Despite her worried look, my father started out by doing our circle ritual, letting me get even more accustomed to my face hitting the water. After we had done that for a while, he stretched his arms out in front of him and told me to lie across them and put my face in the water.

I recall being frightened that I would lose balance and somehow be swept away far from shore, but my father kept encouraging me to keep my face in the water one more second, two more seconds, until it became effortless and I was able to blow bubbles on command. With one arm still balancing me, he took the other and showed me how to cut my hand into the water and push away from my body, one arm smoothly after the other. Then his instructions were, "Kick, kick, kick!"

After many tries, and a good deal of laughter, I somehow managed all of the movements in synchrony and found myself miraculously moving farther and farther away from him, all on my own. With his hands on his hips, standing waist deep in the water, he shouted, "You're doing it! Keep going, keep going!"

As I look back now, I imagine his eyes filling with both pride and sadness as I took yet another childhood step toward becoming independent, meaning, in essence, that I was growing — away from him.

In that moment — as he balanced me with infinite patience, repeated his instruction to cut into the water, and beamed with pride to see me make those tiny independent movements — I learned something powerful: I learned what it means to *teach*.

Fritz Perls, a noted psychologist, has said, "To teach means to show someone that something is possible" (1992, p. 141). The possibilities to that four-year-old on that hot summer day were many: I learned that I could acquire a new skill, that I could chain actions together to do something that seemed to me magical, that my four-year-old body was strong, that I could overcome fear. Aside from giving me those specific lessons, my father was the power of example. He taught me each skill slowly, and he had the patience to wait until I mastered each one.

Was it at this moment, so early in my childhood, that the seeds were planted for me to love teaching and to want to teach? Was the Buddha's meditation instruction to begin and begin again alive in my father that day (even though he had never heard of Buddhism), and did it teach me perseverance?

I sense my father, in all his glorious patience, as I instruct my own students and sit in psychotherapy sessions with my patients, waiting for them to make their own connections, sense their own direction, and swim farther and farther away from shore.

CHAPTER THREE

IDENTIFYING AND RELATING

*T*he psychologist understands the basic importance of learning — through example, instruction, and rewards and reinforcement — and observes it as parents and children play together. Children are learning every minute from what is around them and what they see, feel, hear, and incorporate. We see all of this with our dads and ourselves. It comes close to the idea of *identification*: a feeling of identifying with, or being similar to, our fathers or mothers, such that we take on some of their ways of being in the world.

Identification is an unconscious process — one that takes place outside of our awareness—sometimes we glimpse it and can be shocked, amused, comforted, or confused by it. Identification comes from all those hours together, at the beach or at the kitchen stove, walking around the house or just waiting, absorbing each other and growing a bit more. This holding, learning, relating, and identifying that developed in our childhoods can be a strength and a comfort from which to draw later in life and in facing our father's deaths. We turn to the psychology literature for the importance of this process in the father-daughter relationship.

Psychology and the Father-Daughter Relationship

Few psychologists have addressed father-daughter relationships, and those who have primarily have focused on the negative aspects (for example, situations of abuse or neglect). While these are important stories to be told, it is also crucial to understand the positive influences that fathers can have on the lives of their daughters.

Psychology professor and researcher Linda Nielsen, a nationally recognized expert on father-daughter relationships, has written extensively on the importance of this relationship in many aspects of a daughter's life, including cognitive, academic, vocational, athletic, social, and sexual domains. She has asked the important questions: Why do fathers matter to their daughters? How does a father affect his daughter's life? Which aspects of her life does he influence? (2012).

As Nielsen talks about the value of fathers in their daughters' lives, she cites several myths that distort how we view this relationship and how we behave in this relationship. She explains the importance of releasing cultural stereotypes about dads, and she discusses the beliefs that keep us from recognizing the importance of a father to his daughter.

Nielsen tells us that one of the most destructive misconceptions about fathers is that they affect daughters less than mothers do. Another misconception is that a daughter won't suffer later in life from having a distant or troubled relationship with her father while growing up. Nielsen also contends that if a father tolerates disagreements with his daughter and encourages her independence, he will help her develop an autonomous sense of self.

Peggy Drexler (2011), a psychology professor who studies gender and development, discusses the powerful psychological complexity of the relationship between grown daughters and their fathers. She shows how fathers influence their daughters' choices in love and work.

In a similar vein, Michael Lamb (2010), a psychologist who studies childrearing among various cultures, has examined the impact of fathers on their children, and he contends that more often than not it is the father who instills in his daughter a sense of agency (that is, the daughter's capacity to take an active role in decision making and determining the course of her life). This influence can begin as early as toddlerhood. A woman's sense of exploration, adventure, and delight in the world often has its roots in early father-daughter interactions.

We explore those interactions as we shift now to the stories of the daughters. Cynthia F., a professor of management from Colorado, described adventures with her dad that included both the active and the academic:

> None of [our shared activities] are particularly noteworthy — they're not really amazing things. Just going out and shooting basketball together on a Saturday afternoon. On the weekends, he would take my

sister and me to go ice skating in the winter. He was very athletic all of his life. He loved to be active and to be outdoors, so we would do things like that.

I also remember growing up with him and him doing his homework at the kitchen table, going to school, and what an impact that had on my sister and me.

Madeline Z. recounted her father's role during simple family times as well as adventure — including a near tragedy at their house. She also discussed his mustache — a typical feature of some Italian men:

Sometimes [when I was very young] when he wanted a kiss, I wouldn't kiss him because he had a mustache. I didn't like mustaches . . .

Now in those days, money was scarce, but we had everything. We had a player piano. We got the first television that was ever out.

He loved animals. I remember him bringing home a little dog . . . He had it under his jacket. He was afraid to bring the dog in the house because my mother didn't want dogs or cats in the house. We kept him; that was nice, little Blackie . . .

When the Italians [club] had something going on, we'd go to see the fireworks.

Every Sunday night we'd go to my aunt's house, and we listened to Eddie Cantor on the radio. I remember him carrying me home on his shoulders, because I was small. We'd go by this river in Bristol. The waves and the wind were so high, and I used to be afraid looking down from the sidewalk, looking down on the river, and he'd have me on his shoulder. He carried me all the time . . .

Once in a while he let us help [with making wine], because we used to love to turn the grape. Oh we'd all go down the cellar and he'd let us turn. Of course, I'd stand on the boxes because I couldn't do very much. But my sister and my brother, they used to love to do that . . .

One time my father and my mother and I were on the porch, and the roof of our house blew off, and it landed in the street. Here's our house, and the roof just went over. I'll never forget that. It was the first hurricane that we had . . . That was an awful thing, I won't forget that . . .

On the whole we had a good life, I think. We didn't have much, but we had a good life. We always had enough food. My father was a good provider for sure.

We see even more nuances in the father-daughter relationship when we consider how it is configured in Italian American culture. Traditionally, the mother has been seen as the central figure of Italian and Italian American family life. In Italian culture, "the woman is the heart of the family nucleus, upholder of its values, and vehicle of cultural continuity" (Boscia-Mulè 1999, p. 47), and she is viewed as holding the real power and influence in the family — this in the face of a seemingly patriarchal family structure with the father as the head of the household.

This is even embedded in popular folklore. Esposito (1989) cites a proverb that directly speaks to the sanctity of the mother-child relationship: *La mamma e l'anima, chi la perde non la guadagna* (Mother and soul once lost can never be regained).

But for Italian fathers, there are no proverbs, no stories in popular folklore that elevate his role in his children's lives. Even in Italian American cultural studies, the story of the Italian American father and daughter remains virtually unexpressed.

Co-author of this book, Donna DiCello, together with Cheryl Coletta in their 2009 study, became the first in psychology to reveal the Italian American fathers' influence on daughters. In their interviews of Italian American female psychologists, DiCello and Coletta learned that fathers supported their daughters enormously and strongly encouraged them to become educated. This finding is in direct opposition to the stereotype of the Italian culture's undervaluing of women's education. Our personal experiences bore out this truth. Our fathers cheered us on to pursue graduate degrees, to become professionals, and to make our own living in the world.

We are reminded of the Roman myth of Minerva leaping fully formed from the brow of her father Jupiter. This myth embodies the relatedness and potential closeness of fathers and daughters. Minerva, who has a strong and independent sense of self, is vitally connected to her father. She comes, metaphorically and literally, from inside of Jupiter, and we can imagine that Jupiter lives somewhere inside her strength and independence.

The Power of Example

Children learn — and parents teach — in many ways: often directly, but some of the strongest teaching happens when children observe in those nonteaching moments, when parents are just being, when their actions and relationships say it all. For example, we find out that relationships are key and central to our lives and ways of being or that they are not. We learn how to express ourselves or how to keep things to ourselves. We learn, as little girls, how to become women.

A childhood memory, whose meaning she mused about in adulthood, created a special teaching moment Rosanne B. shared with her father:

> When I was in grammar school, I developed a little interest in astronomy. My father went out and found me a scholar's telescope and he subscribed to *Scientific American* for me, which I couldn't understand at all, but I liked the pictures. He was trying to say to me, "Be what you want." I think it was because he couldn't be what he wanted. Whatever it was, he didn't get a chance.

For some, the simple pleasure of being with her father was enough to forge a bond with him. Watching television with her father was remarkably memorable to Giovanna C.:

> We would watch Johnny Carson together a lot. He loved Johnny Carson. I think that was because of his love of humor. I would watch it with him, and we would stay up late at night, and I think that was sort of my way to get around going to bed early — I was going to stay up and watch Johnny Carson.
>
> We always made hot chocolate and toast late at night and watched TV. I feel like we had a very compatible relationship in some ways. He was very friendly toward me and encouraging.

Providing Protection, Reassurance, and Comfort

Unsurprisingly, fathers were often protective toward their little girls when they were out in the world, providing the comfort and reassurance they needed — and creating lasting memories for the daughters.

Roller coaster rides were a setting where L. needed her dad's reassurance:

I remember going to Playland, going on the rides. When you're a kid, I was between nine and twelve, you're still afraid. When he had his arm around me I was not so scared anymore. I remember if I was on the roller coaster with my dad, if he had his arm around me I wasn't afraid. I have that memory . . .

Adele, who heard about our project through her daughter-in-law and was thrilled to be able to tell her story, was well aware of her father's protectiveness, and this memory stands out for her:

He was very protective of us. He took me to the park one day, Jefferson Park . . . I was walking, and a young man went into me with his bike . . . My father got furious. He went off on the kid, and I remember how protective he was of me. That kind of stuff is what I really, really remember about him.

Laura M. tells of some quiet moments of comfort:

I would always be doing my homework at the last minute, at six o'clock in the morning, in high school. He'd be up. It would just be the two of us in the kitchen, and I'd be doing my homework and he'd be having breakfast before he'd go to work.

When I was younger, I have these memories, I don't know how old I was, of lying on his chest. He had a big puffy bare chest.

Imma, who owns her own catering business, spoke about her father over an incredible Italian spread of homemade pizzelles, sausage sandwiches, and homemade chocolate cake. She recounts an instance from their life in Italy of her father's loving protectiveness toward her:

He used to have some men working on the farm, and when he was going there, my mother and I would go to bring lunch. I would go and spend some time with him. He was very proud of us. As a matter of fact, when I was thirteen years old — I never forget this — this guy came over to ask my father if he could marry me. My father said to him, "Listen, I'm going to the United States to give a better future to my children. Do you think I'm going to let you marry her? No way!"

Early Bonding, Early Memories

A couple of the women's early memories revolve around World War II. Jackie brought history alive as she remembered:

The day that the Second World War ended, there were whistles and sirens and people out in the street. I remember him and me, just the two of us, going someplace together walking, and he was all excited, and I knew that it was a big deal too.

I remember during the war listening to the radio, and we had this special Grundig radio. We would play on the floor and listen to the news . . . there were several people in our family that were killed, so that was a big deal. Some of them were in the war — actively participating — and we were anticipating their coming home, so . . . it was one of the outstanding memories I have.

B. describes her first memory of her father:

I think that I was about a year and a half old, and I was with my mother and uncle going to a train station to meet my father because he was coming home. I remember a really long train and these huge streams of men. I was watching this whole stream of soldiers . . . streaming out of the train, and then it was empty. The station was empty, and my father had not come.

I remember being taken aback because I was expecting him. Then all of a sudden this lonely figure started running from the back of the train toward us, and it was my father. What was quite striking to me is that instead of kissing me first, he kissed my mother! I could not believe that I remembered this! Many years later, but even at that age, that that would impact me [surprises me], that he would kiss her first.

Then he picked me up and I remember being in his arms looking down at my mother and my uncle and just a feeling of complete safety, of being embraced and held. Probably that's the most close, secure moment that I remember of my childhood.

What had happened is that he had a tendency to go to sleep very deeply because he had spinal meningitis as a child. Everyone had gone out and the conductor found him as the last person, and that's why he was late!

Giovanna B.L.M. spoke of childhood memories from Sicily:

Maybe it was on Sunday, he would take me to the pastry shop, and I would get an ice cream cone. To describe something wonderful, my description would be it's like a ball and a cone. As wonderful as a ball is, and as a cone is. I remember that.

He was a cabinetmaker, and he had a shop. He made me a little cutting board, and in the afternoon a man would come around selling ricotta. The ricotta would be sold in — I'll show you one, because I have them — in a form that was made with bamboo. They would fill these forms, and once they were filled, the whey of the ricotta would drain away. So when they came down the street, they would say, "Give me three; give me three ricotta." . . . My father . . . would take this ricotta and put it on the board, and that would be my afternoon snack.

He understood, for instance, Montessori; later we understood the Montessori ideas of making the furniture smaller for children and not expecting them to be little adults but expecting them to be children. He was very attentive to things like that.

While alive, our fathers influenced us greatly, and they have continued to do so even after their deaths; the stories contained within these pages speak to a father's impact and the meaningful reality of the Italian American father-daughter relationship beyond the stereotypes. Fathers *do* matter, and we see evidence of this in the early lives of the women in this book.

ATTACHMENT THEORY

John Bowlby, a British researcher and clinician with a background in the study of animal behavior as well as psychoanalysis, launched *attachment theory* in the 1940s, studying both human and animal babies and children and how much and how they attach to their primary caretakers. According to Bowlby (1973), to feel secure later in life we need to experience secure attachments in our early development. He thought of attachment and loss as foundational to the development of relationships across the lifespan and how these relationships would work themselves out. This theory has a

(Continued)

ATTACHMENT THEORY *(Continued)*

long history in psychology and is also a potent force today in understanding psychotherapy with children, adolescents, and adults.

He describes attachment behavior as our innate need to be physically close to those we feel can help us cope in the world. Whether we immediately need the person or not, when we feel a secure attachment we know that that person is there for us, which drives us to continue that bond. This develops in infancy but can continue well into adulthood and can be especially important in emergency situations, such as when there is a loss.

One of the major attachment researchers (and a colleague of Bowlby), Mary Ainsworth, notes in particular that attachment continues in some form throughout life. She comments, "A person's response to the death of a parent usually demonstrates that the attachment bond has endured. Even after mourning has been resolved, internal models of the lost figure continue to be an influence" (1989, p. 711).

She also considered the deep attachment to parents over the lifecycle and wondered about the relationship over time. She questions whether the relationship can ever be "symmetrical" between parent and child, meaning can we as children ever take care of our parents in the way they took care of us? While reversing these roles during the course of a child's lifetime is usually inappropriate (for example, a ten-year-old shouldn't be expected to take care of a parent's emotional needs), during our parents' elder years we may, in fact, become their caregivers.

A psychological perspective rooted in attachment theory considers the intensity and duration of the bonds with parents and the possibilities for role reversal in caretaking and security needs.

We focus on attachment theory because it speaks so deeply to what a meaningful attachment is and means; in our present society it is easy to forget how profoundly important one person can be to another! It is not only "as if" your very life depends on a certain person, metaphorically speaking; at some point your very life really *did* depend on him! Attachment theory also reminds us that we are all biological creatures, and as such we share something with other mammals: we are born quite helpless, we have long childhoods, and we live and grow in families.

CHAPTER FOUR

DAUGHTERS TALK ABOUT GIRLHOOD

*I*n the Italian American family, early memories often include holidays filled with food, vacations with our extended Italian tribe, and simple moments spending time with our fathers. These moments reflect the value placed on family in Italian American culture, where the father takes his role as head of the household very seriously. Family is central, and time is set aside, no matter what the father's work schedule, to take a Sunday drive, to teach a child how to swim, to watch TV together, or to help with homework.

We heard of these close moments between father and daughter from the women we interviewed. Many of the women, even those well into their eighties, reported not only adventures with their fathers but also quiet moments, such as reading together or watching movies. In these moments our interviewees learned about themselves — they were smart, they were capable, they were loved, their fathers were proud of them — setting the stage for a sense of self-worth and confidence.

OBJECT RELATIONS THEORY

Another way we think about development from a psychological perspective is in terms of *object relations theory*, which shares many ideas with attachment theory. Both of these theories examine the fundamental nature of our connections to others and how these connections inform ("set the stage" for) how we think about relationships in adulthood. We'll see this in many of the women's later stories, when, for example, they heard their father's voice as an "inner critic" or as a wonderful support or considered what he would think when they chose their romantic partners.

(Continued)

OBJECT RELATIONS THEORY *(Continued)*

Jill Savege Scharff and David Scharff, two noted object relation theorists, explain that the psychology of object relations puts the individual's need to relate to others at the center of human development. The infant's efforts to relate to her mother constitute the baby's first and most important tendency.

The dynamic between a mother (or other main caregiver) and her infant sets up a psychological template (a pattern or guide) for how the child will then relate to others over the course of her lifetime; even in adulthood we can see the manifestations of this early relationship as we reach out to others: whether we can trust, whether relationships develop easily for us, whether we feel we can maintain our emotional boundaries with another person (1998).

Put more simply, J. Scott Rutan, Walter Stone, and Joseph Shay, who write from a group therapy perspective, point out, "Object relations theory postulates that everyone is fundamentally trying to be *in* a human relationship" (2007, p. 75) even though it does not always appear to be the case. A person's behavior can often be best understood if looked at in the context of relationships: Why do we seek out relationships? What does our behavior in a particular relationship, with a particular person, mean? What relationship issues influence how we feel or think in our responses to something?

Object relations theory includes the concepts *introjection* and *internalization* to explain how we psychologically connect with others. Through the psychological process of introjection, a person in your life becomes a part of who you are on a very deep level; introjection is how you "take in" others. For example, when you hear the voice of your father saying, "It's not a good idea" and you don't do it, that is introjection!

Psychologists focus on *introjects* and *internal objects* (which are really images of people, not objects) mostly in early childhood, for that is when early caregivers, most commonly a mother and a father, become

(Continued)

OBJECT RELATIONS THEORY *(Continued)*

internalized; these internal templates then live, psychologically, inside of the baby.

These early introjects become a fundamental part of how a baby views and experiences the world. Through the two processes of attachment and introjection, early caretakers and then other significant people become parts of the complex design of our emotional fabric, and in fact they help create who we are to become and how we will respond to others in our later lives.

For example, a child who has internalized a very loving and giving parent may come to expect that same response from others in her life and thus grow up secure and optimistic about how others will treat her and how she should treat others. While this person may at times face disappointment, on the whole she will do fine in her relationships because she has a positive relationship base. On the other hand, someone who experiences punitive or inconsistent parental introjection may go through life not expecting much, not trusting others, and feeling that she has to work harder for everything.

While we don't contend that early childhood writes the final story, we do feel it sets a template for how we view and negotiate our adult relationships and how we approach them. Relationships remain central in terms of who we are and how both our external worlds of real, live people and our internal worlds of introjected traces of relationships grow and change over time.

In this book we have placed the father-daughter relationship front and center as an important relational template, and what we found throughout each story was how the transmuting of this relationship over time set the stage for the daughter's views of both herself and her relationships. You will see this influence as you continue to read how each woman connects to her father over her lifespan.

When we examined the stories the women told us of their childhood memories of their fathers, various themes emerged that illuminated Italian American values, as described below.

Sacrifice and Work Ethic

Many of the women were aware from an early age of the financial sacrifices that their fathers made for them. Adele described this poignantly:

> I remember him working hard but always being home for dinner. I also remember my mom telling me that for one particular Christmas I wanted a Shirley Temple doll. My dad worked all the time, a bunch of odd jobs, just to get me that Shirley Temple doll. That really stuck with me — changed my life — that he worked so hard for that. I know how hard it is when you have kids.
>
> We'd also sometimes go to the movies on 86th Street in New York. We didn't have a lot of money so we didn't go that often, but it was a highlight when we did. We would sing along to the organ music that they would play before the movie. My parents would be singing their hearts out!

Many of the women also described learning about a solid work ethic from an early age, as Giovanna C, herself a writer, did:

> He was always encouraging us to get a job and earn money. I wanted to do that anyway; so even from a young age, twelve years old, I was the first girl in town to have a paper route. He took me to *The Daily Argus* and signed me up. I wanted to work and I wanted to make money, so they let me work.
>
> He would take me every Saturday to the woman who was the representative that I had to pay, because they would give me my papers every day, and then every week I'd have to collect from my clients and turn the money over to the paper. My father would be the one who would drive me to take the money and deliver it, and I would get a pretty good percentage of it . . . Both of my parents taught us about saving money.
>
> They were always harping that if you wanted something you just had to save your money. I bought a bicycle, a stereo, lots of albums. He was good at teaching about money, mostly by example, about being a thrifty shopper and not buying junky things that you didn't need. His big joke would be we'd go into a store and look around, and then there wouldn't be

anything we wanted, so he'd go, "Okay, let's go home; we've spent enough money in this place." We hadn't spent anything!

Jean, a publisher who told her story over espresso in her elegant apartment overlooking the East River, spoke of this ethic being realized in a very humorous and resourceful way:

I remember when I was eleven years old, as we got close to the summer, every year the dinner conversation would turn to, "Now, what are you going to do this summer?" If you didn't come up with a good solution, you had to work at my parents' beauty salon, which I hated. I didn't like touching hair, none of that stuff.

I asked myself, what are you going to do? I told my father, "I notice that everybody who comes to your salon drives a car, and those cars are always dirty. I'm going into the car cleaning service, but I'm going to specialize in doing only the insides of cars . . . The outside of cars is just too much work." I said, "In order to do this, you have to allow me to use the electricity in the garage and let me use the vacuum cleaner and let me solicit your customers."

He agrees. I would come in and the customers would say to me, "How much?" I would reply, "Fifty cents," and they agreed. I would go out and clean the car. I'd come back in and I'd get two bucks for each car. Fifty cents plus a dollar fifty tip.

After I had a few dollars, my mother said to me, "We're going to the bank and open up a bank account." In those years in rural areas, because I grew up in a town of 8,000 people, the banks had the high teller windows with the bars going up and down, and I was a short kid. I told the bank teller I wanted to open a bank account, and he says somewhat patronizingly, "What are you going to do with the money?" I said, "I'm going to buy myself a car."

When I turned eighteen, I bought my first car with the money I started making when I was eleven years old! All summer long that year I cleaned the inside of cars. The customers were thrilled. They'd come in and say, "Where's Jean? We want the inside of our car cleaned."

Anna D., growing up in Italy, had memories of hard work mixed with strong family ties:

At a very young age, I used to take care of my brothers and my sister and some of my cousins. Every time that my father came home from work, I would make sure that I had warm water to wash his feet, for the special touch, to welcome him home and show him how much I appreciated what he was doing for his family.

Then when I grew up a little, thirteen or fourteen years old, I used to go with him . . . I remember during Christmastime, he used to go to people's homes where they had pine trees — huge, huge pine trees — to pick the pines for the pignoli nuts. Those trees were so big. We used to get there first thing in the morning when it was still dark out. We used to climb those trees.

At times, I wouldn't even see him up there, it was so dark. He was small and the trees were so big. I used to cry seeing my father up there . . . It was scary being by myself, down below the tree. And him, I wasn't seeing him because the tree was so big. He used to pick the pine-cones and send them down, and I used to take them. Then, when we were all done picking a tree or two, it depends on how many we had to do, we would go home . . .

Always working. Always providing for his family . . . We would pick just before Christmas, because everybody used pignoli at Christmastime. We would bring the pinecones to the markets, and people would buy them raw. Then they would roast them, and the pine opened up and that's how they got the pignoli out, one by one. A lot of work, but well worth it.

Humor and Playfulness

Although the family work ethic was serious, fathers exhibited a sense of humor that the daughters remembered fondly. Giovanna C.'s father, for example, enjoyed playing tricks:

He'd do silly things. One time my mother was on one side of the store shopping, and he had my brother in the shopping cart on another side of the store, in the wig section; this was some giant department store. He puts this long blond wig on my brother and he comes pushing the cart up to my mother, and she saw my brother and she's like, "Oh my God, who is that kid?" It took her a second to realize it was her son. He'd do that kind of stuff.

Diana F.'s father played tricks too:

I remember when my brother Joey and I were little, we would take walks with Daddy on the weekend. He'd take us around to the neighborhoods, and he'd say, "Gee, we're lost. I don t know if we can get back home." We would be, "What? Are you telling us the truth? You really don't know where we are?" He used to laugh. We'd get a good chuckle out of it.

A high school Italian teacher by profession, Sabrina remembers that during her teenage years her father liked to have fun with members of various religious sects who would come to the door to discuss their religion. Her story was made even more endearing as she recounted it in her father's Italian accent:

He invites them in, "Come in, come in" and says, "You wanna some wine? You wanna some espresso?"

They're like, "Oh no, we don't drink any of that kind of stuff."

He'd look at them and go, "Why? Why you not drink? I no understand. I no see wine, I no see espresso, I no see meat for so many years during World War II. God make wine, God make meat, God make coffee for me to enjoy, and I enjoy."

They would sit there and stare at him and look like they were thinking, "This man is crazy."

Then he'd say, "How old are you?"

They'd say, "Nineteen, twenty."

My dad would look at them and say, "Okay, it's August. You live in California. Beautiful sun, beautiful beach, so many beautiful girls on the beach. You waste time on a bike?" We would just die. They would just stare at him, and then my dad would say, "You wanna know where your priest is? He's home, drinking wine in the air conditioning. He sends you, in the hot August, to come to my house. Go to the beach; have fun. You twenty years old. What are you doing?"

Oh my God, it was hysterical . . . they wouldn't come to our house anymore. My dad was convinced they were at the beach — he had converted *them*!

Her father's enjoyment of play stayed with Joann, one of the first women to contact us to be interviewed, throughout her childhood:

He was always very playful with us when we were children. He was definitely the fuel that could feed your imagination, and he loved fireworks. The Fourth of July was his favorite holiday. He really, really relished it.

Having said that, as children I guess that was our favorite time of year. The summertime, out of school, it's almost a free-for-all. You can stay up as late as you want, and you didn't have to get up for school in the morning.

Every June he would get his pickup, and he would come home with all of these fireworks and lay them all out. He'd pick up a bag of firecrackers and say, "Smell it; smell the gunpowder." He made so many instruments for us to put the bottle rockets in, and [he would] ignite them.

That was a big part of our childhood and growing up. He was a great improviser — whatever he had at hand he made work. Whether it was streaming rain and he rigged some tarp together as a rain cover for the barbecue . . . it was just a lot of fun . . . You want to talk about a kid in a candy store? That was him on the Fourth of July.

Donna C., a professor of psychology who is deeply involved in Italian American studies, also described her father as having

oh, a tremendous, tremendous sense of humor. He would say this outrageous thing in Italian to someone who had no idea what he was talking about. We knew all these outrageous expressions. Those were the kind of things we knew, other than the simple things like thank you that you had to say to your grandparents — basic.

The one I always remember is — he would say in Italian what means in English, "Your face is as pretty as a pig's ass." He would see someone and we would be cracking up, because they would have no idea. I love telling that story, because he would walk up to somebody and greet them and kiss them and say that to them. The kids are like, "Oh my God, what if they find out what he is saying!"

He did have a tremendous sense of humor. He was always telling jokes, and yet in my house I never heard a racial epithet, ever. He never told a joke that ended in anything about ethnicity. And in that era, when I say that was how I grew up, people say, "Oh, no; you're kidding." But no, I never heard him utter anything like that.

Shared Interests and Shared Adventures

A father's vitality and sense of fun often turned time with his daughter into shared adventures. Such adventures helped daughters gain a sense of strength, feistiness, and confidence, as Adele G. describes:

> I remember him swimming in the East River — he was a great swimmer. I remember him teaching us how to swim. We used to go to Long Beach. My mother feared the water and he used to take my brother and me out with him, and of course I was there with him because I was the rambunctious one. My mother would sit on the shore and yell at us to come in, and my father would say, "Let's go out," and I'd say, "Okay, Dad!"

The ocean held a sense of adventure for both Tiziana, an exuberant mother of two children, and her dad as well:

> In the summer we would go to this private beach. My brother and my mother would just sit there, sun worshiping or doing something else, and my father and I would just run into the water and swim out to this big wooden thing. You would just lie on it. It was our time together.
>
> We had similar interests: we loved cold water; we loved to swim; we loved to swim fast. Even when we used to go places, if my father would come afterward, I would go home with my father in his car and my brother would go with my mom. The more I think about it, the more I realize we were just one. We just understood each other. It was those two memories, especially running into the water, because my brother didn't like cold water; neither did my mother. He would look at me and say, "Okay, let's go!" I'm like, "All right, I'm coming!"

LuLu spoke of adventures with her father, which focused on the theater and sometimes involved a sense of the forbidden:

> My favorite thing would be that after a ballgame, we'd go to a bar. He'd take me to a bar. I'd sit high up on a stool, and he'd have a beer and I'd have a ginger ale.

I had all these adventures with him, but my fondest memories were [staying] up at night with him, watching movies. We also had a theater group, and I wanted to be an actress from a very young age. I was at a theater group with him, and I'd have small parts. They did a play called . . . *Ah, Wilderness!*, which was a Eugene O'Neill play, and I played the young girl in that. We had fun.

Linda G. and her father shared a close relationship and adventures with airplanes:

It was very close. He played with me a lot. He literally bounced me on his knee. He would take me with him when he went places. Of course there were no car seats, just kind of hop in beside him . . . I was close to my mother too because I am an only child. But he and I were very close.

He always had an airplane. I thought it was normal. My father had a pickup truck; my mother had a car; my father had an airplane. All his friends had airplanes . . . He would take me to the airport with him. He would take me flying. My mother didn't like to fly, so that actually worked out fairly well . . . If we wanted to fly somewhere, she would drive, because when you get to where you're going, you need a car. So we did that together.

Then I developed an interest in horses and he was not particularly interested in horses. Of course he had grown up on the farm and horses were work animals. So that was a little bit of a split. He would drop me at the barn, and he would go to the airport. But we remained close . . .

One time he took his airplane . . . to Woonsocket, Rhode Island for its annual inspection . . . I was probably seven or eight. We were heading back to Norwood, and I can honestly say it was the first and only time I ever saw him look frightened in an airplane. As we started to take off, even I could tell something wasn't right.

The airplane was skipping. It was like it was coughing. We literally barely made it through the trees. As soon as we were up he started saying to me, "I want you to look for the airport in Norfolk." I'm in the window looking, looking, and I found it. We landed there, and then he had to make a couple of calls, no cell phones, so he had to somehow find my mother and let her know where we were.

That was a big deal. He was very, very proud of me. He talked about it and talked about it. I think every time he talked about it, the trees became a little bigger and I was a little more instrumental in finding the airport, and I grew a little taller with each telling of the story.

Rosanne B., a noted documentary filmmaker, has memories that eloquently express what many psychologists believe — a father is key to his daughter's exploration of the world:

When I was in fifth or sixth grade, my parents bought a little tiny summer house out in Patchogue, Long Island. My mother and I used to stay there for the summer, and my father would drive back and forth for the weekends or maybe once during the week. He taught me how to play badminton; he taught me how to play ping-pong out there.

I don't think he taught me how to ride the bicycle. In Brooklyn my mother would not let me ride a bicycle; she was afraid I would get hurt. I wasn't allowed to roller skate, either. There wasn't much she would let me do. But in Patchogue, it was little country roads, so I learned everything there . . . My father was not about fear of the world. My father was about, "Let's learn how to handle the world."

Shared Connection

Experiencing moments of a shared connection between the women and their fathers was another striking theme we discovered, one that was a consistent thread throughout the stories we heard.

Some of these moments with dad were quiet and sweet, as Sabrina remembers:

I was his little girl. He loved all of us kids equally, but I tended to be the more affectionate one out of all the children, so I was always attached to my dad. I always had to be in his lap, always had to be hugging him. We were really close.

Maria T. recalls a similar sense of physical closeness:

I have some happy childhood memories. I loved going to the library. Sometimes I'd bring home the same books because there were ones that I especially liked. My father would put me on his lap and read to me.

I remember when I was nine or ten, I got into researching day trips. You could take a bus and go to . . . Pennsylvania Dutch Country, things like that, and I remember going with my father. We had just a very warm, uncomplicated, close relationship. When I was a teenager and having constant fights with my mother, he was the voice of calmness.

Maria G. also fondly recalls physical affection:

He was very affectionate. I was definitely Daddy's little girl. It was like that, certainly before adolescence and even after. I'd sit on his lap when I was a little girl. He would pick me up if we were in a crowd, put me on his shoulders. My mother always claimed he spoiled me, but let's put it in the context of the time period, because spoiling then, that's nothing compared to what counts as spoiling now!

Simply being in her father's presence evoked a sense of closeness for Adele:

We lived in an apartment building, and my mother would be cooking and my father would be downstairs in the pool room and she would tell me, "Go down and get your father." My father would be playing pool with his friends, and I remember it was always so wonderful, the camaraderie with his friends. I would peek my head in, and I'd call, "Daddy?" and he would tell me to come on in. He always did like to show his daughters off. That made him feel good, and now that I look back on it, it made me feel good, too, just being there with him.

Time alone with Tiziana's father often involved them walking together:

On Sundays he had his day off, and he would take us to Glen Island. There was a private beach, and that was our time together. On Wednesdays he would pick me up from school, and we would have pizza together, and that was my day with just him and me. I just remember the walk and going in to have the pizza, the whole scenario. We would walk home, which was funny because he had a car, but I guess he just wanted to walk with me. I'm just realizing that now, that we would walk.

Marianna D.T. recalled an incident, which she wrote about in a previously published essay, that demonstrated her father's determination to do his best for his young daughter:

> We were making kites, so we made the kites and we went to fly them. It was just the two of us, and we had a great time. My kite got caught and it was getting dark, but my father kept trying to get the kite down; he kept trying. So then I remember turning around, heading back toward the house, and he put his arm around my shoulder. He said, "Well, we had fun, though," but I probably didn't say it because I was so obsessed about losing my kite.

Families Together

Some of the most beloved childhood reminiscences involved the family spending time together. Including extended family and neighbors could increase the fun.

Karen D., a visual artist whose apartment was filled with colorful artwork and artifacts from her travels, quite humorously described a typical family outing:

> We vacationed together as a family. We would meet at my aunt's on an early Sunday morning and drive in tandem to Maine. You'd think we were going to the northern reaches of Canada! Five, six cars in a row. The neighbors — the Doyles, the Delucas — everybody.
>
> Everybody would meet, and everybody was told, "You bring the meatballs; I'll bring the bread; you bring the salad." Halfway through this trip the cars would all stop; the doors would open; the trunks would open; and we'd all have Sunday lunch. Someone would marvel, "Look, the macaroni's still hot!"

In Giovanna C.'s family, outings included dreaming about what might be:

> One of our fun things we used to do on Sunday as a family was go look at the new houses that were being built. We would all get in the car and drive around, and my father would say, "Let's go look at the houses going up on such-and-such avenue." We'd drive over there and look at them.

We owned our own house, but just like cars, we were always looking at cars and houses . . . we loved doing that. We looked at all these houses and we got to imagine what it would be like to live in this house or that house. My parents would discuss the houses and the prices, and then we'd go to Carvel and get ice cream.

Barbara D. recounts cherished memories that included her father bringing his family into the world he loved and then passing that love on to his daughter:

My father loved the shore. He loved the beach, and each summer we'd all pack up and we'd all go down to the beach. I think that was one of the things that I kind of remember the most. He really enjoyed being down at the beach. He would paint down there. He loved to fish. I think his love of nature and his appreciation of it, I think that's what I remember the most.

For Barbara Q., a novelist whose stories include tales of Italy, the family moments were quieter and simpler:

He was a very good dad. He had erratic work hours; so that was good — he was around a lot. He would often go out on calls at night, after dinner, but he was always home for dinner. We ate dinner early. He would always come home every night with a box of pastries from the bakery and his Italian bread. We would have that every night.

Every woman we interviewed learned so much from her father — by his instruction, by his example, and by simply being in his presence. The memories shared in these stories illustrate what psychologists are beginning to realize: the early connection a daughter has with her father does, in fact, matter — and matter greatly.

The experiences the women had with their dads triggered the construction of a template for relating throughout their lives — which we will explore further in Part III. As the years progressed, their reminiscences formed the tapestry of who the daughters became and what they treasured in their relationships with their fathers.

Pause and Reflect

As you have read here in Part II, the early memories that we have of our fathers are often both dear and endearing and can carry with them the innocence and simplicity of doing modest things together — listening to the radio, having family dinners, or hearing simple words intended as protection. Sit quietly and allow yourself to revisit your childhood and recall some of your own special moments with your father.

+ *Can you remember the moments when you felt safe and secure just by being with your dad or by something special he would do?*
+ *Close your eyes and recall a childhood memory involving you and your dad. Try to envision the place where you are — the sights, the smells, the sounds.*
+ *What do you think you learned from your dad at that moment?*
+ *Did you learn something about yourself?*
+ *Was he trying to teach you about one of the things he valued?*
+ *Is this something that you carried with you into adulthood? In what way?*
+ *Silently thank him for it!*

PART THREE

STEPPING INTO ADULTHOOD WITH OUR FATHERS: CONNECTION AND DISCONNECTION

*W*e all remember our teen years and those just beyond, when we crossed the bridge from childhood into adulthood. As teens, we tried to forge new relationships with our parents that included increased autonomy, a new identity, new freedoms, and new explorations of the world. So much of what happened during those years and how we weathered the storm set the stage for our adulthood relationship with our fathers.

In the Italian American family, the tug-of-war leading into young adulthood may be highlighted for daughters. The father's role as head of the family and decision maker may produce more opportunity for conflict — overt or covert. Historically in Italian culture, daughters, above all else, had to show respect for their fathers and individual interests were to be subjugated to those of the family.

Oftentimes daughters were not allowed the same freedoms as sons or even non-Italian girls their age. Second-generation daughters lived in two worlds — one of traditional Italian values and one of the dominant culture; so depending on the extent of acculturation of both the father and the daughter, arguments could arise over such common parent-teen disagreements as going out, being home for family dinners, and dating — but with the level of conflict multiplied by the separation between old-world tradition and modern ways.

Our stories below integrate these concepts. We have conflict with our fathers, but we manage to weather it, and it is actually through this conflict that the levels of intimacy with our fathers deepen. We learn, as teens, to express our opinions, have them heard, and move on.

Two Strong-Willed Sicilians (Lorraine)

I cannot remember a time when my father and I didn't argue, debate, and have strong — and, at times, stormily opposing — opinions about broad topics, such as politics and social issues, and intimate ones of family, relationships, and life choices. We were "idea people" at our core, and sometimes those ideas clashed.

Yet I also cannot remember a time when that conflict estranged or disconnected me from my father for more than the duration of the argument or a bit of sulking afterward. However, there is family lore that when I was three or four, I said something in anger to my father, who responded that if I couldn't say something nice to him then I shouldn't say anything at all. Apparently, I proceeded to not talk to him for what he felt was an intolerably long time, and he came begging me to speak to him. Maybe that is why our later arguments never progressed to the level of estrangement!

While our relationship involved two strong-willed Sicilians debating their points, I also see us as always talking together, colluding about some event, noticing similar details, sharing a certain perspective. We were negotiating a balance of independence and community; freedom and responsibility; the world of love, family, and intimacy and the world of adventure, striking out on my own, and individuality.

Born in the middle of the baby boom and growing up in the 1960s, those famously comfortable years of childrearing when kids were let out of the house in the morning and didn't come back until dinner, I am still surprised that no one was ever badly hurt, lost, or drowned in "the pond" where we spent most of our waking moments. I had my parents' trust about where I went, the company I kept, and how late I stayed out (my older sister softened them up). My dad had his own sense of adventure and independence and didn't squelch that in me.

On the crucial issues we did not fight, but my father let me know, quietly from the heart, that he disagreed with my path or was concerned how it would affect me or the family.

During my sophomore year in college I embarked on many changes. I applied to transfer to a larger school, farther from home. A friend and I were gleefully undertaking the proverbial "backpacking trip through Europe" during spring semester, and I was home to earn money for the trip — no small challenge mid-recession!

My dad, not usually a worrier, worried about all this and let me know, and we had time together that winter to talk: Could I earn enough money to make the trip and still help with college expenses? (Yes, I would be back to work in the summer!) Could I keep getting financial aid despite taking time off from school? (Yes!) Could I still graduate on time? (I had taken extra courses!) Would I be okay in Europe? (The last time he was there, they had been shooting at each other.) Would my mother worry? (The only thing my mother asked of me was to not go to Sicily because she was afraid they would marry me to someone.) Would I really return to school, or would I lose my motivation? (Not a chance!)

In the end, he handed me extra cash and kissed me good-bye on the platform as I waited with Thea for the train to Montreal (for student airfares) in a late March blizzard.

He swallowed his sadness and was proud of me for going off on the adventure of a lifetime and for connecting up with family in Italy. When I returned months later, he listened more raptly than anyone else to my stories of Europe, the details, the people, the art, the food, the churches, the amazing cultural differences, and the telling moments with people from Greece, Italy, Spain, Germany, the Netherlands, Czechoslovakia, and France. He nearly came to tears when I told him of his uncle he had never met, who wept at my arrival.

He was proud that I had traveled to Prague at a time when no one was traveling to Prague, a few years after the Prague Spring, and that people in that broken city had embraced me. He saw that I knew what it was like to have my Hermann Hesse novel and my journal grabbed and scrutinized by scornful border guards. His daughter had needed to see the lost side of Europe and her homeland of Italy, returning safely with new visions of our world and history. I became some kind of a grown-up to him at that point, although I would stay in school and live mostly with my parents for many more years.

Taking Flight (Donna)

The dynamic with my father during my teen years was much as Lorraine describes above. My father was second-generation Italian, and although he was in many ways assimilated, he brought to his family the Italian prescriptions of family loyalty and obedience and the idea that daughters are to be especially protected.

My sixteen-year-old self had very different ideas about freedom, so of course I chose a few friends who seemed more daring and outspoken than I was at that time. Interestingly (and probably much to their later chagrin), for my sixteenth birthday my parents gave me a ten-speed bike, my ticket to freedom and exploration.

One summer night, a friend invited a few of us over to play cards and hang out. When I asked my father about spending the night, he asked if her parents were going to be home. They were not, but of course I did not see the issue with that and told him so. He predictably said no, I could not go; so I argued and then sulked in my bedroom for a few hours — until I remembered my bike in the garage.

When my parents were safely tucked in on our upstairs porch for their usual after-dinner coffee and cigarette, I tucked pajamas under my shirt and sped off down my driveway, down the street, and to my friend's house on my chariot of freedom — the ten-speed bike they had given me. After an uneventful night of playing cards and then a huge breakfast the next morning, we rode our bikes to the beach to watch the sunrise and stayed the day — and then I decided that it was time to go home and face the music.

When he saw me come into our apartment, my father became angrier than I had ever seen him before. He sat me down in the living room and pronounced that I was going to be sent to military school. He told me, his face wearing a grimace that I will never forget, what a disrespectful daughter I had been to do such a thing. I remember crying and saying to him, "It doesn't matter how good I am [I was a straight-A student and never really gave them any cause for concern], you don't understand who I am!"

My father looked at me as if I had three heads — as if who I was in the family left nothing that needed to be known. I cannot recall exactly how this argument ended (although there was certainly an apology on my end), but I did not go to military school, and my father and I resumed our weekly Sunday afternoon movie watching together shortly thereafter.

As I moved into adulthood, the thought that my father did not know me seemed like a foreign idea, one that no longer applied to the relationship we had built. The conflicts of my teen years ultimately settled into a collegial relationship in which I sought out my father's opinion about work matters, movies, and skeletons in the family closet — the growing pains long behind us.

CHAPTER FIVE

THE TIDE SHIFTS: RENEGOTIATING CONNECTION

*A*lthough a period of new discoveries, the teen years are also a time of mourning: a father must say good-bye to the little girl he once knew, and a daughter must say good-bye to the image of her dad as infallible, as well as to the child that she once was. While Western culture focuses on the teen totally separating from his or her parents, we consider it more a time of *renegotiating* these relationships. Arietta Slade, a psychologist known for her work with children and adolescents, speaks of the need for this different *type* of connection — one that includes newly negotiated freedoms that honor the attachment between parent and child (Slade 2004). Her research indicates that teenagers still depend on their parents for help in making major decisions and remain in need of parameters, boundaries, structure, and connection.

Because of the ongoing changes in their relationships, fathers and teen daughters may find themselves at odds with each other. He may fight to retain control of his daughter in a way that no longer fits, while she fights for more independence and a voice in her destiny. The once compliant child may become a snarling, contradictory alien; Dad may be unreasonable and old-fashioned. If not managed well and with a great deal of flexibility — that is, "renegotiated" — the teen years can be a painful time for everyone involved.

The stories of the women we interviewed reflect the mingling of pleasure and turmoil of the teen years. Themes of protectiveness vs. freedom and mothers vs. fathers emerged, and experiences varied according to the generation of the father and his level of acculturation.

Protectiveness vs. Freedom

The fathers of many of the women we interviewed increased their vigilance in keeping their daughters safe during her teen years. This heightened vigilance, of course, coincided with the daughter's burgeoning sexuality and growing identity as a woman.

In many Italian American families, it was important that daughters remain virtuous and not bring any shame on the family. So, for some of the women we interviewed, going out of the house in a short skirt was seen as jeopardizing her honor!

The generation in which a daughter went through her teens had a bearing on which of her behaviors brought on conflict. Helen, for example, was a teenager in the 1930s, so a boy even coming to the house caused quite a stir:

> Oh, I had one bad episode in the teenage years. Before I went to the convent school I was in a regular American high school. I think that I was in my sophomore year, and one of my classmates, a boy named Jerry, drove up to the house to call on me. My father charged out of the front door, yelling, "What are you doing? Get out of here!" And that was not good!

For Barbara Q., a teenager in the 1970s (the era of free love!), the conflicts took on a different form:

> His "Daddyness" really came out when I was sixteen. He was very against me piercing my ears. He said I would look like an immigrant. All the immigrant babies had their ears pierced, and he was very much into being Americanized and melding into society. I kept saying, "Everybody has pierced ears. I'm the one who looks strange." I didn't pierce my ears until I was in law school, living away from them.
>
> I also remember I wore a minidress once, and he was totally shocked. He said to me, "You're not going out like that!"
>
> I said, "Dad, everybody goes out like this; if I don't go out like this I'll look strange."
>
> He replied, "I don't think you should go out like that."
>
> I did go out like that; my mother backed me up, and it wasn't that bad. I know that he was just worried about me; he was a man, and he was

afraid of what might happen to someone who was young and attractive. He said, "That's not how people dressed when I was growing up."

It is not unusual for Italian American families to draw a circle of proximity around their children, especially during the teen years. A few women described this circle as their fathers' rules on being out in the world. These rules often resulted in conflict, but it was conflict embedded in connection, and the daughter often came to understand her father's good intentions.

While it raised difficulties in her teenage years, as an adult Adele had some understanding of her father's position in retrospect:

My relationship with my father was very good until my teenage years. Not that I was rebellious, but I was not allowed to do a lot of things. For example, I wasn't allowed to have anyone sleep over. I could go to dances, but my mother took me and my mother picked me up.

I think that my father was very strict because he saw his sisters run around — they had a couple of husbands and got divorced, which was a no-no — and I don't think he wanted that for me. He didn't mind me bringing everybody home for dinner on a Sunday or a Saturday night — everyone would come to our house because I couldn't go out. My father and I butted heads a lot, but I understand now what he was doing.

L. had a similar feeling of both irritation and understanding:

Oh, we used to fight all the time! We were always fighting. My father was very strict, so he kept us on a short leash. He had four of us born within five years, so during adolescence he had four teenagers going in every direction. As I said, he was very anxious about us getting hurt or something happening to us. I think every Italian family was like that; it was the way it was then.

Imma also reflected on understanding her father's position:

Oh, I've got to tell you a story. I was eighteen at the time and was going over to Peter's house. At that time he was my boyfriend [now her husband]. He lived maybe a mile away. I was friends with his sister, and then when they knew I was going to marry her brother, I would visit at their house.

One night there was a huge snowstorm, and you could not even walk. My father wanted me home. He would not let me stay there, even though these people were my future in-laws. They had to take me home in the blizzard, walking — three men and myself. It took a couple of hours! Like I said, I loved my father, but he was strict. Maybe sometimes they loved you too much that it was wrong, but in his mind he was right.

Karen D. describes a scene that was equally frustrating for a teen girl:

We were required to be home for dinner every night. We had to be there before my father got home, and in high school that became more difficult: we had our afterschool activities.

I remember getting yelled at one day for getting home late because I was in the art studio making family Christmas cards, and I got tied up with the cleanup. As soon as I walked through the door my father yelled, "Where were you?"

"I was doing the Christmas cards, Dad. I was silk-screening Christmas cards."

He said, "Well, you're late!"

I said, "Yeah!"

So he was rigid in that regard.

Some of the women's teen years were somehow managed despite significant difficulties. This may indicate the enduring bond these women had with their fathers, as Donna C. so matter-of-factly expresses:

During my adolescent years my relationship with my father was very turbulent. I was a tough adolescent with a lot of concerns. It seemed to me that we were always battling over something. Then, I don't know, we just sort of woke up one day and it was over.

Despite the protectiveness that some women experienced during their teen years, they also experienced some very tender moments with their fathers, particularly as young adulthood loomed on the horizon, as Donna C. continues:

When I was about sixteen, I essentially ran away to get married and got pregnant. We were somewhere in the Midwest and my father called me, and he was in tears. It was the first time in my entire life I had ever heard my father cry. He said, "Look, I understand. Come back; we'll work it out." We did go back, and it was quote "worked out." The marriage didn't last, but that changed my relationship to my father.

She goes on to say:

> Even though we were at loggerheads, I felt he made tremendous effort to understand who I was and to speak to me. Some folks talk about Italian fathers who were working all the time and closed the door to you — absolutely not. We had a conversing relationship throughout our adult lives which I really cherish and, I always say, I miss.

These tender moments often included very concrete loving gestures, gestures that spoke to an understanding of the needs of the daughter, either real or perceived. Sabrina describes such a moment with her father:

> In junior high and high school, my mom never drove so my dad would have to run all the errands and go grocery shopping. It was always me doing those things with my dad — it was our routine.
>
> He would also do things for me; he was such a sweet man. When I was a teenager I was working and going to high school. I would come home from school sometimes and just run upstairs to finish homework really quick because I needed to work or needed to do something, and a lot of times I'd come downstairs and find my car in the driveway washed, with a full tank of gas. He was the best dad. He was amazing. He really was.

Her father's sensitivity is hidden in Rosanne B.'s example; even years later her father hid the softer reasons for his actions:

> I went to an all-girls Catholic college, and the people who went there were more middle and upper middle class at that time. It was the college for moneyed Catholic girls. We could just barely afford to send me there. My parents both had white-collar jobs. My mother was a bookkeeper and my father, when I was growing up, was an insurance broker. I don't think they identified themselves that way.
>
> Comes father-daughter weekend and, of course, my father came, but he didn't say a word the whole weekend because he was afraid he would

embarrass me. We were there sitting with the other girls whose fathers were, for example, the head of public works. He came to everything, but he didn't want to embarrass me. Years later, when I asked him why he wanted to send me to Catholic schools, he answered, "For control." I think that's pretty interesting.

Jackie's experience showed how her parents trusted her:

I know the times were very different, but I will always be grateful for the fact that my parents — they gave me a lot of liberty and freedom — they just trusted me. I did things that it surprised me that they permitted, like going out with boys. They did know the parents of these kids too, so that probably had a lot to do with it. But dating, I think that they just trusted me, and it was nice. It kind of translated to the relationship I had with my daughter.

Louise finds the humor in her dad's occasional disciplining:

My father had very big hands. He never, ever, ever would touch us because he was always afraid he would hurt us.

I have a funny story for you. I forget what I did this time, but he chased me in the house with the broom. But the funny part is . . . I ran into my bedroom and went up onto my bunk bed. He had built these great bunk beds for us . . .

He went to come after me with the broom and he hit the side of the bunk bed that he'd built, and the broom snapped in half. Well I started laughing hysterically . . . My mother said the minute that he closed the bedroom door he cracked up laughing. He was just trying to scare me. Whatever I did was a bad thing, but it was just poetic justice that his broom broke on the bed he built.

Christine P.'s father warned her about boys when she was fifteen:

He said, "Well I want to tell you about boys. When you kiss boys and you're with them and they lose their head, you can't control them." Meaning that you can't blame the boy for what happens. He let me know that it was my responsibility to be in control.

Mothers vs. Fathers

Another pattern emerged, which shed light on the differences between a daughter's relationship with her mother and that with her father. Many of the women described much more conflictual relationships with their mothers, with their fathers often undoing rules their mothers had set.

This was, perhaps, owing to strains within the marriage, the result of which was increased emotional bonding between father and daughter. For some of those we interviewed, the mother's role as the "gatekeeper" of the daughter's relationship with the father in childhood began to unravel as adulthood approached. We do not intend to diminish the impact of a daughter's relationship with her mother but to shed light on the often unrecognized relationship with the father.

Maria T. had some idea of why her relationship with her father was the way it was and thought her parents' relationship played a role:

> My father basically wasn't any kind of disciplinarian, so maybe part of it was just the dynamic between my parents that made it easier for me to have an easy relationship with him. He was never the one to say, "Your skirt's too short." That whole era, the coming of age — go braless and wear a mini! — it really was fraught with craziness between my mother and me, but my father just didn't get involved, for which I was grateful.

Conflict with her mother often led to a daughter's ceasing to identify with her, which brings into question the impact of gender role development. What does it mean if a daughter identifies with the qualities of her father? And how might this change the balance of the Italian American family? Tiziana's experience was very different from those of her Italian American friends:

> It was never turbulent between my father and me. It was just the opposite. My mother would give me a hard time about my curfew. He would say, "You know what? Just let her go. I have complete confidence in her, that she's not going to do anything wrong."
>
> They would fight because of this, because he would give me permission, and she didn't want me to go. He would say, "I'll wait up for her. Go to sleep; I'll wait up for her." He'd fall asleep on the couch. I'd have

to come in, wake him up. I'd say, "Okay, go to sleep." He'd be, "You home? You okay?"

So different, because when I talk to all my friends who are Italian, their fathers were the worst. They were so strict with them, like what they wore, how they dressed, who they were allowed to date. My father never gave me that problem at all. He trusted me.

I did not want to be like my mother. I wanted to be more strong. Excuse my language, but I grew a set of balls being around my dad. He molded me to be strong, and to be tough, and not to take crap from people. He was also compassionate and would be there if I needed him.

Giovanna C.'s experience also reflected a more conflictual relationship with her mother:

My mother and I got into really big arguments. Sometimes she would agree with me — she's the one that politicized me, too — because she was very progressive in many ways. My dad would mostly listen; occasionally he'd say something, but mostly he'd make some joking remark that turned the whole conversation into laughter. He was good at that.

In some cases, a father's alliance with his daughter even resulted in an overt dismissal of her mother, as in Sabrina's situation:

On Saturday and Sunday mornings, before my mom went to work, she would come in my room and wake me up early to tell me I needed to do the chores. She would remind me that I needed to get out of bed and wash the floors . . . and my Dad would walk in behind her, close the blinds again, and put the covers back on me and say, "You can sleep another two hours. It's early; your mom's crazy."

Giovanna B.L.M.'s father was protective

but not overprotective. When I was admitted to Bronx High School of Science, my mother complained because I had to take the subway. My father sat her down and said, "Yes, she has to take the subway, but this is the best school in the system, and it's an honor to go to this school, so she will learn to take the subway. I'll go with her the first time." Which he did, and then I went to school by subway.

P.B. called her father when she had a car accident in college:

Somebody rear-ended me. The first thing you do, of course, you had to go to a pay phone. I called my father. He used to joke that I was so upset, I was so afraid to tell him, that he's going, "Hello, hello," and nothing was coming from my end because I was trying not to cry.

My dad, whenever anything was wrong, he would say, "It's going to be all right. Don't worry; everything's going to work out." We kind of had an understanding; he was my best pal. We had kind of a bond that I didn't have with my mother. I love my mother, but I can't even explain it, something unspoken with him.

Sometimes daughters directly saw unfair or sexist attitudes toward their mothers, as C.N. notes:

As far as my parents' relationship being complicated, I think that as much as I loved my father and always felt close to him, I would say I became a feminist because of my father's attitudes toward women. Feminism was sort of a reaction against him because he was extremely sexist then.

I do think this is sort of an Italian trait. I don't know if it is a stereotype, but I think some Italian men have an attitude that their mothers and their daughters are sort of saints. Their wives, well, not so much. Their wives are there to serve them. I don't think that all Italian men think that, but I think that was definitely my father's attitude. I know that he loved my mother, but he did kind of treat her as a servant to some extent.

We compartmentalize things, and so I was able to. Although there were times when I was upset with the way my father might treat my mother about something, it didn't make me not love him.

In this chapter you have read stories about how the father-daughter relationship shifts during the teen years. Sometimes these years were marked by conflict between fathers and daughters; sometimes respect developed, which led to a different level of understanding; and sometimes, the mother-daughter relationship changed, as well.

What clearly emerges from these stories, however, is the maintenance of the connection between father and daughter — the weathering of the storms, the tenderness in times of difficulty — with the fathers learning who the daughters were and (to paraphrase Donna C.) how to speak to them in the language of adolescence. Whatever the boundaries between father and daughter during childhood, the teen years caused them to be made anew.

CHAPTER SIX

FORGING AN IDENTITY

*T*he teen years and early adulthood are the developmental periods when we begin to find our own way in the world and to separate from our parents. During these years, we can follow a number of paths: we can develop our own ideas about careers and relationships, we can adopt our parents' views, or we can remain psychological children and, like Peter Pan, never grow up.

According to the work of renowned developmental psychologist Erik Erikson (who developed a theory of psychological stages of development throughout the lifecycle; 1950/1994), adolescence is a time of identity vs. role confusion. During these years, a girl often asks herself the big questions: Who am I? How do I fit in? Where am I going in life?

Erikson believed that if allowed to explore, an adolescent would form her own identity. However, if her parents continually pushed her to conform to their views, she would face identity confusion. According to Erikson's theory, an "identity crisis" can occur if the young woman cannot resolve who she is in the world. Carol Gilligan, a social psychologist who focuses on women's development, noted that for women, Erikson's stage of intimacy vs. isolation (or the importance of developing relationships as opposed to avoiding them) may in fact be a period that stretches across the lifespan and consistently holds great importance (1982).

When all goes well (though we know that it often doesn't), this time can be an exciting one, with parents and teens relating to each other in new ways: parents and daughters having in-depth discussions about current events, daughters sharing their newfound opinions and ideas, or parents supporting daughters' newly discovered creativity.

For the father-connected daughter these processes tend to run smoothly. The ability of a daughter to separate from her parents and renegotiate the closeness of that connection as she develops her identity results in adaptable decision making, self-direction, and a sense of agency.

Negotiating Cultural Ties: Following a Career Path

Because of the close-knit nature of many Italian American families and some Italian American fathers' wish to protect their daughters from prejudice they experienced, issues of control between father and daughter often dominate a daughter's decisions about education and career, as they did for Karen D.:

> I wanted to go to art school, and he discouraged that. He wanted me to do a more commercial venture, commercial art. My dad said, "You should go to Northeastern." He didn't want me to go to any of the state schools; he thought I probably had more talent than that. Northeastern had a cooperative program so you could work and go to school, so that made it affordable for him. I applied the summer before my senior year in high school and I got accepted . . . so that meant I was enrolled in the School of Business.
>
> Here I was, the August before college was starting, enrolled in the School of Business, studying marketing at a school that I didn't really want to go to. No one said to me in my senior year, "You know, you read a lot; what about a liberal arts college?" I just never got any guidance, which probably was not atypical. I mean for my father to send his daughter to college anyway was unusual.
>
> But the light bulb went off in my head when they sent us our registration packets. I thought, I don't want to take these classes! And also in my senior year I got a letter from the Art Institute of Chicago, saying, " . . . We'd be interested in your application." I think that was because of my art awards in high school. I thought, this will never fly with my father because (a) it's art school, and (b) it's Chicago.
>
> He said to me, "There's no need for you to go outside the city of Boston. You can study in Boston, and you can commute from home." That was the part I didn't like. I commuted from home. I resented it at the time, but I realized it was just his own fear: his fear of losing me, and his fear of what that world was, and the fact that that world hadn't been kind to him or his family.

Christine P. speaks of her father's attitude toward her career choices:

> He was not supportive, I can put it that way. He was loving, affectionate, but he was not supportive. He wanted things his way. I remember in my

late twenties, in an impulsive moment, I applied and got into Harvard Business School. Oh God. I said to my family, "Maybe I want to go to Harvard Business School?" My father stopped talking to me again. Of course I didn't go. No regrets on that one.

Rosa's experience spoke to what she describes as the conflict between immigrant and mainstream values:

The relationship with my dad was very close, but in terms of education for their kids, immigrant families had different aspirations and values. I would say to my father, "You sent me to the best schools, you sent me to Europe to have that experience, yet where you want me to be is in New Haven."

Without question he had a hard time with me getting my own apartment, doing those things that moved me in a different, nontraditional kind of direction. That was hard for them, and it was hard for me. He was looking for me to get married and have kids and so forth.

While LuLu was able to pursue the career she wanted, she felt the need to create a sense of separation and did so through the identity of her name:

I know that when I was starting to do art, I was thinking of using another name. I think that was my little act of separating myself because I grew up here. When I went down the street it was always, "That's Pete's daughter. That's Rose's daughter." I was, in a way, making my own identity by changing my name.

For Jean, while her father "found his way" to helping her pursue an education, there were parameters for keeping in contact once she was away. She describes her need to push back against his wishes regarding her graduate education, illustrating a daughter's need to follow her own path:

Somehow my father found his way, after arguing with me relentlessly about always having my head in a book, and I ended up at American University. I remember when we went down to enroll me, he said, "Look, the deal is you've got to stay here for four years. It's not optional that you drop out or transfer somewhere else. I don't want you to call — write." I never kept the letters from our continuous stream of correspondence over the years.

I did graduate four years later. When I finished, I won a scholarship to Ohio State to do graduate work. I think he was very pleased — one, that I finished; two, that I got a graduate degree. But, when I received my undergraduate degree in government and public administration, he wanted me to enter a school of business! The more he pushed, [the more] I went in the opposite direction, ultimately getting a graduate degree in journalism.

Romantic Love

Conflicts with dad about the choice of a romantic partner often had a good outcome among the women we interviewed. A strong sense of self, which resulted from the daughters' identification with their fathers, helped them negotiate this conflict.

Cynthia F. was ready to separate from her family if needed:

Probably the worst conflict I had with my father was regarding my husband, who is Japanese American. We met when we were freshmen at the university and started dating. I came home for vacation and said, "I'm so excited. College is so cool. I'm meeting so many different people, and the guy I'm dating is Japanese."

All of the forks dropped at the dinner table, and my parents informed me that they considered this to be an interracial relationship and that if I didn't stop they would pull me out of school. I told my dad that he [my father] was not the man he always told me he was, but we all got around it and we all figured our way through it.

At some point I said to my parents, "This is who I'm going to marry, and you can either accept it, and that's great, or you can decide you don't want to see me again, and I don't want that but that's what's going to happen." They grudgingly accepted it, but it took quite a while.

It actually took until my father lived with us, and my husband was very good to him. My father continually reminded us of what kind of mistake he had made, and we'd say to him that we have daughters, too, and we understand completely what he was trying to do. Everything turned out okay!

Joann's strong sense of self influenced how she handled the problem of dating:

There really wasn't much conflict, because my dad really didn't know the daily goings-on. Not that I was a rebel or anything like that, but he didn't know the day-to-day.

I can remember there was one huge argument. At the time it was earth shattering. I wanted to date a boy he didn't like, and that was the end of the world then. I can remember tears. I think my mom may have intervened a little bit; you know, "The more you push, the more you push her toward," so the reins were kind of loosened. It [the relationship with her boyfriend] just kind of petered out and disintegrated on its own.

Linda G. described a romantic conflict involving a major sociocultural issue of the times, the ill will between Italians and the Irish:

He was very, very protective when it came to boyfriends — almost to a point where it was not a good thing. I'm sure I'm not the first person to say this. When I was sixteen or seventeen I had a boyfriend who I probably didn't really like all that much, but it sort of became a conflict between Dad and me. That was very difficult.

We argued and I don't think at that point my father was able to articulate his dislike and his reasoning. I do remember Dad saying that he had bad teeth . . . and that he was Irish. I was just beginning to understand the Irish-Italian enmity that existed, partly because of growing up in a town where there weren't many Irish people . . . The way that resolved is I married the boyfriend, and it was a terrible marriage and I got divorced. And everything my father said was correct.

Evolving: Becoming Our Own

Karen D. had her own inner critic, which was embedded in her need for her father's approval, and some conflicts with her dad remain unresolved:

I think that some conflicts I weathered, but the one that I don't think I weathered the best is the need for his approval and the underlying implication that there's a criticism or not meeting standards. I think that I've carried that to adulthood.

I think when you first told me you were coming over and I began to think about things, one thing I thought to myself was, had he lived another ten years, which we all thought he was going to, I might have been able to work through some of that.

He died when I was forty-five; my children were still young. I had moved away to Mexico . . . when I was thirty, and my twenties were tumultuous years for me, so I don't know that I had an opportunity to kind of go through some of that.

I drew and painted a lot when I was a kid, and he was critical of that. I don't think he was critical of it with bad intentions; I think that he was just trying to get me to be good [at it]. Since that was something that he did — he also painted — it became an area of conflict.

We see B.'s identity evolving with input from her dad:

I was a counselor in training at a YWCA camp in Maine and . . . my father came up for Sunday visitation, and he sent me one of the few letters that he had ever written to me. He had been extremely moved to see me all dressed in white in this position of leadership, and accolades like that from my father were few and far between, even though I knew that he loved me and appreciated me . . .

One of the key instances which still reverberates in my life is that when I was a junior in high school, I was getting straight As in math . . . geometry, which I loved. Of course, I've become a sculptor . . . it all makes sense . . . It was the year of Sputnik. He insisted on taking me to MIT to meet the dean of admissions because he wanted me to be an engineer.

I was thinking of being a social worker or a nun. Of course, artist was in there but I had already decided that artist was too selfish, that I wouldn't be able to help the world, having grown up with a social worker mother involved with many immigrants, displaced persons after the Second World War . . . I had a very strong social conscience at a very early age because I met survivors of concentration camps who had lost their whole families.

I remember the dean looking at my grades and saying, "There's no reason why you couldn't come here if that's what you would like to do." . . . Although I felt really embarrassed in my Easter suit with my mom right beside me and my father, I have often reflected on his faith and his strong belief that it never made any difference that I wasn't a boy . . . There was always a strong belief that I could do whatever I wanted if I just went for it.

Developing political beliefs divided some daughters and dads. Christine P. gives an example of this:

I went to college. That's when the conflict began, because I demonstrated against Vietnam and he thought that was awful because it was un-American. He had fought in World War II. You have to support your country. To demonstrate, be against the war, was not the role that I should take.

College was a time of tension as C.Z. figured out who she was:

I'm sure, as a parent, I have total understanding now for what they experienced, the shock of it. I explained what I was planning on doing, which was to move across country, study modern dance with my best friend. They said to me, "This is a mistake. Don't do this." My mother said it, but I think they both felt it, "You're going to be a failure." I was shocked.

I had no real strong dance background, and I was going into a field that I knew very little about, but on the other hand, it makes a stubborn Italian, a strong-willed Italian shall we say, even that more determined to prove them wrong. I had to fall back on anxiety-driven performance. You're going to make this happen and shut off feelings of being unloved, unsupported, afraid. And I did. I just did it.

I am here today doing what I wanted to do when I had that notion back in 1972 . . . I always felt that my parents would never give up on me. I mean I would have to murder somebody before they might consider it . . . Blood is thicker than water. I felt it . . . knew it.

CarolP's father had difficulty with her gay friends:

Until that day [the day of her mother's funeral] he was always disgusted when I went with my friends for dinner or dancing or whatever . . . But that day after John dropped off the tray of lasagna, he turned around and said, "I'm so sorry I misjudged your friends. You pick good friends."

R.L.'s evolving identity required telling her parents she was gay and would be living with her partner. Although her mother did not accept her partner for many years, her father seemed to go out of his way to make her welcome:

ɪhere'd be times when she would come over, and my mother would just get up and leave the room. My father was so shy and so silent, and actually he started making small talk with her. It was shocking! He was just shy, and he really liked her.

She felt he was more sensitive because of his background:

I think it was the immigrant experience, because he would tell stories about how the nuns would not let him and his sisters speak Italian to each other at school and how he was very good at math but he was probably fourteen and with nine-year-olds and couldn't fit under his desk.

They'd have to go to the public bathhouse in south Boston, and the teachers would say negative things about the Italians needing to bathe more, so I always figured he was hypersensitive because of being a foreigner. America was not embracing diversity like America claims it is now.

Or [the reason for his kindness was] that he was just a compassionate heart.

Holding One's Own

These next two women — at odds with their fathers around significant life crises and differences — experienced extreme challenges attempting to negotiate through serious conflict. In one case the bond deepened; in the other it stretched and strained.

Andrianna describes a time of family medical crisis with her twin sister, when she had a big disagreement with her father:

My sister had an operation, and my brother went to Rensselaer Polytechnic Institute and he was going to a ballgame [with my father]. And I remember going over, and I said, "You know what, you're going to a ballgame and you have a daughter being operated on." And he looked at me. I said, "I don't mean to be disrespectful saying it, Dad, but why?"

He looked at me and he said, "Honey, you know why? Because I can't handle going in that hospital and seeing her like that." And he started to cry.

I said, "Please, I'm so sorry."

He said, "Don't apologize. Whenever you feel you got something to say, you say it. And if I think you're being disrespectful, I would say so."

Certain things that stay with you, and that was one big thing right there . . . That gave me the answer, which I was glad. I had thought, "Oh, because we're girls, because boys were always the number one thing." Anytime you did get mad and you did say something, he'd say, "You're right." But he was so strict and didn't change his mind. He would bang his hand and say, "This is what I say, and this is what you do." Yet he also listened.

For Christine P., becoming an artist meant somewhat of a leave-taking from her father:

All my life all I ever wanted to do was be an artist. My father wanted me to be a schoolteacher or secretary. I won scholarships when I was, I think, seven or eight to study art at Carnegie Mellon. They had a children's program. My father wouldn't drive me into Pittsburgh. Number one, he had his own things to do on Saturday. Number two, not what he wanted for me.

So I would go with another family, and I got carsick. I was so nervous, because this is what I wanted, and at the same time it was not what he wanted . . . So I was always this wonderful artist. When I was exhibiting in shows in high school, my father wasn't interested. Of course he'd go to the sports games. I was a cheerleader. But anything to do with art he was not interested in.

Then I wanted to go to art school. He didn't want me to go to art school. So I got a scholarship to the University of Pittsburgh, where I was studying Spanish, French, Portuguese, and Italian. I was studying four languages. I liked languages, too. After one semester I realized I really wanted to go to art school. I applied to art school . . . and my father stopped talking to me. He just completely cut me off, the slamming doors and brooding. He completely cut me off, really forced me to do something I didn't want to do.

Now the sad thing was, my sister went to art school. He let her go because I think he realized he had made a mistake because I was alienated from him. Anyway . . . he didn't talk to me until I decided to return to school in Pittsburgh. That was a big tumultuous time when I was demonstrating against Vietnam and trying to pull away and go to art school in New York.

He thought he raised me wrong because I wanted to do something that was outside of the circle of what he thought was acceptable, and [he thought] that I would ruin my life and be living in some attic somewhere, being a bohemian with no money, or who knows what, smoking marijuana, being wild. He didn't want his daughter to do that.

Her father embraced Italy's language but not its post-Renaissance art:

Hearing the Italian language was great, and some of the songs were great. He didn't focus much on the art [of Italy]. He kind of put out the message that the world art scene peaked and ended with Michelangelo. It was a class thing. I've come to realize that. Probably number one, he didn't want me to become that class: an artist. Number two, maybe he thought I would never be successful because I wasn't from that class. And number three, he didn't want me to be alienated from him.

Once she became an artist,

he hated it. I taught at B.U. [Boston University] for thirteen years. He would tell me that's not a job. That was awful. That's when everything was sour . . .

I was an artist and a writer. I had worked at other things for a while. I had my own business. That was all right. Then I worked as a journalist. That was all right. But as soon as I started writing fiction and not going to a regular nine-to-five job he'd say, "You're going to spend your whole life in a room and have papers going up to the ceiling all around you. You're going to fill up five rooms and you're not going to make any money."

The stories in this chapter illustrate how the daughters managed the process of growing up and out. As Nielsen reminds us, the daughter who is connected to her father is able to grapple with the issues of identity and relationship and manage them well. Even when the father's influence was great, many of these daughters were able to think critically and mindfully about how to craft their lives and make decisions that took them away from their fathers' own hopes and dreams for them. Whatever the external conflict may have been, the connection remained.

CHAPTER SEVEN

BEING SEEN AS AN ADULT FOR THE FIRST TIME

*I*f connections are rocked during the teen years, they are often healed during young adulthood. This period can be the "calm after the storm," and it is often during this time that you hear people say, "My relationship with my parents is better now; they treat me like an adult." Conversation may take on the tone of that between peers rather than between parent and child (although it may at times revert to that!). As you will hear Helen simply state below, "It was a much nicer relationship."

This transition can take many forms in Italian American culture: reaching a traditional milestone, such as marriage or children; being allowed to become more independent through traveling; or weathering a major life event with their fathers. A paradigm shift in the United States toward more closeness between parents and late teenaged/young adult children (Setterstein & Ray 2010) and toward "emerging adulthood" (Arnett 2006) has become popular, yet these are practices that many Italian American families have long embraced (Giordano et al. 2005).

Edging toward Womanhood

Because many of the women we interviewed were aware of their fathers' protectiveness during their teen years, we were interested in when they felt their fathers first saw them as adults. For Diane G., having children was the watershed event:

> I think when I had my son, because I was seventeen. At first when my husband wanted to get married, my father said, "No, you're not marrying her." He refused. My husband had to beg him to get married. I feel once I

had my son, he treated me more like an adult, because I took on so much responsibility.

He was always there for me, even in the hospital. He had someone come from Spain, one of his associates that he dealt with, and he brought the man up to the hospital. Mr. Polo his name was, Antonio Polo, and he came to visit me in the hospital. My father was so proud; he was just so proud of me as an adult, not like his child.

If he also gave you a responsibility, he trusted you even more. He would give me little responsibilities that he didn't give somebody else. He could trust me. I used to have to go to the bank for him once a month and clip coupons for him and deposit the money, and he trusted me to do that. I also held all of his savings bonds.

When she got married, L. entered adulthood in her father's eyes:

He always called me L___, and that was what he called me when I was a little girl. He was the only person. I don't think I ever grew up for him, except maybe as I was taking care of him that last year.

Actually, I think he did see me as an adult prior to that. I got married. We lived in the area, but he never expected that I was going to be there [his home] all the time, only coming for Sunday dinners every once in a while. It wasn't going to be every week; it wasn't going to be every weekend. I think he did see me as being grown up when I got married; I was twenty-three then.

It was the same for Maria T.:

I got married young, when I was twenty. It was between my junior and senior year of college. That forced my father to see me as an adult.

It was actually her brother's marriage that changed things for Barbara Q.:

When my brother got married, we drove my father back home . . . and he just broke down in tears. He was so upset that my brother was growing up and I was growing up, and he was crying about that in the back of the car.

I think that was the only time I saw him cry. I was twenty-two at the time. At that point I was engaged, so he knew I would be next. I was just struck by how much he cared, and I thought it was touching and sweet, and I started to understand the cycle of life — how you let your children go.

The psychological tension between holding on and letting go that the fathers felt was evident to some women, who say their fathers saw them as an adult for the first time when they went out into the world: traveling, getting their first professional job, making adult decisions about their lives. Sabrina describes her experience with this:

The first time my dad saw me as an adult . . . I think it probably was a little bit earlier than usual, because when I was sixteen, my parents asked me if I was going to get a car and what I wanted to do with my life, and I told them I didn't want a car, but I wanted to do high school in Italy for a year. I think that maybe then my dad probably looked at me for the first time and thought, "Okay, she's responsible. She's a big girl, and she's a good girl."

They let me go. They let me do it. It was amazing. It's kind of hard to answer that question completely, though, because I think my dad always saw me as his baby. At the same time, my dad got really sick when I was twenty-three, twenty-four. They had already moved to Italy, and he never really got to experience me as an actual adult.

The shift in her father's perception also came early for Tiziana:

I had my first real job at TWA when I was seventeen. When I was about eighteen [co-workers] planned a three-week trip, with the intention of touring Europe. When I wanted to go, my mother said, "Absolutely not; you're not going anywhere for three weeks . . . go ask your father."

I went right to his restaurant; I just knew he was going to say yes. I walked into the kitchen and said, "Papa, Mommy won't let me go around Europe for three weeks."

He said, "You have your passport?"

I said, "Yes, I have my passport."

"You packed?"

"Yeah."

"You need money?"

"No."

"Then bring me back a T-shirt from Spain," he said. "Have fun; be safe."

There you go, that's when he thought I was ready to be an adult.

The establishment of Barbara D.'s career was the marker for her dad:

He probably saw me as an adult when I got my first job. Up to that point I think he thought I was just nuts! Then when I started teaching, I think he finally figured out, you know, "She's going to make it. She's going to settle down, and she'll be okay."

Diana F.'s father let her make her own decision regarding a romantic relationship, which was the decision her father wanted her to make:

It was so funny, I was in my late twenties and I was going out with this guy who ultimately I thought I was going to marry. My father's remark to me was, "Well, you're old enough, but I'll tell you, you'll never marry this guy, because he's just all about himself and not you. You're old enough to know — you make a mistake, it's your mistake." I never married the guy.

For Joann, it was a college degree that did it:

After I graduated college — I was the first one in my family to graduate college — I think maybe that was a culminating moment when my father said, "Okay, she's an adult now."

Andrianna's movement into adulthood came as she was married, with her father seeing her as an adult but also reminding her new husband that he was still her father:

That's when all of a sudden, the love got even stronger. When you're a teenager, the strictness is there. But when I was eighteen years old and my in-laws to be wanted us to go to a Yankee ballgame, my fiancé came to my dad and said, "Mr. Renna, is it okay if I take Ann with my parents? We're going to stay overnight in New York." He looked at him and said, "Jim, I like you very much and Mr. and Mrs. Riley also, but no. Once she gets married she can go wherever."

Once we got married, he sat down with my husband. He looked at my husband and said, "There's only one thing I'm going to tell you: if

Anna ever does anything wrong, I want you to come to me. Don't you ever lay a hand on her or do anything that could make me upset. Because if she does something real bad, I will take care of her." Now even though Jim was going to be my husband, my father still made that point. I don't know if that means anything, but that to me was [that I was an adult], and still he was number one. My husband respected that.

R.L. was propelled into adulthood by letting her parents know she was gay:

I did come out to my parents as a lesbian right after I graduated from college, and I was not going to set a precedent by pretending my partner was my roommate and spending holidays apart . . .

I went over after work, then I said to my parents, "I'd like to talk to you in private. Can we go into your room?" Which was shocking, because I didn't know what they thought. I said, "I just wanted to let you know that we are gay, and I just want to be honest with you." My mother started crying and was all upset. And my father just hugged me.

In B.'s life the recognition of her adulthood came later and made up for something that was missing earlier:

When I was thirty-seven, I was living in California. My family was extremely upset that I had gone to the west coast. When my daughter was graduating . . . I begged my father to come out because I'd had a recent separation with the man I was sharing my life with. And I only got him there by saying, "Her dad's not coming; we just need a man from the family to be there."

He came on his own, which was extraordinary. I felt that we encountered each other as two individuals in a way that we never had before, because my mother was always in the middle. My mother was very loquacious, very generous, and really the head of the family.

I had been teaching classes and started an art program . . . I had gotten together a huge three-town art exhibit of children's work . . . My father met many of the parents, and he saw this extraordinary accomplishment that had never been done before and took a lot of coordinating with these three very disparate communities geographically separated by fifty miles.

I think that he really saw me, in a way, very differently than he had before. We spent a lot of time driving around together . . . We had these long conversations, and he shared thoughts with me, even private things about the family that he had never, at home, spoken of.

I felt as if I fell in love with my father in a sense. Those are just the words that came to me when he was leaving. That we had just really encountered each other in a very, very deep way. And it was a great gift . . . because I always felt like my father was missing somewhere. He was missing, physically. He was always working his two jobs. But I now realize that he was very present in my life in deeper ways.

Giovanna B.L.M. had trouble eating breakfast as a child, and her father always fixed breakfast for her:

I got married. If I talked to my father he would say, "Did you have breakfast today?" I would say, "Yes, I had breakfast." Six months passed before I decided that I'm now an adult woman, and I don't have to have zabaglione in the morning if I don't want it. I remember one day when he said, "Did you have breakfast?" and I said, "No, I didn't." He was wise enough to know that I am a married woman now, and if I don't feel like having breakfast, I can't be forced. I had grown up. He had pulled me through to adulthood, and I was all right now.

Turning Points

We were interested in turning points in the daughters' relationships with their fathers. We found that almost all of those who reported a turning point were positive about it and felt that the relationship changed for the better. It also often culminated in the daughter understanding what her father was attempting to do as a parent: teach a lesson, set an example.

Interestingly, this also often coincided with the daughter's marriage, a rite of passage in Italian American families, although for a few it happened after a divorce, either theirs or their dad's. For Helen, it occurred when she advanced in her career:

A turning point in our relationship? I became less in awe of him as I got older. I had my own family then; there wasn't that same kind of fear, like, I'd better be good or else. No, it was a much nicer relationship.

I think another turning point was when I was in Italy and began to write the articles for the *Syracuse Herald-Journal*. He wrote to me and said, "Send me what you are writing and I will take it to the paper." I think he was very proud of that. I think that that meant something to him, that I would write and send it to him. Then he would go down to the paper and say, "Here is my daughter's latest." So at that point things began to mellow out.

Adulthood was the point at which Adele felt that she finally understood her father:

Adulthood was wonderful. I finally realized what my father was trying to do. He was always so loving. He came to see me every single day of his life — stopped by my house — not a day would go by that he wouldn't come to see me when I was an adult.

I went from being in my parents' home to my marriage home, but he would come every single day and our relationship just got so much better. I didn't have to prove anything anymore and we were on an even keel.

Seeing L. as an adult was the result of a physical separation that engendered anxiety in her father but that he came to terms with after many years:

I worked in Manhattan, and my father always thought of Manhattan as "Sin City." He was always worried about me being down there; then after 9/11 he was even more worried that something was going to happen. I was working from early in the morning until late at night. I think that was a turning point for him, my going to the city. He tried to talk me out of it.

I worked at M_____ for twenty-three years, so I was always in the city, and that disturbed him. He finally got used to it, when nothing happened to me. Ten years later and nothing had happened, so then he thought, "Oh, maybe it's okay."

Several women noted moving, often because of a job or her spouse's job, as a turning point involving loss and sadness for both daughter and father but also sometimes new appreciation for the relationship. When asked how it felt to move to Boston from New Jersey for a job, Jackie responded:

> That was a little bit of a wrench, but again it was another thing that they never said, "Don't do it." I know my neighbors thought I was crazy: "How could you leave your parents?" And I just said, "I'm not leaving them."

She was growing up and out but not leaving on a deep level.

When the fathers saw their daughters as adults for the first time, the lens through which they viewed them shifted. No longer rebellious or identity-searching teens, the daughters were now young women with relationships, embarking on careers, sometimes even physically moving away from the family. These literal moves often could be seen as metaphors for the psychological changes that occurred in the relationship, which helped the fathers see their daughters in an evolving way.

PAUSE AND REFLECT

In this part you have read stories of transitioning from the teen years into adulthood. For some fathers, seeing their daughters grow into young women was a bittersweet time, as they watched their daughters, with both delight and sadness, form their own opinions, develop relationships outside of the family, begin careers, have children, or come out filled with gay pride. For other fathers, this transition was marked by tumult, perhaps because it was so difficult to let go.

We suggest that you recall your own passage into adulthood with your father, using the stories here as points of reflection.

+ *How did your relationship with your father during your teen years influence your passage into adulthood?*
+ *When did you feel your father first saw you as an adult?*
+ *Was it similar or dissimilar to the experiences you have read about in this part?*
+ *What were the turning points in your relationship with your father?*
+ *Did any themes emerge that still seem relevant to your life today?*

PART FOUR

Holding On, Letting Go: Our Fathers through Illness and Death

*W*e lose our fathers in different ways — some in prolonged illnesses such as Alzheimer's disease or cancer, some in a quick, unexpected incident such as a heart attack or an aneurysm. Some of us have nursed our fathers through their final days with all-night vigils in the hospital, multiple doctor appointments, or hands held in hospital beds at home. Some were one minute talking to him in the living room and the next minute calling an ambulance and watching his face for signs of life. However the deaths of our fathers come to us, we are never prepared for that moment when we hear the words, "He's gone."

The relationship we had with our fathers may shift during those final days, weeks, or months, if we are fortunate enough to have them. For those of us who had a close relationship, the bond may become even stronger as we reverse the roles of parent and child and take care of our fathers as they once did us. If our relationship had been strained, it may remain so, or impending death may bring with it the opportunity for forgiveness, healing, and newfound closeness.

We may read to our fathers in their hospital beds, make promises to take care of our mothers, feel anguish as we watch our once strong and vital fathers become tired and weak in body and spirit.

The good memories we have of our relationships with them may become the backdrop for what we see before us: our worlds shifting as we face the impending reality of a life without our fathers. Yet sometimes there is no time for shifting, and our expectations, hopes, assumptions, and connections come cataclysmically crashing down, as though jolted by one of the many earthquakes that strike Italy and disrupt life as it has always been known. The vibrant man is just gone, and we are left in the aftermath to emotionally piece ourselves and our lives back together.

As we lose our flesh-and-blood father, we are also losing years of history, relationship, and meaning-making. We are losing all that he has been to us and has meant to us in so many different ways, for so many years, which is why two or three siblings can lose the same father yet experience the loss in very different ways. We are not just losing an individual; we are losing a *relationship*. Who and what each woman's father has become to her will show up again in her loss and grieving in a very personal and at times indescribable way.

All through our lives we have taken into ourselves the critically important people around us, and they have impacted us and helped us become who we are. As we discussed in Part II, we carry the images and experiences of our early relationships with us into adulthood, and these even influence how we experience grief.

Joe, You're Back! (Lorraine)

The Fourth of July in my childhood friend Debbie's lush backyard saw my dad making his party debut after a year of medical horror and near-death experiences. He sat in his wheelchair, spoke with everyone (even poking fun at some of his worst travails), had a beer and a hotdog, and wore his special Fourth of July straw hat, as Debbie's brothers and husband exclaimed, "Joe, you're back!" as if he had risen from the dead. Which, in fact, he had.

A year and a half earlier, as my dad, my daughter, and I sat together one winter evening in the fireplace room, little did I know that the odd round sore that I noticed on his calf would end his life. We were in a better time of our lives than we had been for years since my mother's shocking death had absorbed us in grief. That little girl playing with a train set on the rug had connected us back to life and delight.

Now he was getting out more, visiting, playing the horses at off-track betting with friends, and we were living in a marvelous cocoon of love across the generations. We still missed my mother terribly, every day, but we were living once again. My dad would cook rotelle with peas and onions, lamb chops, or clams white when we visited, and we'd eat and talk and talk, just as we always had. But that little round sore meant it was all about to change.

We entered the world of peripheral artery disease, which included possible arterial bypass surgery and likely leg amputation. We visited doctors, talked, cried, talked, and visited other doctors. When it seemed the only options were amputation or death, my father chose death, not wanting to be maimed and perhaps unable to ever walk again. As he explained his reasoning to me, very carefully and movingly, I actually understood his choice and could accept it. He wanted to leave this earth as a whole person, as he had always lived. We made yet another visit to another doctor and found a prominent surgeon at a prominent medical center who offered the arterial bypass, and we were, for the moment, spared.

Then the next nightmare started, as complications settled in on top of complications, and my dad ended up comatose in his hospital bed and transferred to the ICU. He had been administered too much pain medicine without proper monitoring of his response. He didn't see his home again for five months, when he was released home to die. During those months, I could never relax, sit still, or rein in the constant emotional catapulting. I just could not be at ease with him in the hospital or at the rehab center, particularly given his pain, his reactions to OxyContin, and the hospital staff's inadequacy. (I filed complaints to state accrediting bodies afterward.) It was as if a part of me lay imprisoned and vulnerable too.

At one of my dad's most critical points, he was worried that my family was in danger. A physician friend of mine commented, "Even in the worst of moments, your dad is still your dad. He's still taking care of you." Yes, he certainly was.

My daughter and I would go, alternating with my brother Joe and my sister JoAnn, to his room to visit, play, talk, choose food from the menu or bring food (ziti! eggplant!) from home, help him eat, work on exercises, and just be there.

One night when we were leaving the rehab facility, a fire truck pulled up and I panicked, running back to see what had happened. My dad's dedicated nurse told me that in the case of a fire, he would personally put my father on his back and get him out of there. I believed him.

With a gorgeous November sunset as backdrop, my brother Ciro and I finally brought my dad home, to his own home, ecstatic despite the poor prognosis. This began our last nine months together, months that included unremitting pain and unrelenting frustration but also closeness, conversation, laughing, favorite foods, friends and family, and sharing care with our family friend Cathy, a persevering visiting nurse, and a devoted physical therapist. My dad came back to us with the fullness and vibrancy of his personality and presence, even though, ultimately, he suddenly "up and died" when we least expected it.

It was a warm August night at my dad's, a week after Ciro and Jacque's marriage celebration that is pictured on the cover of this book. My dad had made stuffed clams for a hundred guests and had been hugged and hailed by all. Now Ciro and Jacque were on their honeymoon, my sister was in Germany welcoming my dad's first great-grandchild, and my brother Joseph had just gone home after a wonderful dinner of spaghettini with red clam sauce, with plans for an excursion to the shore for a fried clam dinner the next day. My daughter, my nephew, and I were settling in for the evening as my dad got into his bed in the living room, said something to his granddaughter, and closed his eyes.

He was gone. As simply as that — just gone. The child who had come into his life when his wife had left it was sitting at the foot of his bed, waiting for him as he had asked her to do. I was on the phone with my husband, a physician who was a huge help in my dad's recovery and was now helplessly long distance. We screamed and called 911 and rushed around, the kids quite able in the crisis.

Looking at my dad at the moment of his death and later that night as things quieted down, I just knew that he was definitely gone, already on his way to another land, flying from the face of this earth, not lingering in the corners or eaves. His departure was peremptory, decisive. We had gotten him back only to lose him again. For real. For now.

Opening to Strength, Defining Courage (Donna)

I did not expect my father to die in 2003. Life hummed along until the diagnosis came one summer — lung cancer. My father had privately complained to me the previous spring that he was very short of breath and was having pain in his shoulder. I urged him to have it checked out. He did — and that act ushered in a chain of events that proved to be the beginning of the end.

When I say that I did not expect my father to die that year, it does not mean that I was in denial. I knew that he was very ill, though he never lost his fighting spirit, his lovable sense of humor, or his will to live. I saw all of those things in him each time it was my turn to take him to chemotherapy, as he sat in the chair and the poisons that were meant to prolong his life (for we knew, at this stage, that there was no cure) surged through his veins. It was actually on one of his good days that he made the final trip to the hospital, the trip from which he never returned home.

One of the things that haunted me the most about my father's death was being there the moment when he took his last breath. He was still conscious in those wee hours of the morning when my family and I finally said goodnight to him before he went to the ICU. When I called the hospital a few hours later to check on him, the doctor explained just how grave the situation was, and my family hurried to get back to his side.

To see my once robust father lying in the hospital bed, on a ventilator, seemingly unconscious, and on medication that paralyzed him to aid in the dying process broke my heart. The reality of the situation — that my father was dying — was difficult to grasp, and I could barely stay focused. Yet I also felt that I had to be there for him, to help usher him into the next part of his journey.

By his side, I took deep breaths and laid my head on his arm, the arm that taught me how to cut the waves when I learned to swim, the arm that worked hard in the yard of our childhood home to make it beautiful, the arm that hugged me and made me feel truly loved, despite some difficulties over the years. I had my head on that arm when he took his last breath, when the hospital machine signaled to us that he was, in fact, gone from this world.

In the months following his death, I felt traumatized by that scene. It would wake me in the middle of the night, would come unannounced when I was driving, would arise in my mind during a meeting. I could not resolve that the father who told a good joke, who was always a good sport, who was a lovable curmudgeon was the man in that hospital bed. I worked hard to push that image away, which I think in some way was my attempt to deny what had happened.

One day, shortly after my father's death, my oldest and dearest friend (who had lost her only brother a few months before my father died) gave me a stone for my Zen garden. Though it did not make sense to me at the time, the stone was inscribed with the word "courage." Prior to receiving that stone I had, surprisingly, never considered that dealing with death required courage and resolve, strength and resilience.

As I contemplated how I would incorporate courage into my experience, I deliberately let the image of my dad in the hospital bed come to my mind. With deep breaths I would gently let this experience touch me in a different way: how fortunate I was to be with him when he died and what an honor it was that, on a spiritual level, he had let me experience his passing with him. I allowed the scene to become a healing vision for me. No longer afraid, I found deep wells of strength within myself, strength that I was able to bring to other situations as well.

In his life, my father was afraid of very little; I like to think that my acquired courage came from him.

CHAPTER EIGHT

IN GRIEF:
THE DAUGHTERS
SAY GOOD-BYE

*J*ust as we lose our fathers in different ways, as Italian Americans we also experience grief in our culture in various ways. Italians have a strong desire to make the passage from this world to the next the best possible. We put an emphasis on the community of mourners: death is never experienced alone; it is a family event. And death is not a cognitive experience: it encompasses the whole self, in a community of loved ones. Our ethnic culture gives us so much of what we need in the raw moments when we are face-to-face with the loss of someone we love so much.

When it comes to death, many Italian Americans do not subscribe to the "get over it" or "find closure" approaches, and when we considered how we grieved the death of our fathers, neither did we. The quotation "Italians tend to keep their dead with them" (Giordano et al. 2005, p. 623), an idea central to this book, helped us to normalize and depathologize grief and loss as Italian Americans and alerted us to the possibility that others are in similar situations — caught between the Italian American world of relatedness and connection and the mainstream American world of endings as final. We may still carry some of the sense that Mangione and Morreale (1992) describe about southern Italians, "Ever present death is bound up with a love of life and a love for those close to one" (p. 44). Maybe we hold some deep collective knowledge of the closeness of life, love, and death that infuses our grieving.

In addition to our individual feelings regarding our fathers' illnesses and deaths, we may have to deal with changes in our family dynamics. This may be particularly salient for the Italian American daughter. In Italian American families, often the eldest daughter is expected to become the caretaker.

If our mothers are still alive, we must often simultaneously take care of them and begin grieving for our fathers; taking care of our mothers may even delay our own grief. We may have overt conflicts with siblings who do not agree with our decisions regarding our fathers' medical care or who may be having difficulties of their own as they deal with our fathers' illnesses and deaths. Underlying conflicts may rise to the surface. The closeness of the Italian American family may be taxed during this time, as the members struggle to make meaning of their own grief. You will get glimpses of this as you read the stories in the following pages.

GRIEF

When we lose someone significant in our life, the grief we experience can make us feel a multitude of things: deep sadness, shock, being overwhelmed, confusion, despair, relief, anger, being lost. Grief can also eventually show us the way to resilience, gratitude, meaning, and joy in our memories. Whatever we feel, grief has the potential to internally change us forever — for good or ill. As the experience of grief is embedded in our connection to those we love, we cannot discuss grief without discussing how we lived in relationship to that person.

To better understand the context of the women's descriptions of dealing with their fathers' illness and death, a summary of what has been written about grief and mourning may be beneficial.

What exactly *is* grief? Psychologists have described it as a reaction to loss. John Archer, a British psychology professor, suggests, "Grief . . . is the cost we pay for being able to love in the way we do" (1999, p. 5). As people love in myriad ways, they also experience and express grief in many ways. Loss is unique for each person and even for the same person at different times.

How the experts conceptualize grief has evolved over the course of history (see Granek 2010 for a comprehensive overview of the literature). Sigmund Freud (considered to be the forefather of modern psychological thinking) was the first theorist to introduce the concept of grief. In his first writings in the early 1900s, he suggested that the emotional energy of grief had to be transferred to other areas of one's life; otherwise a

(Continued)

GRIEF *(Continued)*

psychiatric illness could result. He acknowledged, however, that this could take a great deal of time and that grief was never, in fact, truly resolved.

Stage theories of grief, which began to take shape in the 1940s, say that if one "resolves" one stage she can pass on to the next stage and so on until all stages have been completed. The most widely known grief stage theorist was Elisabeth Kübler-Ross, who identified five distinct stages of grief — denial, anger, bargaining, depression, and acceptance — that even today remain in the grief vocabulary (1969/1997). It is important to note that Kübler-Ross based her theory on work with dying patients, although over time these stages began to also be applied to individuals who were grieving the death of a loved one.

Stage theories such as Kübler-Ross's lost favor over time, being considered too linear. Journalist Ruth Konigsberg, for example, cites these stages' inability to reflect the resilience of the bereaved that more current theorists have highlighted (2011).

George Bonnano, a pioneering researcher in the field of bereavement, reiterates, "The empirical fact is that most bereaved people get better on their own, without any kind of professional help. They may be deeply saddened, they may feel adrift for some time, but their life eventually finds its way again, often more easily than they thought possible" (2009, p. 24). He is quick to admit, however, that professional help may be essential in helping those who suffer from more "complicated bereavement" return to productive and meaningful lives.

Grief is still very much on the minds of the general public. The number of books on grief (more than 15,000 hits on Amazon), Internet sites that focus on the bereaved (a Google search resulted in 2,000,000 hits), and the rising number of grief counselors and organizations send the message that grief is increasingly kept on our radar.

Why has grief become such a popular topic? Konigsberg suggests that a "grief industry" has developed in our culture, with the assessment and management of grief becoming a commodity to sell. Despite how American culture has appeared to sanitize death and adopted the idea

(Continued)

GRIEF *(Continued)*

that we should "get over" our grief, a number of theorists (e.g., Hardy-Bougere 2008; Parkes, Laungani, & Young 1997; Rosenblatt 2008) have stressed that divestment from our cultural roots has contributed to our sense of isolation, perhaps allowing the grief industry to prosper.

The idea of "breaking bonds" with the deceased (or getting over our grief) has dominated how we view the mourning process in the United States, although the idea of maintaining bonds, or "continuing bonds," with the deceased (e.g., Field 2008; Field, Gal-Oz, & Bonanno 2003; Klass, Silverman, & Nickman 1996) is becoming a more popular view, particularly as we consider how culture may impact how we grieve and maintain those bonds.

This idea of the continuing bonds of grief focuses on the potential positivity if we maintain an internal picture of the deceased. Simon Rubin, director of the International Center for the Study of Loss, Bereavement, and Human Resilience in Israel, eloquently writes, "The greater the comfort and fluidity with which one can relate to the representations of the deceased, the more one can refer to 'resolution' of the loss" (1985, p. 232).

We would argue that both the internal *and* external representations of the deceased aid in this resolution; so thinking about your loved one as well as perhaps keeping photographs or items special to him around may bring comfort, evoke happy memories, and be reminders of a life well lived.

This idea of continuing bonds forms the warp and weft of how we view grief in Italian American culture; however, readers from any culture can recognize how their culture might influence their need to grieve, how they grieve, and how their deceased loved one becomes integrated into their life after death.

The Nature of Death

How we experience our fathers' dying processes is impacted by the circumstances of his death: Did we have an opportunity to say good-bye? Did we have to watch him suffer over time? For Cynthia F., a seemingly interminable process led to relief at the end:

He was with us for ten years and so it was a very, very slow decline. He was really quite active, lived on his own, and drove until the last year. He bought his own groceries, cooked his own food. The only thing I would do was take him to his doctors' appointments and things like that.

He did pretty well. Then he literally hit a wall. He was parking his car, and his foot hit the gas instead of the brake, and he went into the wall of the parking lot and the airbags deployed. He called me up and he said, "Have them take the car away; I don't think I can drive anymore." That's the end of that. Then he just seemed to sink.

He moved into assisted living and then had some mental health issues with depression and paranoia and a whole number of things that we worked through, but then December — he died right before Memorial Day — the December before he died he decided that he wasn't getting out of bed anymore and that was it. He wanted to die; he had had enough and was happy to be going.

The night before he died my husband and I were with him, but then we left him and went home to bed and got woken up. It was one of the nurses at assisted living. My father had a very high fever; we knew he was going to go at any minute.

He would have just turned off a switch if he could have, and he just had to wait for God to decide to take him. And he fought all the way to the end — fighting for breath.

It was so hard but also a release. We believe he went to a better place. I would not have liked to live the way he did those past six months; there was no quality of life whatsoever.

For others, grief was exacerbated by having watched a father not take care of his health, as in Giovanna C.'s case:

I wasn't prepared; we didn't expect him to die. What happened was he was having a lot of spiking with his blood sugar; he was a diabetic. He was starting to get where he shouldn't be driving anymore, because he would get forgetful, but also he would get moments where he would have very low blood sugar. My mother would try to hide the keys so he wouldn't take the car.

This one day he came home, and a police officer had followed him home. The officer had thought he was drunk, but he was getting woozy because his blood sugar was low. She found out he was diabetic, so she followed him home to make sure he got there.

It was maybe a week or two later, he was out, trying to sell one of his cars, because he knew he had to start getting rid of his used cars. He got into an accident and fractured his leg. He got worse and worse, and he wasn't able to talk at that point. I think that's what was going on with my father, lots of side effects from the diabetes, because he was beginning to drag his feet and he had neuropathy. He was also not careful about what he ate.

He wasn't that old; he was only seventy-one when that happened.

The death was often etched in memory, even when many years had passed. Rosa can still recall the details of what happened when her father died; and his death left an ever-present void in her:

My dad was sixty-eight — he's been gone forty years now. The relationship with my dad was very close. You know, it was just such a void. You wish that you had more time. You're thinking back from this perspective. It was just an amazing loss.

He died the day after Easter Sunday; it was April 1971. He had chest pains that weekend. We went to the doctor, who said not to worry. My dad was helping my mother make a pizza again for Easter Sunday; you know cutting the prosciutto, and doing all that. We did have Easter Sunday with him, with the extended family. Then Monday morning she called and said, "Meet me at the hospital. Your dad has had a heart attack." I went to the hospital, and he was gone . . .

Donna P. worked in administration for the state of New York and has been connecting with old friends, family, and heritage through the West Albany Italian Club. She was twenty-three and about to get married when her father died suddenly and dramatically. Although diagnosed with heart disease, he was living a fairly normal life:

In September the year before, we were at the church for a friend's wedding and he didn't feel good and didn't look good . . . My brother insisted, and they took my father to the emergency room. He had had a heart attack [that he had not acknowledged] and was having another heart attack . . . That was scary because he was our rock. When he was in the hospital (we were engaged), I remember him saying that he probably wouldn't be here for his grandchildren. I said, "Daddy, don't say that."

But he got through it . . . He was only fifty-four. My mother would try to keep him on a heart healthy diet, but he loved food. During recovery he said, "Some people eat to live; I live to eat." He did quit smoking, but he really enjoyed food. And he was so angry . . . He couldn't work, and he started to go back part time in June . . .

I can remember the day. During the day, calls were coming in for my bridal shower, and I remember him on the phone. It was a Saturday, and I heard him say, "I went to the doctor's yesterday and he put me on a new pill, and I'm really feeling good."

Then he and my mom went to visit my aunt and uncle. The West Albany Italian Benevolent Society (of which he and my uncle were members) was having a feast. The women stayed home, and my dad and uncle went to the club. I remember trying to make sense out of it all. He had seen all his old friends that night, and he probably ate a sausage and pepper sandwich.

So his last hours were good. But when he and my mom were coming home, my father saw this house on fire and he pulled over because there was a lady standing on a roof over a doorway . . . and he was running to tell her, rather than stay in a burning building, jump . . . [and then] he just dropped dead in front of my mother.

A few women reported situations in which their fathers never let on that they were ill, and they were shocked when suddenly confronted by their inexplicable deaths. Joyce speaks about going into denial:

Then after he passed, I had to go to a psychologist because I just did not accept his death at all. I was so mad that I was miserable to everyone. My poor husband, he is a saint because he put up with me. I was going to the cemetery every day, decorating his grave for all the holidays. Things didn't go right, I'd go down there and talk to him. Don't think I'm crazy.

Both Giovanna B.L.M. and her father were very young, and suddenly his "bursitis" had really been cancer. She was filled with anger and would ask, "Why did it happen? Why did it happen to me?" To deal with his death, she smoked. Probably I listened to music. I continued to go to concerts, and I became closer to certain friends. You know the anger. I dealt with the anger, but I felt lonely, I felt very deprived.

When asked if she understood how young he was, since parents can seem older, she said:

I know parents seem old. No, I was very aware.

Finding Peace in Death

For some of the women whose fathers suffered from difficult illnesses or for many years, the deaths of their fathers evoked a mix of emotions. They missed their fathers exceedingly, but death brought relief not only for their fathers but for them as well. How they recounted their experiences speaks to the complexity of their fathers' deaths and the aftermath.

Barbara Q. remembers the difficulty of watching her father's slow decline, but she found peace with him in his last moments:

His death was of course very difficult. He passed away five years ago now, this past August, and I went through a lot with him. He had a few ministrokes. That's what first started, in his late seventies. Then he started having gall bladder problems, but he was so weak that he couldn't really have the operation. They put stents in, and that caused him great pain.

The last maybe six months or so were very difficult. He was in Calvary Hospital for the last six weeks of his life. They are really angels there. It was very hard for him. I'd come in, I'd bring the paper, I'd read to him, he wanted to hear funny stories. He would perk up as soon as he saw me, and he never, ever complained.

We finally figured something out, some pain medication that worked for him, but he didn't like it because it made him groggy; he wasn't able to talk as much as he wanted. I'd read the paper and he'd be dozing; he didn't like that. He was basically the one who checked out. He knew when he didn't want to put up with it anymore. They told me he said, "Increase the morphine; I just don't want to do this."

[When he passed away] I was with him; I got to be there with him.

Dealing with her father's Alzheimer's diagnosis ushered in a period of mourning that lasted for some time, preparing Maria T. for what lay ahead:

I worked at Hunter at the time, and they had this Brookdale Center on Aging. They had this whole Alzheimer's project, and I was very aware of what it really meant when somebody got a diagnosis of Alzheimer's.

With all these various signs with my father, that things weren't quite right, we were praying it was something else that could account for it. When he ended up going to a neurologist at New York University, and he did diagnose him as having it, even though it was just the very, very beginning, I cried every night for a week. That was my mourning. It continued, but to me, that was the death sentence. I knew my father was going to slowly, slowly die to me, and die to himself. I knew what was ahead.

My father eventually ended up going into a facility. I would go once a week, and I would come home a good part of the time, just crying. This was the way it went for a couple of years . . . the pain was just terrible.

Then toward the end, he was put in the hospital. He was in two days, and he just passed away there. At that point it was a blessing, because he was just a shell of himself, and it was torture to see him like that. My father's passing was liberation.

Other women had time to plan for their fathers' passing, as difficult as that was for many. There was also a sense of family and connectedness that seemed to ease the burden of saying good-bye.

Karen B., a nursing professor, speaks of the complexity of watching her father suffer, while simultaneously wanting him to be in a better place:

He was such a determined person; he knew exactly the way he wanted to die. He knew, rather, the way he wanted to live, and he did not want to live incapacitated. He didn't even want to live the way he was with the stroke; it did take away some of his dignity.

I don't know if this is possible, but during that whole period of time he was sick, which was eighteen months, I was already mourning — probably because of my knowledge as a nurse, knowing that it was the end of his life as he knew it, because he was no longer able to have an independent life. He had been so ferociously independent.

We didn't use IVs either, because that just adds to the delay of the dying process. It was a beautiful death — he just did everything by the book. He was alert for days, and all my cousins showed up to say good-bye to him one by one with their families. He got to say good-bye to everyone and he could still talk a little bit, which was amazing.

He just kind of faded away in the last couple of days, and we stayed with him. I just had this second sense that it was going to be just a few hours, so we were all there with him when he died. The dying experience was very difficult and yet so beautiful. I felt happy, proud to have experienced it and also to have been there for my brother, my sister-in-law, my mom.

My father was alert for most of it, so the memory he went out of this world with was the idea that his family was together. That for him was by far the most important thing. When he actually died — this is really weird — I was actually happy.

When LuLu's father began the dying process, it was similar to how he lived — large and full of life:

I was in the room with him. I brought my father's book of poetry. I went there, and I knew that he was dying. I could sense that. I was there with my dad and two of my sons. I had to tell him that it was okay to go, to leave. I told him that and I read him his poetry. I wanted him to know it was okay to die. My two sons said, "He's waiting for Alex," my other son. As soon as my other son came, he passed away. After that, I felt his spirit in the house for a long time.

There is a funny story from when he was in the hospital. He always played lottery numbers. He's in the hospital and he wins the lottery, and he says, "This is hot shit. I'm in the hospital and I win the lottery!" It was almost $2,000! We all said, "You know, you won the lottery. Let's have a procession, and we'll get a band — a Dixieland band!" We prepared his funeral and decided to have a procession from Mt. Carmel Church here, down the street, band and all.

L.'s father, too, retained a core sense of who he was, despite his illness:

He was in the hospital, and I was very lucky because I started my vacation on the seventeenth to have right through the holidays in December; so I was there every single day. He found out that he had lymphoma and that he was going to die. He had tumors in his liver. He told the doctor not to tell us, that he was going to, and he didn't tell us.

My sister had come down from New Hampshire, and it was the twenty-ninth of December, and he was failing. Everyone was in the house, the grandchildren, the great-grandchildren, the children. It was the first time we had to give him the Percocet and the other drugs for the pain. Two days later he was dead.

Everybody feels good that they were able to say good-bye to him, and he was able to talk to each one. He would call the kids "monkey," so he'd see them and he'd say, "Hey monkey, how are you?" He couldn't talk much. Or he'd slap five with one of the little great-grandchildren as he always did. He related to everyone as they always remembered him . . . and after that he went into a coma and that was it . . .

Verna L. is an administrative assistant at a college and has a unique collection of articles and artifacts about her father that she brought to the interview. She was the only one with her father when he died, which meant a lot to her:

Here I am, his only daughter, and my sister-in-law said, "He waited for you, Verna." I guess he did. This is what made me have closure, because I thought being a girl in an Italian family, boys were so important. Then I said, "Okay, he waited for me. So maybe I'm important too."

Devotion

The support, love, and connection that many of the women reported feeling in their families manifested in their own devotion to their fathers throughout their illnesses and deaths — as they cared for them in ways that often exceeded expectations for a daughter.

Such an example is poignantly described by Sabrina:

My dad taught me so much from the time I was a baby until the time he passed away. Even when he couldn't talk or really do much for himself — taking care of him and watching his expressions, me doing the talking — I felt like we were having a conversation, and I kind of became the parent.

He taught me a lot about being a mom and being patient. I think he knew that. I really believe that. He kind of looked at me and knew like, wow, she is totally taking care of me; she knows what she's doing.

His doctor had told us in the year before he passed away, he told us maybe five times, "This is it. Say your good-byes." Then all of a sudden he'd be home. It would be months later and there would be another emergency room episode.

The last one was he got aspiration pneumonia because he couldn't swallow anymore, and that was supposed to be the end. We were in the hospital, and then he got better. My mom and I went to pick him up, and as soon as I walked into the room, my father was breathing horribly. He could barely breathe, and there was nobody in the room.

My mom and I stopped dead in our tracks. I ran to one the nurses and said, "Why isn't anyone watching him? He is not breathing correctly." Within minutes there were about ten different people on top of my dad. My mom is hysterical, and I grabbed one of the nurses and I told her, "Take my mom; get her out of here."

I stayed with my father and they wheeled him into the ICU. My dad grabbed on to my hand and wouldn't let go. They said, "You need to leave." I said, "If you want to take my arm with you, fine, but I'm not going anywhere." They were like, "You can't go in." I said, "Well, I'm not letting go, so deal with it." I did not leave. They rolled me in with him all the way to the ICU and I just looked at my dad and said, "Don't worry, Pop, I'm not going anywhere. I'm right here."

For Anna M., who spoke in the kitchen that she and her father had shared for many years, the devotion went two ways: not only did she make many sacrifices to care for her father at the end of his life, but her father continued his caring gestures toward her:

He always said that he didn't want to go to a convalescent home . . . I was afraid of that happening because I knew how he felt. He was able to stay home. As a matter of fact, up until the last time he got sick and he went into the hospital for three weeks and then he died there . . . he would make my breakfast in the morning. I'd get up and he'd have the coffee on and toast. Then he died.

The Influence of the Mystical

A connection to spirit, to a world beyond, transcended some women's upbringing and strengthened their ties with their fathers. The mystical helped Sabrina deal with the harsh realization of her father's death, and her experience with it again demonstrates the level of devotion that she speaks of in the passage above:

> My mom was really afraid to be in the room with him if anything happened in the night. I gave my mom my room, and I slept in her room with my dad, and my sister came too. For the last three nights, we slept in his room with him and for the first two nights we did not sleep at all, not even for a minute.
>
> I don't know where that energy comes from. I have no idea how they explain it, but it just happens. We were just up, and there was a nurse, a hospice nurse staying there too. On the third night, which was the last night, again we were sitting up on the bed talking. My dad was right there next to us, and it was the weirdest thing. I'm not very superstitious, but this is something I cannot explain.
>
> Only my sister and I know. There was a certain point when we were sitting there, and we were talking, talking, talking, and we looked at each other and we both just fell into a deep sleep — a deep sleep, at the exact same time. It was the weirdest thing. All of a sudden, at the exact same time, we opened our eyes and woke up. We both get up, shoot out of bed, and at that moment, the nurse is standing over my dad, and he took his last breath, like right when we woke up . . . It was really bizarre.
>
> Later my sister and I talked, and we had only been asleep for about an hour, but we both felt like we had slept for, like eleven hours. We both felt completely rested. It was really, really weird.
>
> That last night, he was completely out of it. I looked at him and I said, "Pop, can you give me a kiss?" The nurse looked at me like I was completely crazy, there's no way this man can even lift his head. He puckered his lips, and he kissed me on the cheek. The nurse, her jaw dropped to the ground. She was like, "I cannot believe he just did that." I was like, "I can. Of course he's going to do that. I'm his little girl." That was the last night, and he passed away that morning.

Karen D.'s experience also demonstrates a link to beyond the here and now:

During the time he was in the hospital, I dreamed that my father and I were standing in the church where my younger brother had gotten married several years earlier. We were waiting for the family, and I looked over and my dad came over toward me, and he was dressed in . . . he usually wore this sort of beige jacket and slacks. He came over and I said, "Why aren't you dressed? Where are you going?"

He said, "No, I have to go. I can't wait around anymore."

And I said, "Where are you going?"

He said, "There." I looked over and you know how they have a little door on the side of the altar to take you to the sacristy? There was a door, and the door opened, and there was this white light there. He said, "I have to go."

And I said, "No, don't go yet, Dad. It's not time. Don't go yet."

Another time, I woke up in the middle of the night, sat up, and felt like I couldn't breathe. I settled down, and I had a glass of water, and then I fell back to sleep. The next day I called my mom and asked how's Daddy doing. She said, "Oh bad. Last night in the middle of the night they had to take him from the nursing home to the hospital." I asked why. She said, "He pulled that trach out again; he couldn't breathe." I said, "What time?" She told me, and it was the same time I had that experience of my breath being taken away.

A dream came to Louise the night her father died:

The weird part was, right before the phone rang, I had a dream that my brother was at the hospital picking up my father. My mother called and she said, "The hospital just called. Your father passed." I said, "Oh my God, I just had a dream that Bobby picked him up." I couldn't believe it. It was the freakiest thing.

Patricia R.'s father's death also had a mystical feel to it:

I had just come back from Sardinia and I had a whole group of pictures and things to tell him about that part of Italy. I was in Pittsburgh and I spent two nights with him, and he was all distressed because he had these battles with raccoons because they came and ate the grapes. When I was trying to go to sleep, he's telling me this story that he has to get this raccoon. He said, "That son of a bitch is a heroic enemy." He's got very poetic language, my father. I sat up in bed, "What do you mean heroic enemy?" He told me that this raccoon came to life after he killed it.

The next day . . . I heard that my dad had died. He was under the grape arbor with a baseball bat, fighting with the raccoon. He died of a heart attack in one corner of the grape arbor, and the raccoon was in the other part and was dead. He died protecting that piece of Italy. Amazing, right? Fighting the heroic enemy . . . I left that morning, not thinking anything, and later that day he died.

It was devastating for me. I felt unmoored. Somehow, he grounded me in a way. I probably would never have described it that way up until after he died.

Daniela felt her father pass through her a moment after his death:

I was always sad that I didn't get there in time to hold his hand while he was dying. But I had this experience, and I'm not a religious person. My sister called me and said, "Daddy is dying; you'd better get here right away." I had a friend that I called, and he was going to drive me; and while I was waiting, my sister called and said, "It's over; don't rush."

I just stood by the window, and I felt this tremendous light walk through me, as if my father's spirit was passing through me and going off into the great beyond. It was such a vivid experience. And I'm not religious. I don't believe in the occult, so I don't know what that was. The sun came out, and I felt it was my father. I just felt it was him. Of course, it was all my own emotions I suppose; but who knows? I don't believe in an afterlife.

Like my father, I believe in Einstein's theory of the universal mind that we all get a piece of and it goes back into the great pool of mental energy or light. But I had that experience when he died, that he walked through me as light, as pure light, and I felt what was strange is I'm standing there, at this window looking out into this little garden, and I felt light walk through me, and a sense of incredible peace came over me, like his spirit was released from torment or something. Now he was at peace.

Maybe I felt that he was not really happy when he was alive, as he suffered so much all of his life with illness.

Regrets

Despite the deep connections with their fathers that the women spoke of, they also experienced guilt — for time not spent, for decisions made — even when their fathers were reassuring, as in Rosanne B.'s situation:

> When I went down to Florida, I told my parents that I was getting divorced. My mother said, "No!" My father said, "I knew it was just a matter of time." You get a really good picture of how my father was inside me.
>
> My father was diagnosed with esophageal cancer about a year and a half before he died, and they did an operation and, theoretically, that was supposed to be the end of it. Then it showed up in his stomach. There was a constant deterioration.
>
> My biggest regret, really, is that I didn't spend more time with my father when he was sick. I mean, I went to visit him, you know, a few times. I was just not in it. I was only thirty-eight, thirty-nine. I didn't want to accept the fact that he was dying. I'm somewhat ashamed of how I handled that. I didn't spend enough time with him. Before that happened, I sat in his room with him, and I said, "What do you think about while you're here in the hospital all day long?"
>
> He said, "Oh, I think about my life."
>
> I said, "Well, what do you think about it?"
>
> He said, "I did what I was supposed to do; I had you."
>
> I said to him, "I'm sorry for anything that I did that was wrong."
>
> He said, "You never did anything wrong." But I don't know how much comfort I gave him in his last time.

Grief made Diane G. question what she did in her father's final moments, despite what she had done for him throughout his life:

> He had the first stages of non-Hodgkin's lymphoma and he was living in Florida. We told him, "Why don't you come here? We'll take you to a

hospital in New York, and you'll get the treatment." He said, "No, I'm fine." He was the type, you're sick, get over it. He would get certain amounts of radiation treatments, and it would be done.

They put him on a respirator. I was getting ready to go there for Christmas. My nephew, who was in Florida, called me and said, "Aunt Di, nothing can help Poppa, only divine intervention." That's what the doctor said. I let out a scream on the phone, and it felt like my heart burst in my chest. To this day I feel so bad, because my nephew was trying to be strong and hold it together, and when I lost it he lost it.

When I got to Florida and walked in the hospital room and saw my father on this machine, and I didn't expect it, I fell backwards. My brother was behind me and he picked me, literally lifted me, up off the floor.

I just kept saying, "Daddy, Daddy, please, Daddy." I just kept talking to him because they said he could hear us. They then came in, and they showed us his X-rays, and they said there's nothing they could do for him, that we had to take him off the machine slowly. They were basically asking us, "How do you want him to die?" I was crazy. My mother decided to take him off the machine slowly, and that's what they did.

I did not want to sit there and watch it. Sometimes you say, "Should I have stayed in the room?" because I felt guilty that I wasn't there holding his hand. But would he have wanted me to suffer like that? I don't think so.

P.B. has only one regret:

My mother, my brother, my husband, and I were all there one night, and my dad, his office was in the basement and he was in the den in the hospital bed. He was still talking, a couple of days before he died. He sat up and he goes, "I've got to go downstairs. I want to go down to the office." My husband and I are looking at each other; we're going, "Let's carry him down there." My mother and brother didn't think it was a good idea . . . So we didn't out of respect for them.

My husband and I still to this day say, no, we should have . . . just to give him that satisfaction. Whether it was crazy talk or not, maybe there was something there. Maybe it would have made him feel better. Maybe he would have talked for another day.

Carol A. regretted that her dad had not seen her children or her grand-children grow into adulthood, as her mother did.

Linda G. spoke about the hard issue of not being able to say good-bye to her father and what might have changed if she had:

> It's huge [not being able to say good-bye] . . . I wonder if he had gotten to the hospital sooner if he might have had more time. I'm told that he started not feeling well on Friday, and he didn't get to the hospital until Monday. I didn't even know he wasn't feeling well . . . If I had been there, he'd have gone . . . He was in his eighties, and despite the stroke he was usually in really good health . . . I don't have any fantasy that he would have lived for another ten years or anything like that, but I just think it might have been different.

The Nature of the Relationship

Sometimes the relationship that was warm in childhood is no longer warm at the time of a father's death. Christine P. and her father had had conflict off and on for several years and then a rupture a few years before his death, illustrating that deep estrangement is sometimes intertwined with deep connection:

> By the time he died, I felt like he had already been dead. I had grieved my relationship with my father for three years. He wasn't talking to me. He was disappointed with the choices I had made in my life. I had to go through grieving while he was still alive.

He died unexpectedly:

> He was on his way to Florida with my mother. He'd stopped en route at my sister's house. They had dinner. He went upstairs and died. Just had a heart attack. I was very sad. I went to the funeral. But I felt like I had already grieved the man who I loved so much and who I had been so close to. I had already said good-bye.
>
> I think my novel *The Virgin Knows* came out maybe six months after he died. I remember thinking, "Maybe the worst thing that can happen is that my novel is going to be published, and he's going to die before it comes out." And that's exactly what happened.

CHAPTER NINE

THE ITALIANNESS OF
OUR FATHERS' DEATHS:
RITUALS AND PRACTICES

*E*very culture has its own rituals surrounding death and grief. These practices evolve over time, as each generation shifts and shapes them to adapt to current times. For many cultures, there is a communal aspect to death and grieving, and as we noted earlier, the community is there to provide solace and support. Some of the practices are meant specifically to bring comfort and a sense of order in the face of the senselessness of death.

Thinking of death and grieving for Italian Americans brings certain images immediately to mind: the tradition of wearing black, the flow of visitors to the house, the importance of cemetery visits, the professional mourners, faith and prayer, or trinkets in the casket. Like many cultures, Italian American culture places special emphasis on death and the journey after death, both the journey of the one who has died and that of those left behind.

The women we spoke to reported a variety of rituals and observations regarding the Italianness of death.

Funerals as Ritual

The funeral or memorial service is such an immediate and integral part of grieving. Many women spoke of the importance of the gathering that took place after their dad's death and the way it honored their dad while bringing family and friends together to support each other. We come together in times of great need and great loss, and we find some strength in that coming together.

For many the funeral itself was an elaborate affair. Lulu's father was a community icon, as she described earlier,

We had a procession for my father's funeral. We had many really big political people march in it. We had the band start to play a slow dirge — like Dixieland — going out and playing some of his favorite songs. Oh, he loved to dance. Tiger Rag. He loved to do the Peabody. We'd go to these weddings and he was like, "Kid, you've got to dance with me." I'd have to dance.

Anyway, we started out walking. We had these men, who were mainly black and Hispanic men that he had mentored, as part of the procession. They wanted to carry his coffin, and the funeral director thought, "We can't have this." We said, "No, they're carrying it."

We just did this procession to the Settlement House. We played some music, and somebody started dancing. It was really sweet. Then we closed the door to go to the cemetery, and we played "Take Me Out to the Ballgame," because that was my father's thing.

What was also touching was, as we walked through the neighborhood, people took off their hats. They were kissing his picture. The street was named after him, quite shortly after his death . . . We had nothing to do with it. It was mainly the black and Hispanic people of the community. They went down and did all the work. We knew my father would say, "Nobody's going to know who I am, like, five years from now."

It was, to me, a beautiful, beautiful funeral. Personally, I had a tough time. I was in a crazy denial that he had died because he went to the hospital and he was supposed to come home, and he died on Father's Day. You know when somebody's in the hospital and they're going to come home? I kept thinking he was going to come home.

Adele's father's funeral was much simpler but no less meaningful:

Oh, just the wearing of the black, no television, no radio, being quiet and mourning silently. That's what I did. I don't know about anybody else.

After the funeral they had a big dinner. We had a big dinner for my dad. People milled about and talked, and my mom had it in a restaurant. We talked about the things he did, the things he built. More or less everybody talked about the things he built in different people's houses. A lot of people had had stuff built by him. It was a social thing.

Now I see people at funerals and they wear red. They would have you thrown out. It's different today. They think of death differently.

L. and her family grieved in their own way:

We didn't have professional criers, but having a tear, shedding a tear. Not hysterical falling all over the casket or anything, but having a tear during the funeral. Having a tear during the burial, I think was the way I grieved. After it, having my own personal tears at home was important.

My father died on a Friday. We had the wake through the weekend, which was New Year's weekend. We had the funeral on Tuesday, because Monday was the holiday.

I took the three days off. After such a tragic event, having to face people again was hard. I wanted to do that. Having people extend their condolences, to be able to appreciate what they're saying and not fall apart totally was also important to me to do. I think having to go back to work and getting my mind on something else, and yet having my family on the weekend and my own private grief at night, was what I did.

Donna P. was still in shock in the days following her dad's sudden death:

The priest came to the house, and he said, "Oh, you must be the girl getting married next month."

"I'm not getting married now." I didn't want to because I didn't think you could celebrate.

He said, "Oh no, you will get married. It's what your father wanted." So we did.

It's the hardest thing; it's very hard to lose a parent. I remember going into the funeral parlor, the first day, back when you had it three days. I just remember screaming, "That's not my father." I remember the funeral. There were a lot of people because he was so young and he was so well liked by everybody.

We went back to the house with all the family and friends. I think it was the first time we were going to have my husband here and they had made a huge batch of sauce. That's what was served to the family and friends. I remember getting home, because as I said, I lived at home. I never lived outside on my own before I got married.

Andrianna was also young when her father died at age fifty-one. He was one of several brothers who all died young and within a year or so of each other. The family was already reeling when her dad died:

> My grandmother was in Italy. We had to hold his body for four days to get her back from Italy. It was awful. It was horrible, the screaming, the yelling [at the wake]. My sister never made it to the cemetery. I remember taking a pill because, what do you call something for your nerves? I was able to get through it. My sister never made it because she tried to get him out of the casket. I mean it was a nightmare, being young.

ITALIAN AMERICAN CULTURE, RELATIONSHIPS, AND DEATH

Four aspects of Italian American culture — family as central to life and to survival, a comfort or familiarity with religion and spirituality, resilience tempered with fate as a framework for living, and the power and transformability of ritual and symbol — underlie our thinking about Italians and their relationships to each other and death (DiCello & Mangione 2013).

Family as Central. Family, including extended family and close friends, is considered one's greatest resource in life and critical to survival in an often harsh world (Alba 2000; Gambino 1997; Giordano 2005). The deep level of connectedness is at the center of one's psyche and life. Outsiders are often eyed with suspicion.

Italy's recent celebration of the 150th anniversary of unification is a reminder that Italian history includes invasions by other countries, battles among different groups of Italians, the military campaign for unification, and involvement in both world wars (Mangione & Morreale 1992). Given this discord and distrust, Italians formed a fierce connection to the land and smaller communities, encouraging Italians, particularly southern Italians, to rely tremendously on family as their primary social unit (Gambino 1996).

Religion and Spirituality. That family life includes an emphasis on religion and spirituality, whether through Catholicism and its more mystic, ritualistic aspects (Giordano, McGoldrick, & Klages 2005) or through folk wisdom. And certainly in Catholicism, death and rebirth

(Continued)

ITALIAN AMERICAN CULTURE, RELATIONSHIPS, AND DEATH *(Continued)*

are central. Images of Christ seen in homes and churches eloquently tell the story of birth, life, death, and redemption and resurrection.

Religion for early southern immigrants was "based on awe, fear, and reverence for the supernatural, 'a fusion of Christian and pre-Christian elements of animism, polytheism, and sorcery along with the sacraments prescribed by the Church'" (Mangione & Morreale 1992, p. 326). These influences fostered an openness to otherworldliness, a mystery to this life and the next, and answers that are not rationally defined.

Resilience and Fate. Coming back after defeat, seeing the glass half full, practicing optimism despite setback — all define the resilience that, together with adaptability, Giordano et al. (2005, p. 617) note "became ethnic trademarks" for Italian Americans. The early immigrants' ability to adapt and compete in a strange new world showed in their work ethic, capacity for labor organizing, and creation of mutual aid societies (Mangione & Morreale 1992).

Historian Jennifer Guglielmo (2010) documents Italian immigrant women's involvement in "resistance and radicalism" in the labor movements of the early twentieth century, surely a manifestation of a fighting spirit and resilience. Yet Italians often believe in the power of fate (Giordano et al. 2005), with resilience perhaps residing beneath and both influencing our grief and mourning. Grief is integrated into life, and loss is a part of living.

Ritual and Symbol. In a culture imbued with rich visual arts and architecture, expressive hand and facial gestures, a mystical and ritual-laden religion, ancient beliefs in oracles and soothsayers, and stories of gods and goddesses, symbols and meaning-making abound. Perhaps because life was inscrutable and mysterious, Italians developed the practice of drama, symbol, and ritual as important vehicles for life events and their religion (Giordano et al. 2005), particularly regarding death.

Symbol and metaphor resonate in a culture in which the unconscious, the unknown, and the unknowable are freely at play. Bona states, "Like Persephone returning, writers of Italian America portray death as a story

(Continued)

ITALIAN AMERICAN CULTURE, RELATIONSHIPS, AND DEATH *(Continued)*

of continuity, a story about how things change, but don't end" (2010, p. 208), reminding us that grief and relationships may be more fluid and less straightforward for Italian Americans.

Some of the above material originally appeared in our chapter in the first book published on Italian American mental health, Benessere Psicologico: Contemporary Thought on Italian American Mental Health, *edited by Dominick Carielli and Joseph Grasso (2013), a groundbreaking book that includes issues of identity, stereotype, families, gender, and culture.*

Laura M.'s father died suddenly and unexpectedly. She had just visited him at his home about six hours from hers at Christmas, and on New Year's Eve day she received the call that he had died. She felt like she was "in a daze" yet knew she had to have a service that would honor him and fit with what his family would consider appropriate. She was moved by all the people who came and by the "big guy at the wake, tears streaming down his face" who told her that her "father was like Mickey Mantle to him, a real star." She held on to that image.

Daniela felt that given her father's stance as a believer in science over religious dogma, she wanted to create a ceremony specifically for him:

My father always used to quote to me Gray's *Elegy Written in a Country Churchyard*: "Many a flower is grown to blow unseen and waste its sweetness on the desert air." He felt a little bit like that about his own writing, his own poetry — that he was something special but the world would never know. So oddly, this place where I buried him by chance has a little cottage called Gray, inscribed with Gray's *Elegy Written in a Country Churchyard*, and it's made after the little building in the real country churchyard in England . . .

For his memorial I devised a special ceremony. My aunts are religious, so I had to, even though my grandfather and the men in the family weren't. So I thought, well, I'll have a priest for the old Italian aunts. The only priest I could find was Irish. My father would have been turning over in his grave because he always felt wounded by the Irish. When the Italian immigrants came, the Irish were the police, and they used to arrest and beat up the Italians for no reason, call them dagos, and throw them in jail. They kept them from getting ahead, because they were the police and the priests who were here first.

So we had the Irish priest . . . but he was very nice. I only gave him a very short while, because most of the ceremony was everyone got up and said what my father had meant to them . . . I actually played tapes that I had taped of his immigrant history, of his trip on his steerage passage journey to America and his time hospitalized on Ellis Island.

When people walked in they could hear my father's voice, and they were all freaked out. In those days, 1981, it wasn't so usual to do a funeral that way. Now it's more so. I was playing tapes of his immigrant story for the grandchildren, because I wanted to preserve this story . . . Sort of a bit of ancestor worship. I think ancestor worship is a very real thing, because after all, if we are anything, we owe it to the people who raised us, and the people who raised them, and the people who raised them.

Part of honoring Anne P.'s father meant giving his eulogy:

This is what I had written for his funeral, but I had forgotten that I had found a poem that I put at the beginning that, I don't know where I found it, I just thought it was really appropriate. It made me think of him . . . I would say it fell to me because I wanted to do it, but it's sort of my way of dealing probably more than either of my siblings.

The Cemetery: A Place of Solace

The ritual of going to the cemetery was significant for many, as it was for Cynthia F., who had a rather striking story about it:

One of my earliest memories is going to a cemetery — they loved going to the cemetery — and putting flowers on the grave. You would always go through and you would hear all the stories of all the different people. One was my father's Aunt Magrina, and the story that he always told was that Aunt Magrina — we never knew if it was a real name or a nickname — jumped into the grave of someone who died and people were holding her back and she was weeping and wailing. That's always been the kind of thing . . . about Italian funerals and the wakes.

There were so many people I know that have never been to a wake and we started going when we were very young, and observing all of that was quite interesting, And the drinking in the bathroom. Everybody kind of observing and praying and going on and on. It was really quite a cultural thing. I think that the Italian rituals around death are pretty interesting. My dad loved to read the obituaries — and when he was in Chicago he went to as many wakes as he could — that's what they all did — that was part of the system.

Community of Friends and Family

Central to the Italian American way of grieving are the acts of family and friends surrounding the grief stricken, as Giovanna C. describes:

Grieving is such a mixed bag for Italians. It brings up so much stuff. I remember my siblings were fighting, and I was fighting with my mother, and a lot of that was grief and shock. But definitely there's a lot of coming together. People really turn out for wakes.

There were a lot of people at my father's wake. It was a big family reunion. People from his old neighborhood where he grew up came, people in our family, relatives, and friends. I think the grieving is mixed because you're happy to see people you haven't seen in years, so it's a reunion, but you're uniting over losing somebody. That's the sad part.

Grief in Catholicism: Last Rites

In the lives of some of the women, Catholicism played a role in how their grief was experienced. Anna M.'s father struggled with the dictates of Catholicism and his own beliefs:

And the last time he was in — and I know the priest went to see him, because he'd always say to me, "I told you not to put down Roman Catholic." So I said, "Well, I'm going to put it down." So I said to him, "Don't you want to, you know, say your confession? Isn't there something you want to say?" He said, "No." And I'll tell you something . . . Maybe I'm wrong, but I admired him for that, because I've seen people who, you know, lead a really dissolute life and then, at the end, they get religion. He wasn't like that. I said, "Don't you want to say something to the priest?" He said, "What am I going to say? I never killed anybody."

Barbara Q. saw the religious aspect as embedded in the culture:

There's always the religious aspect. I think that's ingrained in a lot of Italians. We had a Mass for him. Of course we had a big meal together. We made pasta, and we had strawberry shortcake, which he liked. Nuts and figs, that was his other big thing. All those things, but that's all part of him and that's all related to him being Italian, I think.

The hospital priest was involved in R.L.'s father's death and decisions:

The priest was very compassionate . . . His wife had died of cancer and then he became a priest — so he was very knowledgeable in what it was like losing a family member and very compassionate — so my father had about four or five last rites. I travel a lot for work so I had to resign myself that I might not be there, so I was at a few of the last rites . . .

They had never talked about end of life decisions. So my father was eighty-three, his body with the Parkinson's is going downhill and his mind with dementia, and my mother would always say, "Yes, take extraordinary measures," and they were putting tubes in him . . .

The priest was so helpful. He would say to my mother, "What do you want to do? Do you want to take these extraordinary measures?" The doctors would ask us and all of us sisters wanted to say, "Just let him go, let him go." My mother would say, "What's your opinion," so we'd say, "Our opinion is you should let him go, but it's your decision" because we didn't want to disrespect her decision. The priest would say, "Well it's your decision, but you might want to think about letting him go."

[At one point] the priest did the last rites. He anointed my father and then had us all take oil and anoint part of my father's foot . . . We were saying prayers. I guess we were saying "Our Father" but I guess we were praying for . . . St. Joseph is the patron of a happy death. We weren't praying for a miracle of recovery. We were just praying for his passage. It was just being together and praying for us all.

The priest was so compassionate. He was so nice to my mother. Because it took a long time for my mother to be able to let my father go, that once she made the decision we surrounded her with our support, and the priest said, "God has been calling him home for a long time now." We all held hands and started to pray, and we all spent the night in vigil in the hospital room with him.

He died the next day when many of them had briefly left, something that seems to happen often.

Easter became a bittersweet time for Joann P.:

I think Easter was the toughest. My dad passed away the Sunday after Easter, and he actually went into the hospital on Good Friday. So I remember sitting on the chair and laughing to myself, thinking, "My father could be the second Jesus. He could be the Resurrection!" But that's my warped sense of humor . . . it was very painful.

Wearing Black

For all who are Italian American, the ritual of wearing black for a period of time after the death of a loved one is probably the most recognizable sign of grieving. This period can last a few months or many years. Several women reported some wearing of black. For Imma, who came to the United States as a young girl, acculturation outweighed the influence of the old country:

I wore black, but not for long, because I used to work. You feel bad if you wear it for so long. I wore it maybe for a month, for respect. My mother wore it, too, but then we talked to her about wearing dark clothes.

My father-in-law died when he was forty-seven years old . . . My mother-in-law, she went crazy. She wore black for how many years, because they were really close, in love, whatever. That was a way for her. I guess you think different. You don't bring anybody back by wearing black.

Gifts for the Departed

A lesser known custom is the placing of gifts for the departed in the casket. A last reminder of the personality and soul of the departed, it speaks to the sweetness of the connection that many of the women had to their fathers. Joann stated:

> For some odd reason, my family always put little trinkets in the casket with the deceased. If it was a woman and she was a sewer, they would put in a needle and thread, something that they liked. For my father, there was a whole cigar, a deck of cards, some poker chips, some bullets that we had to take out because he was cremated. I think my mom wrote him a note, and she may have put his dog's bowl or something significant of the dog in there.

Verna speaks of her son's response to his grandfather's death:

> My son took it quite hard. He asked me, "Do you think Grandma would mind, because Grandpa loved Regina Pizzeria (in Boston), if I put a Regina napkin in the casket and hot pepper?" Because my father would put hot pepper, crushed red pepper, on everything. Michael took a Ziploc bag and put hot pepper in, and the next morning at the funeral, he slid it in on the side of the casket . . . That's how my kids remember him, because we used to go to the Regina with them; we'd all go.

Giovanna C.'s family also observed this custom:

> In my immediate family, people were very private about not crying in front of each other and they didn't necessarily sit near each other. My mother was afraid I was going to throw myself in the coffin. I guess she thought I was more emotionally expressive than some of my siblings.
>
> She tried to hold me back when I went up to the coffin, when my dad was in his wake. She tried to hold me back, and I said, "Why are you pulling me back? I want to go up to the casket." She let me go, and I just said a prayer and put something I had written in the suit that he was wearing.
>
> We all put something in that meant something to us. My brother Donald, who used to watch baseball games with my dad, put some baseball cards in there. My sister Roseanne put a little wallet with five bucks in there in case he needed a coffee, in case he needed to get somewhere. We all put something in there. I think we all tried to personalize it, but we all were very private in our grieving.

Of all the parts of this book thus far, this one probably stirs the most emotion in us. Here you have read how the daughters experienced their fathers' deaths — from hospital room visits to final phone calls to funeral processions. These descriptions speak to the relationship, both tangible and intangible, each daughter had with her father — the devotion she might have felt, the way she said good-bye, how she managed the relationships with remaining family members, the dreams she may have had that alluded to his death.

How we lived with our fathers informed how we prepared for and coped with his death and, ultimately, how we said good-bye.

PAUSE AND REFLECT

In this part you have read the Italian American daughters' poignant stories of the deaths of their fathers. Although some fathers had died many years earlier, the daughters' memories of preparing for the funerals and dealing with their grief remained alive for them. You also read about how Italian culture shaped many of the death and grieving rituals for these women. Take a moment now to consider what your good-bye rituals were.

✦ *Is there anything you would have wanted to say to your father or anything you would have wanted to do for him for which you didn't have the opportunity at the time of his death? Write it down.*

✦ *Does something still bother you from the time of your father's death, perhaps about how he died, the reason for his death, or the timing of his death? Can you talk about it with someone else who was involved or write about it and see how your thoughts and feelings have evolved?*

✦ *Were there moments around your father's death that reflected a sense of the spiritual or the mystical? Allow yourself to sit with them a while and contemplate your relationship with your father and with a larger sense of reality.*

✦ *Is there anything you felt particularly good about regarding your father's funeral service?*

✦ *Is there anything you would have wanted to change?*

Let go of your regrets!

PART FIVE

AFTERSHOCKS: MISSING OUR FATHERS THROUGH TIME AND SPACE

*I*t is human nature to try to control things that we cannot control: the weather, other people, our sense of security. We want things to stay as they are, or we want people to see the world through our lens, so that we feel the world is both recognizable and understandable. The death of a loved one is one of those life experiences that shake us to the core whether or not it is anticipated.

We might go through our fathers' funerals with a sense of depersonalization — this is happening to someone else, not us — or we might have every word we hear seared into our souls. We may not have much memory of who we spoke to on that day, or what the weather was like, or who came to the funeral home to offer their condolences, or some of it may stand out in sharp relief.

In the immediate days after the death of someone close to us, we are usually surrounded by many people; friends bring us food, offer to do errands, hold our hands at the funeral home. We may have a gathering after the funeral to celebrate the life of the person we just lost. And then life seemingly returns to "normal." We go back to work, we walk the dog, we do our own grocery shopping, and we are faced with the loneliness that death brings as it catches up with us in the dark hours of the night when we are alone, on our car ride to work, or as we wait for a train.

As we traverse the days, weeks, and months immediately following our fathers' deaths, we go through our process of grief, which may include not believing that we have lost them, feeling extreme pain or guilt, being angry, or experiencing depression and loneliness. We may find our emotions expressing themselves through physical symptoms as well, with waves of nausea, headaches, backaches, or unexplained body pain adding to our distress. We may experience the dichotomy of both enduring one of the most difficult things we can go through in life and life continuing as it was in the days prior to our loss.

The loss and its ramifications continue, which is why we think of this as the time of aftershocks. The major earthquake has jolted us, but there are many more subterranean, unknown seismographic events yet to radiate from that initial quake. The shifting of our lives and ourselves that the poem "Shifting the Sun" spoke of at the opening of this book continues in the days and weeks and even long after our fathers have died, just as the earth shifts subtly after an earthquake.

We inhabit a world in which many of the traditions of mourning have been lost, such as assuming a year of mourning in which the community respects the mourner's process; so many of the aftershocks are now borne in private as the world around us rushes along with its business.

When it is a parent who has died, the loss can shake us on a much deeper level and these experiences may be more intense, more painful, even if the loss occurs when we are adults. Our parents provide our first relationship template; we learn from them, as earlier chapters have shown, how to form relationships both in childhood and in adulthood. No matter what our relationships are with our fathers, their deaths sever that first early bond, both literally and figuratively; we become untethered, often feeling like a bereft child despite perhaps having children of our own.

To navigate the loss of the person who helped bring us into being, who took care of us when we were most dependent, who has known us the longest in our lives is no small task. At times the pain feels unbearable, but it is certainly not insurmountable.

To continue our journey, Lorraine shares journal writings and Donna offers a koan she wrote, both from the first months after their fathers' deaths. The aftershocks rumbled on in new and surprising ways, bringing us further and deeper through grief and loss.

The Long and Winding Road, or: What Is the Sound of One Heart Breaking?* (Donna)

Death is mysterious — it has a way of paradoxically making time stand still and also pass at the speed of light. Immediately following the death of my father, time had that quality to me, resulting in my days feeling surreal and shrouded. If only I part the veil, I thought, this will have been a bad dream. Hours would pass, and I would think that it had only been one. Or conversely, when the pain felt the greatest, I would watch the clock, certain that it had not moved one second and that the batteries must be running low. But that was not the case, of course.

Sitting in my office at work, I would look at the phone and think, "My father is not going to call me today." I tried hard to remember the last time he had left me a voicemail, and I agonized over the fact that I had not saved it. I would never hear my father's voice again. Never. Gone were his belly laugh, his opinionated view of things, his attempts to remember the Italian he had spoken long ago with his mother. In my mind I would strain to hear his voice, but after his death it so quickly became ephemeral, like a vapor rising from the grass in the early morning — rising, rising until it becomes one with the air, nothing of it remaining in the midday sun.

When my father died, my mother became a widow after fifty-one years of marriage. My parents came as a matched set — always together, finishing each other's sentences, a sense between them that they really liked each other. It certainly was not a perfect relationship, but together they had woven the warp and weft of a life that worked for them.

My mother took my father's death hard, often telling me that she still thought she heard him talking to her in bed at night, and we would laugh over cups of tea that even in death he probably still had a lot to say. I knew that it was not the voice of psychosis that was speaking to her but the primal emptiness that comes from losing someone who was in your pores, who was your other half, who you could not imagine a life without.

When her birthday came only three weeks after he had died, it was difficult to celebrate. Even that soon after my father's death I could feel the foundation of my relationship with my mother shifting, something I had not anticipated. I missed my father immeasurably, but her feelings seemed larger than life and required more attention, and it was difficult to balance the two. I would find myself getting angry at her for no apparent reason, secretly wishing that she would feel better more quickly, or be less needy, or reach out to friends. At the same time, my heart would ache for her and love for her would rise to the surface, every fiber of my being wishing that I had the power to take the pain away from her.

I realized how much my father had attended to my mother, and now with him gone the baton had been passed to me; both my mother and I were straining under that metamorphosis, neither one of us sure how to fathom these new roles. My father had always said, long before he became ill, "When I'm gone, make sure you take care of your mother." I would try to brush it off, telling him that of course I would, but that he would probably outlive all of us. But now I was confronted with that task, in the face of my own heart breaking.

My sister and her children and I came together for my mother's birthday that first year, trying to make it festive for her with cake and presents, but the elephant was in the room — the grief that frequently overtook us in quiet and not-so-quiet ways, reminding us that life was fleeting and that things between us would never again be the same. We would now have to deal directly with each other and face the fact that our roles would need to be born anew.

I remember many days in the months following my father's death when my physical self felt tenuous. I would think about losing him and my voice would catch or my chest would tighten, and it would feel difficult for me to catch my breath. I tried to remind myself to breathe through each moment, as I did when I meditated, knowing that what I was feeling would soon transmute into something else, something more manageable.

It was at these times I would try to remember a funny story about my father. Once, many years before his death I was away on vacation and sent my parents a fruit basket to cheer them up, as my mother had not been feeling well. I called to see if it had arrived safely, and my father answered the phone. After a bit of chitchat, I asked him what the fruit basket was like, expecting that perhaps he would say it was nice and that they were enjoying it. But my father, in his inimitable way, started out, "Aaagh, the pears are *lousy*."

That became a signature line for him in my mind, and even years later I would chuckle about it with friends who knew and loved him. In the dark moments after I lost him, it still brought a smile to my face when I thought of it — the bitter with the sweet.

I also struggled with the fact that everyday life continued, despite the immensity of this loss. A few weeks after my father died, I was driving on the highway in the late afternoon, directly facing a beautiful sunset. It was one of those red suns that you usually only see in the summer; the clouds were magenta and violet, and the air held those first subtle sweet smells of spring. I remember thinking, "How can this be?" I had just gone through one of the most intense experiences in my life, and the sun was setting, just like it always did. I was looking at it and realizing how incredibly beautiful it was and how lucky I was to see it.

It was then that I realized that both experiences could in fact exist simultaneously: I could be raging against the fact that I had just lost my father *and* I could find joy in this beautiful sunset. Ignoring the sunset would not make its beauty go away. Wishing my father alive again would not bring him back.

Zen principles teach that suffering is an opportunity to awaken spiritually. It shows us our attachments, enables us to feel empathy for others, and helps us to develop the courage we need to continue living. In that moment, I knew that I had to let go of my attachment to wanting things to be different, that if I didn't it would keep me from my life. I heard my father's voice in my head, sounding as I knew it would if he had seen the same sunset. I imagined him in the passenger's seat, looking out through the windshield with me, a slight smile on his face. "Donna," he would sigh, "isn't this *bee-YOU-ti-ful*?"

Previously published in Benessere Psicológico: Contemporary Thought on Italian American Mental Health, *edited by Dominick Carielli and Joseph Grasso (2013).*

Where Are You, Daddy? Why Did You Go? (Lorraine)

After my father's death, I was confused and brokenhearted, holding fast to my connection with him wherever I could. Journal writing sustained me, and reviewing those entries now gives a sense of my grief and what emerged as salient: spending contemplative time at our family home where the memories would just pour through me, holding my child and remembering her exceptional relationship with my dad, connecting with friends and family who loved him, and asking why he had to go, over and over. I offer a few entries here that started the month after his death in mid-August.

Early September: Two dreams, the first was in Boston and I was trying to find my way to some school program near Filene's [department store]. I was in the T-station and people were helping me figure out what I had to do. I hurried down to the train but wasn't fast enough, and it closed decisively as I tried to get on. Then I was left in a strange place — somehow nothing was in English anymore — all by myself.

I woke up with the distinct feeling of being abandoned by my parents. I fought so hard to keep my dad alive because I had *so much* to lose. The train to heaven takes on new meaning. I was definitely shut out of this one.

[The] second dream involved chaos at Daddy's house, bad weather and things going wrong, and then Daddy wheeling out from down the hall, dressed and ready for the day, and asking if we still have hamburgers from the ones he had ordered. He had the typical good humor he has had during this whole trial of illness and healing. His remark and demeanor changed everything; we got past the problems and into discussing dinner.

This is my first time "seeing" him. He looked great and was just himself.

Days later: Last night I was up, anxious and searching. I looked out at two a.m. and saw us all out there at a picnic table in the moonlight. I just watched us — the original family, as if it were their backyard. I was not nervous to see spirits there. It seemed normal.

Days later: Alessandria [my daughter] and I spoke of the night Papa died, having spaghettini with red clam sauce with Uncle Joe and Papa and some goofy ice cream for her and Anthony [my nephew], how she wants to do it over again. She wishes you could "rewind" to a part of your life. It was important for her, very big, even fun in a way, the police and excitement and how she and Anthony were such a part of it.

I told her I'd like to rewind but with a different ending — Papa breathes again. She wants to do it exactly the same way — he dies at the end still. That was part of the whole night for her — can't change it. She said, "Mama, sometimes when you die you just die."

After September 11, 2001: It is staggering to me how much I have cried, how utterly inconsolable I feel, and how I both wish for my dad (would have been my first phone call!) and am grateful he has been spared this. He would have grieved for the rest of his life. He would not have been able to die "in full bloom." This would have so deeply distressed his soul. Instead he is in heaven to welcome our innocent martyrs, perhaps cooking great quantities of rigatoni for them. Maybe with some eggplant on the side . . . He would have been here to comfort us in our grief, even through his own despair. He would still have been our dad.

End of September: Good moments, when we invoke "Papa Memorial" and we are sad but something is funny too; my girl brings me to those moments every so often. Suddenly his presence is so big, so present, if only in our hearts, which are breaking. "Papa Memorial Egg Salad Sandwich," like the overstuffed ones they shared in rehab, and she just ordered at a diner in upstate NY.

Mid-October, my dad's house: Things were going so well here; we had a good life going. Why did it have to end? I sit here in the emptiness on this radiant fall day, sun streaming in and leaves falling, and everything seems to be the capriciousness of some uncaring god. I eat provolone and hard roll, his favorites. Everything is still here and he is just gone. The flag Ciro painted in 1976, Mommy's beautiful maple tree, the lilac bush, the old stools from the snack bar, the heart pillowcase Alessandria made him.

Everything is here, waiting for him; yet he is definitely gone. His beloved deck where he spent time since Easter, talking to his niece Mary on the phone. This glorious time of year! All gone. No one to talk to. No one to love me as he did. No one who knows so much. No one who could have told us how to handle ourselves in these dark days.

Later, at home: A few friends came by at my dad's. Debbie said that the house was just too quiet. It was really hard for her to stay. My parents were her parents for so many years. Laurie just sat and stared around, not saying much. Had a long talk with my niece in the Army from Germany, who's scared and on high alert since the attacks and wants to be home with her husband and baby, who wanted to be here when Papa died. Tonight I spoke to Cathy, who was with us every week of my dad's last year. *I feel as if I have cried with everyone today.* Daddy filled the house and now the house is empty.

Then I look at how happy he was in August, his health returning and Ciro's wedding, and I am glad he could die in a euphoric state.

CHAPTER TEN

IMMEDIATE AFTERSHOCKS

$\mathcal{W}$e see the same themes in our lives that we see in so many of our women's experiences: great sorrow; the intensity of the loss and all its ramifications for home and family, being known and being loved; deepening or questioning one's spirituality; sometimes relief and sometimes regret; the importance of how and when our father died, his age, and his health status; the focus on family and close friends; and at times the immediate and drastic reconfiguration of family relationships and dynamics.

In this chapter we look at the many ways women coped with the power and the immediacy of the loss and talked about that coping as well as the ways their fathers might have lingered, or returned, to be with their daughters.

The Enormity of Grieving: Tears, Reflection, Action

Anna D.'s immediate aftershock caused her to be somber, reflective:

> I was quiet, to myself. Crying all the time . . . Very personal. Very hurt. There was an emptiness in my heart. You lose a parent, you have another; you lose both, you are an orphan no matter how old you are . . . When you lose the last parent that you really count on and you have that kind of relationship, it is devastating.

For Joyce, anger was dominant:

> In the first two years I just was angry, mad, mean. I think nobody wanted to be around me. People would talk and I would just start crying for no reason at all. It took me three years to clean out my father's house. I couldn't go in the house, because every time I went in there I would do a little bit and I'd say, "I've got to get out of here." It was like the walls were closing in on me. I had to get out.

I talked to the priest and I told him, "I was angry with God. I'm just outright angry. Why did they take him? He was in the prime of his life." For his age he was, I thought he was; but his sickness he kept to himself. He just didn't want to burden anybody. For the first two years after he died I was just angry. People would pass and it's hard to say, but I didn't have, it's not that I didn't have remorse, but it was like I wasn't here. I wasn't in my body. There was no feeling. How can I say it, numb? . . . I had to go to the psychologist, then to grief counseling. That helped.

In a traditionally Italian gesture, Patricia R. brought figs to our interview in her office, sharing the fruit along with her sadness and her need to keep the connection:

There were a lot of tears. Then I had to leave. I had to go back home. I was teaching, living in Boston. I was extraordinarily sad. I tried to figure out what I needed to do to keep that connection. Then it came to me. I needed to plant things. I live in a condo, so I got this money and said to the guy that takes care of the grounds, I want a tree, I want an azalea bush. So right outside my condo are these, I call them Pasquale [her father's name] bushes . . .

I don't go to the grave. I mean after the funeral, just not my way.

Every summer you have the figs and tomatoes and all that. What he used to do is save the biggest tomatoes, the best tomatoes. I would come home from Pittsburgh looking like a packrat, when you could still take things on the airplane . . . He would be mortified now that I couldn't take these things home . . .

I used to go to the North End on Saturday mornings, because all the old guys were sitting out there in their undershirts, talking, drinking coffee, and I just wanted to sit down there and have espresso or cappuccino and watch them. I didn't really talk; I would say hello to them or *ciao* or something . . . It just seemed like I needed to be there.

Sometimes grieving involves trying to find ways to distract or comfort yourself; one of the daughters painfully related that

coping was drinking. I drank too much for probably the first year after his death. I cried a lot . . . I had to be there for him after my mother passed away. In hindsight, and I told a friend this, I said I never cried after my mother passed away. I was extremely close with her, but it was time I suckered up to be there for him. But I think I cried every day for a year after he passed away.

For Barbara Q., coping took the form of music:

I listened to Chopin's Nocturnes, which really helped me. I would put them on in the car, and they would calm my mother down, too. They really work . . . it was phenomenal. I just kept playing them over and over again as I was driving, and that would help.

Physical work helped Sabrina move forward:

I built a garden in my backyard and I would spend hours and hours back there every day after work. Just gardening. I started growing and jarring tomatoes and growing broccoli, and eggplant, and just everything you can imagine. I still have the garden and spend hours back there every day . . . I painted the kitchen. I painted a bathroom. I started keeping myself really busy. Anything I could do, any activity, I would just start doing it.

Sometimes other events take precedence, as with G.D.F.:

Almost immediately after that, my mom's sister in Florida fell apart . . . and I've had to take care of her . . . I found her a place, assisted living, and I feel guilty to this day when I didn't keep her with me. So . . . I never mourned my father. I didn't have time.

I had my work, and then that following summer, I took a vacation and a writing workshop on the Vineyard. I found that through the writing I was doing I was mourning my dad . . . That started the process of, I guess the mourning process where you start regretting things you never said, the things you did that you wish you hadn't. And I cried a lot . . . suddenly out of the blue I start thinking and crying.

The Family: Intersecting Connections and Our Fathers

The context of other deaths in the family stood out for R.M., as did the feeling that she had done all she could for her dad:

I grieved more my mother and my sister. I felt, my dad was eighty-six, he had a good life. Don't forget, it was not sudden. My mom at sixty retired from work; three months later she was dead. That was tough. I still grieve for her. I still cry for my sister. I still cry for them because they were women that didn't see their whole life.

But my dad slowly got [worse], progressively, so that's part of the grief. It's a process, whereas . . . I saw these women just go . . . I did everything that I could possibly do [for my dad], that I was capable of doing. I didn't feel guilty about anything. I knew that he had a long life. Of course I was sad. I try to tell funny stories and things like that of who he was. But it was tough with my mom and my sister. It was terrible.

The loss of Andrianna's father affected her children and husband:

We had to wear black for nine months. That's a very big thing. It didn't bother me or my sister because we loved him so much that, who cared about the color? . . . My kids [were so upset that] they didn't want to go anywhere, do anything . . .

[Then] it was Christmas and I didn't want to go out for toys. My husband finally said to me, "Anna, I loved him as much as you did, but you've got three children and you've got to go on. He wouldn't like it to be any other way." We used to pray that, "Dad, you've got to help us to get through it." It was just devastating . . .

I stayed at my parents' house for a month and then I said, "I can't do this any longer," because my children were suffering . . . My husband would come here mowing the lawn . . . it was getting harder and harder coming up here. That's when it was decided . . . about us taking this land and building on it . . . So we moved up here.

She heard her father's voice through her brother:

My brother lives right in back, and after my dad died and we came to my mother's house, he was at her house more because my mother was so upset. We'd sit and he'd talk. We just laughed about so many things . . . especially living with the grandparents and how my grandfather would always tell my father, "You gotta do more; you gotta do more."

Giovanna B.L.M.'s intense sadness led her to search for information on her grandfather:

I think it took me a long time, a very long time to think about the many wonderful memories I had without breaking down. I miss him. Where is he? Why did he leave me? Taking it personally. The memories are the afterlife . . .

I went on a search for my grandfather, who died in the United States and we didn't know the circumstances. In the process of doing the research I came across a document, a citizenship paper maybe, but it had my father's signature on it. It was so moving to see.

But you see now I don't break down; I don't cry. I can think of these things and remember.

Many women spoke of the comfort that family connection provided. Madeline Z. spoke of her kids bringing comfort:

If I didn't have little David, I'd have been lost because my husband had to go to work during the day. David was a lot of help. [She felt relieved] because I knew my father was paining, not that he showed it. But you don't like to see anybody in pain. I thought it [death] was a blessing for him. I didn't like that [her children lost a grandparent], because I thought, I never had a grandmother or grandfather. I know I had them, but I never met them . . . They were far away. But it was always nice [for the children] to have a grandpa and grandma. I think that the kids must have missed that.

The loss reached into many levels of Daniela's own identity, bringing up existential questions about who she was and what she was striving for:

When he died, I felt that my entire reason for being was gone. I was living to fulfill his dream, and now he wasn't around to see me do it. So I felt like my life had no purpose when he died, and I was totally bereft.

I had these nightmares of wanting to talk to him. Every time I would publish a poem or a book I would feel bereft because I couldn't show it to him. I couldn't show him the book; I couldn't show him how I was continuing to put his Italian name in the U.S. Library of Congress . . .

I got the New York State Sons of Italy Award and the American Book Award. I have these plaques hanging here. He would be absolutely thrilled to see that I was the first woman with an Italian name to be widely published in American poetry . . . I was a clone of my father and living his dream and fulfilling his dream despite not being the son he always longed for . . .

As a psychologist, you can say that's terrible: why should you have to fulfill your father's dream? But if you look back through history, a lot of great achievers were fulfilling their fathers' dreams, from Mozart to Beethoven. They were really trying to please their fathers, to be somebody.

My father couldn't be a writer. He never got enough credit for his scientific discoveries. He never had enough money to really get ahead, and he didn't know how to hobnob with the WASP world. He always had this immigrant humility.

Our Fathers Return: The Richness of Dreams

While several women reported not dreaming at all about their fathers, some reported very poignant or vivid dreams.

Donna P. speaks of waking up angry from dreams about her father because they were so real, and then it would feel like she was losing him all over again.

Carol A. seemed to look out her window to the ocean's great expanse as she noted:

In a way I mourned him for three years. The way the mourning occurred, he would come to me in dreams in a very positive way. They were not scary at all. They were very positive, loving talks we had. Not even saying things we hadn't said in life, just conversations. And a few times I felt his very presence in the room, and again not frightening, but as a very happy presence.

Dreams contribute to the sense of solace for Linda G.:

I dream about flying with him a lot. I'm always waking up and saying I had a dream about him. It's comforting . . . As I think about it, he's usually younger. The dreams are very vivid . . . He's very active.

One of the things he used to like to do, he was a little bit of a wise guy. He liked to take his cousins up in his airplane and do acrobatics and make them sick. He thought that was just the funniest thing.

P.B.'s father had written down all of his dreams of his parents, and now her dreams of her dad leave her with the most wonderful feelings, even though he doesn't stay:

When I dream of him, he's always smiling but never speaking. This is so weird; I don't know a lot about dreams, but I think every single dream that I have of him . . . it's like I know that he's dead, but I'm amazed that he's here. In my dream I'm saying, "My God, Dad, when did you get here, how long have you been here, how long can you stay?" He smiles and he hugs me. He's always wearing his plaid sports shirt. He doesn't talk necessarily, smiling all the time.

I always remember being filled with this feeling. It must be like when you, if you get to heaven, this is what heaven is like, this euphoric feeling inside of me.

CarolP says she dreams about her father

all the time. What do they call it, point of indecision, or what's the right direction? Maybe I'm finding it from inside, but it comes to me in a dream where we'll have a chat. The same thing with my mother, she'll come to me when maybe I'm having a moral dilemma or how do I handle this at work, they come to me. I guess it's your subconscious. I mean that's how I diagnose it. We'll just talk through it: "What do you think is right? What do you think is wrong?" I know what the decision is in the end, but having that kind of discussion helps.

Though writing was the creative vehicle for Marianna D.T.'s grief, she also recalls dreams about her father following his death:

I had a number of dreams in which he appeared. It was usually as I was waking up and he was usually about to tell me something, and I'd be convinced, "Oh, this was going to be good; I've got to hear this," and every time I would wake up. Sometimes he would be a younger man, but sometimes also an older man . . . My father always said the ghosts were nothing to be afraid of because they were your relatives coming back.

Verna continues to speak with her dad and have dreams on occasion, and he often will tell her what to do about something. Such visits felt like gifts to the bereaved daughters.

DREAMS: VISITS FROM AFAR

In the introduction to his book on dreams in psychotherapy, *Nocturnes: On Listening to Dreams*, psychoanalyst Paul Lippmann describes a summer day canoeing in a saltwater marsh, drifting along lazily, when:

> Suddenly, a hidden great blue heron startles us from our dreaminess with a rush of beating wings, as it explodes from the tall grasses, whooshes up and away, then turns and soars off, graceful wings spread wide, to a further part of the river. Perhaps we'll meet again later. How much like dreams are birds. They float in and out of our awareness. They fly where they will without our will involved. They float in air . . . But at times also, dreams are like fish. Fish live outside our immediate awareness in all layers of the sea, from the surface to the depths. Sometimes we catch one, mostly they go their own way, like dreams. (2000, p. 5)

During the aftershocks of our fathers' deaths, dreams are one important element we encounter. They are the classic doorway to the unconscious and are a way of communicating to ourselves, to others, and perhaps to and from those who are gone. Dreams can show us much about ourselves and our world, where we have been, and how our psyches are moving. Dreaming is often very active in grieving; many people report having vivid dreams during this period that may be comforting, upsetting, inspiring, or painful. You will encounter many dreams in Part V and perhaps in your own grieving process.

Dreams have their place of honor in Italian culture, in myth, in religion, in the ancient world, and in the ancient parts of us. They connect us to our

(Continued)

DREAMS: VISITS FROM AFAR *(Continued)*

fathers who have passed on and to a larger, sacred tradition from many cultures of honoring important dreams.

Giordano et al. (2005) offer this view: "Death . . . has historically been met with impassioned grieving by Italian women, which is deemed appropriate, as women are understood to be expressing grief for the whole family . . . [they] may relay dreams they have had of the deceased or speak of an occasion when they felt the presence of the deceased person, receiving comfort from such experiences and sharing that comfort with other family members" (p. 623).

A dream is a creation in and of itself. It does not have to mean anything in particular. A few simple questions are valuable in helping us understand our dreams: How did it feel? How did it speak to you? Does the dream bring a message or a sign? Can this dream be helpful? We do not assume there is one specific meaning to dreams and do not subscribe to any particular theory of dreams; rather, we are interested in the experience of the dream and the dreamer.

You may have had a special type of dream, particularly vivid and intense, that felt more like a visitation. This type of dream offers a deep feeling of connection with your father and is singularly important. You may have woken up feeling you had actually just been with your father.

Dreams are part of us. We create them, and we can work with them. Dreams can be an integral part of working through our grieving after we have lost our fathers. They can help us cope, remember, love, grieve, move forward, and understand.

Lippmann goes on to wonder about how dreams connect up the generations, given the long history of the importance and even the prophetic nature of dreams. He asks, "Is it possible that dreams glimpse long-ago and far-future experience? Do the generations touch in dreams?" (p. 6).

It is as if another level of reality, one more psychic or spiritual, is playing out when we dream, and on that level, the generations still visit, touch, talk, and, at least for Italians, maybe even share a meal.

Patricia R., whose father died in his grape arbor, commented on current dreams that remind her of the anniversary:

What is interesting was when this [interview] date came up. When I made this date with you, I thought, did I make it on the date he died? Is there some unconscious thing going on here? I had to go look it up, which I did this morning. But I knew [the anniversary of his death was near] from my dreams this week, nightmares really . . . disturbing dreams, where you need help and can't get it, anxiety dreams. I never know the real date. I know it's September. I don't pay attention to the actual date.

September, when the grapes are maturing.

A recurring nightmare spoke to Daniela's agony over losing her father:

I would cry every time I thought of him gone and my inability to speak to him. I had this dream. You see, he had read Shakespeare to me, and there's this song in *Hamlet* that Ophelia sings after her father Polonius is dead. She walks around bereaved, singing, "Full fathom five my father lies, of his bones are coral made./These are pearls that were his eyes; nothing of him doth remain but doth suffer a sea change into something rich and strange."

The song kept running through my head, so I would have this nightmare that I was a diver in a black rubber suit, with flippers and a tank on my back. I'd be diving in the ocean to find my father, and he would be sealed in a glass coffin, and his eyes were pearls, and he was becoming something rich and strange. What I think it meant to me was that he was becoming my poetry. I wrote a poem about that: "American Sonnets for My Father."

I had all these horrible nightmares about trying to talk with him, and I've recently written a poem . . . called "No Longing So Complete": "There is no longing so complete as the desire to talk with the dead." A lot of people appreciate that line . . . because they identify with that line. So I had this longing to talk with him, to tell him how much I appreciated him, to tell him how I understood the sorrows of his life.

Belief Systems: What Happens Next?

Our belief systems — which tell us what happens when we die, such as whether there is an afterlife and, if so, what the afterlife is like — can take many forms and can include religion, a broader concept of spirituality, and philosophical or existential concepts. What we think or hope happens can definitely have an impact on our grieving and sense of loss!

For some of us, the idea of an afterlife and what we do or do not believe suddenly becomes much more important, critical even, with the loss of someone close. We may need to know where our beloved family member or friend *really is*, and we may hope for, or experience, contact with the spirit of the dead. We may suddenly scrutinize our early, comfortable ideas, or this new experience may reaffirm our beliefs.

Our participants mentioned many different beliefs about what happens after death, ranging from absolutely no belief in the afterlife to a firm belief in the Catholic ideas of heaven and hell, with a lot of variation and nuance in between.

Donna P. strongly believed that her father went to heaven:

I do believe that he went to heaven . . . When we had our son, I was sad because my dad was not here, but I knew my dad saw him and knew him. I couldn't see his reaction; that's why I was sad . . . Yes, absolutely, my dad saw him.

Louise also felt that there is something beyond, and that was a comfort to her:

I think that they go on to a better place, whether they're buried or whether they're . . . cremated. I believe that my parents joined my brother and some of his family. That's my belief. I always believe that you're going to see somebody later. You're going to be rejoined somewhere along the line. I believe that when I die I'll see everybody.

Belief in heaven helped Pat M. accept her father's death:

I think probably that [my mother accepting the death] helped us. I really can't say that I didn't accept it. I knew it would happen. I just felt, "Well, that's it. He is in a good place." I knew he was in heaven because he was good all his life. He never would steal a penny from anybody. He worked hard, and he brought up his family the right way, and he went to church. I mean what else? . . . We missed him. There was a big space there. We really missed him a lot. I always thought on Easter, "Oh, my God. He is up in heaven with all the beautiful choirs of angels and the Easter lilies."

His legacy has boiled down to my grandchildren. I think he gave me a lot of faith so I could project it to my children. They loved my father. We talk about him all the time. We just talk about him like he is still here. It's happy.

R.M. describes a vision in connection with her religious beliefs:

I am Catholic. I do feel I'm spiritual. I do feel that there is a presence, I do . . . Every now and then I'll get a sign from my sister . . . , my mom [both deceased]. When I went to the hospital to find my father in the emergency room, we had stopped at a light, and the funny thing is, my husband and I, he always thought I was nuts when I would tell him, "Gee, I feel like I have a sign or feeling of Mom." He sloughed it off, the scientist, the doctor. Anyway we both turned around at the light and we saw an image of my mother. It was really wonderful. I was so happy . . .

I got the phone call that said he's probably gone. We had to go confirm that. But I was so happy. My husband looked at it like, "What?" I said, "Well I told you, every now and then. When you're lucky enough to get it . . . " Of course, I really felt Mom was there to take him, to call him, to be part of his life. She appeared in a dress and an image that was just about the time she died . . . I just smiled and felt so full.

Andrianna links her Catholicism to St. Anne and spoke of the vicissitudes of feeling helped and not helped with her father's and sister's deaths:

For St. Anne there was a novena every year to go to. Now, my dad died on St. Anne's [Day], July 27th. My sister gets cancer. She gets operated on [on] St. Anne's day . . . We had a lot of faith in St. Anne. St. Anne got her through that operation and everything was great. October 27th my sister died. I never went to St. Anne's for the novena after that because I felt as though it isn't a good omen, yet I'm very religious.

When my sister was dying . . . she'd say, "Daddy is coming every night talking to me." I mean the love that we had for this man was beyond. She says, "I'm not afraid anymore because Dad is waiting for me." So I always think of her up there with my grandparents and the way they cooked. I know it sounds funny, but that's what gets you through . . . my sister up there cooking and them all sitting around a table.

(Our interview was near Thanksgiving, and Andrianna's menu for dozens of friends and family members sounded incredible: *cavatelli*, *bracciola*, wild mushrooms, antipasto, . . . in addition to traditional American foods.)

Beliefs in an afterlife are complicated, and belief systems change over time, as Carol A.'s discussion illustrates:

At that time, I think I was still a believer in heaven and hell and I'm agnostic now; it's just a little too mysterious as far as I'm concerned. I don't know if I ever even thought about where my father would go.

Actually, maybe I was troubled by it, because I remember one time my father said to a priest that he practiced birth control . . . and the priest wouldn't give him absolution. He said you'd have to stop doing that or go to hell. Maybe the reason they were practicing birth control was because after having me, my mother almost died. My father said that would be a hell of a thing — to expect a man to give up his family.

At the time I was a believer, so maybe I thought he was in hell. I don't think I really believed that he was in hell . . . But in those visitations I thought he's somewhere out there and he obviously wasn't in hell. I think of it as more like heaven.

The Catholic religion can be complicated too, and several women expressed a "pick and choose" approach to Catholicism. This seems to fit with the view on Italian Americans and their relationship to Catholicism noted by Giordano and his co-authors: that the ritual, drama, and family elements are the centerpieces of Catholicism rather than dogma or church authority.

Madeline Z. seemed to cast a glance over her whole life's experience when she commented:

We were brought up Catholic: if you're good on this earth, you go to heaven . . . Oh definitely, he [her father] was too good a guy to go down below. I mean that's what we thought in those days. Now it's a different story; you think different, the way the religion turned out, especially the Catholic religion.

Lisa expresses it this way:

I'm Catholic but I'm the kind of Catholic that interprets things their own way. I went to Mass every Sunday . . . I find the Catholic part is a cultural thing, but I'm more interested in the spiritual side, and it's not necessarily related to all the dogma of the church. I use it as my environment in which I can be spiritual . . .

I honestly feel that death is not the end . . . I believe in the soul, whatever it is. I don't know where it goes or what it is or whether it's just pieces of consciousness . . . I'd like to believe that there's some . . . whatever God is . . . a person or . . . I'd like to think that ultimately pieces of this whatever can connect to . . . other pieces . . . I felt that the spirituality has helped . . . not necessarily the Catholicism, but the spirituality piece.

I obviously feel there's something there that goes on and it's somewhere, and I'd like to be able to connect with that again . . . Even though I'm Catholic, and that doesn't sound like a Catholic thing . . . I felt it more when it was early on.

Some women moved from Catholicism to another practice or worldview that incorporated Catholicism, such as B.:

I wouldn't say that I have a belief system about that in any formal way. However, I don't think we disappear. I left Catholicism because it was so dogmatic, but I never left the spirituality of Catholicism, the deepest part. I always felt the one important concept was . . . one must love thy neighbor as thyself, and if you really lived that you really didn't need anything else. I would say that the last thirty years, I've followed a more Buddhist tradition, and I have a sitting practice, but I'm not a dogmatic Buddhist. I don't think anything "post-Catholicism" can be dogmatic!

I had to deal and will have to deal more with death of people who are very close to me. I feel that they are still with me . . . even the things that we've talked about today are not things that are very absent from my everyday life, frankly. The gifts that I receive from different people . . . I think I always feel him kind of on my shoulder . . .

Especially as I'm getting older, I'm going to be sixty-nine, now I have grandchildren, there's a sense of continuity and an appropriateness of passage . . . and that we're all here as *rondini di passaggio*, birds of passage; we're here just passing for a while. It's not always easy and I have to work on trying to accept my place in this too. It means accepting the people who have gone before me. I am looking forward to seeing them at some future point . . .

Some of the [art] pieces I just made are *rondini di passaggio*. The [Italian] immigrants were always called the birds of passage because they, more than any other immigrant, went to Italy back and forth. It's funny because even the show that I just made . . . it's about life's passage.

Giovanna B.L.M. feels that memories are the afterlife — rather than a specific place, such as "heaven." Adding to this sense of complexity, she also commented that she believes Italians are anarchists and as such need to create their own versions of things. Therefore, as an Italian, you can be a communist and still get your child baptized without it feeling like a contradiction.

Anne P. spoke about her parents being reunited after death:

Immediately I think it was the comfort of knowing that he wasn't struggling with the health issues anymore, that his life had just not been the same after my mother died. As much as he loved us and his grandchildren, it just wasn't the same . . . I think there was comfort in knowing that whether it's what really happened or not, he certainly believed that he was going to be back with her. In fact whether I believe it or not, in that last phone call I said to him, "Say hello to Mom for me." So there was that.

Anne P.'s hopes sum up a feeling that we saw in many daughters:

I certainly grew up believing. My beliefs have changed over time, but I think there's still that hope . . . that there's something after, that it may not be the way we were taught in the Baltimore catechism, that there's something, that there's a way of staying connected. Right up until now, I continue to feel connected. I still talk to him, to my mother as well, or make comments. I'll be talking, especially to my sister, and one of us will say, "Dad would have said such and such." I think there are ways in which he certainly is still alive for me.

We grieve our fathers in many ways and with many feelings. We may be unbearably sad, intensely angry, or a bit relieved. We may listen to music, drink more than usual, or emulate what he would have done. The longing to hear and see our dads can be huge, and the subsequent silence and emptiness can be daunting. Yet our fathers do often return to us in different ways, through dreams and words and images and the things we find ourselves doing. What a wonderful gift to ourselves and our fathers if we can accept and even welcome these moments of returning, these priceless visits.

CHAPTER ELEVEN

LOSS OVER THE YEARS: COMFORT AND COPING

*A*lthough it may seem that the initial loss is all encompassing, at times overwhelming, and will never subside, our feelings and thoughts do change over time, perhaps slowly or perhaps quickly, sometimes in a comforting direction and sometimes toward greater distress and feelings of aloneness or regret.

As the daughters spoke about the months and years following their fathers' deaths, certain incidents stood out as having had an impact on their relationships with, and images of, their dads, or on how each daughter sensed her father's presence as she was grieving. We look at these incidents here, as they powerfully evoke our lost fathers and hence affect our grieving process.

What Brings Dad Back?

Emotions crept up unexpectedly on R.L. one day:

> I would have to say the only thing that has really pulled at my heartstrings is that at my office they hired this guy who was Italian American. At the first all employees meeting, he was up there and he has very Italian American features: his hair is very thick, curly, and jet black like my father's hair was when I was a kid. And so all of a sudden I'm sitting in the meeting and I start to feel really sad. I'm like, "Oh, his hair reminds me of my father's hair." It was just him introducing himself and what visions he had for our office, and I said to people, "I found that really emotional" and I realized why.
>
> I said, "His hair is exactly like my father's hair was when I was little." That's the only actual emotional . . . my father died in '07, and that was probably 2010 that I was staring at his hair and really, really missed my father.

Being at his house also makes her miss him:

> Every now and then I would say to my mother, "I miss Daddy. Do
> you miss him?" and she says, "Oh yes, every day." I go over there and he's
> not around, and then the pillow he used to lie on on the sofa smells like
> him. I still check to see if it still smells like him. It does . . . I'll notice my
> father's loss when I go over there . . . but no one sits around and talks
> about it.

Sometimes the dad comes back through those who are most closely
related, either as family or neighbors, as Linda G. describes:

> When I see people who are related, I look for similarities, physical
> similarities. One of my cousins has hands that are exactly like my
> father's. I found myself one day, just reaching out. I grabbed his hand
> and was looking at it. He was fine, but he asked, "What are you doing?"
> "Your hands look just like my father's" was all I could say. It was nice . . .
>
> I look for him in other people and other circumstances. I look in
> particular where he and my mother both grew up, in Needham . . . a lot
> of stores have old historic photos and I look at those and imagine what
> it was like. He has one surviving sister who is ninety-two, and I take her
> out to lunch . . . We talk a lot about family and grandparents.

Seemingly small things bring us back to our dads. Anne P. describes
these:

> There are little things . . . my father loved corny jokes. If someone tells a
> corny joke I always think, "Oh, he would have really enjoyed this."
>
> He was sort of a mild Red Sox fan, whereas I'm a more rabid Red Sox
> fan, and . . . I'd make a comment to him about it . . . I've thought, "What
> would he have said?" He would have said, "Oh those bums."
>
> Holidays, certainly [make me think of him]. Or if I'm looking
> through pictures or talking to the kids, if one of the kids brings
> something up . . .

Sometimes family issues compromise one's ability to grieve and remember.
R.M. feels her memory of her father is colored by complications of relationships
and property that arose at the end of her father's life and continue:

I think about him. I try to think of happy times. I don't think of the sadness. I really don't. The only thing is, my dad did not marry a very nice woman . . . she's given us an incredible amount of headaches. To this day honestly, I felt my dad should have resolved his financial affairs. He left the house to us, but he also gave us a lot of money that she took from him, which I only found out a few months ago . . . It is a big headache.

In that sense, when I think about my father, it is tainted by that . . . It's very difficult to separate the love and affection and then the grief . . . He did not resolve certain things in his life . . . Because he was afraid of this woman. He needed her to take care of him. He was diabetic. I could only do so much. I was living miles away. She was caring for him day by day . . .

It's a burden on me because I have to take care of his house. I don't want anything to do with it. I have beautiful memories there of my mother, but I just want to sell the house and get rid of it, but I have to wait till she dies . . . I have help from my husband. It does require financial assessment and making decisions, going down there. We spent all last summer cleaning it. It's been a lot.

So does that have an impact on grief? Yeah . . . You strive to create emotional distance and do what you have to do. I cope knowing that I'm trying to save it for my brother and his son.

Anna D. recalls her father when she hears his name:

And, his name, every time that name comes up, my father's, it's like my heart opens . . . I feel it, right away, as soon as I hear that name, it is my father. You know what I mean? . . . He is right there.

Sense of Presence

A sense of presence, a feeling that he is here, with us, is very precious when we have lost someone we love. Linda G. has a strong sense that her father is nearby:

I do believe that a spirit lives on in some form or fashion. I do feel like he's with me, whether it's something involving nature — he was a huge lover of nature and animals, especially dogs — or the weather. He was always bringing home some hurt animal.

Sometimes when I see a beautiful butterfly on a flower, it just makes me think of him . . . that déjà vu thing; you do something and you're sure you've done it before? I mean sometimes not only do I think *I've* done it before, but I almost feel like I can turn and say, "Haven't *we* done this before?"

I do feel his presence around a lot . . . Sometimes his wisdom, his wit, and his humor.

Louise also feels her father's presence:

I think about my father all the time. We think of him every Christmas because we have to designate somebody to hand out the presents. I think of him when I look around the kitchen and I know that he painted it and took great pride in helping us. We have great stories. We get together and we'll tell stories about, "Remember the time [he did this or that]?"

It's funny because for years we didn't talk about my brother [who died young], even though I felt that I wanted to. Then one day we started. *It is cathartic. It really is a good thing to do* . . . But we were nervous because my parents aged ten years right in front of us when he died, and we did not want to bring those memories up.

Her father brought Lisa a loud and clear message about what to do with her life and her grief:

After he died . . . I just couldn't deal with it. I went to a bereavement group. It was really helpful and they did things like write a letter to your father and have one written back . . . It was very therapeutic. It really helped a lot, because I just missed him so much.

I really felt like he was with me all the time. I used to say that, and I remember to this day, I said to my boyfriend, "I think he's with me . . . " and my boyfriend would be like, "Whatever. You wanna think that, yeah." You know because he was totally unspiritual . . . So that was . . . horrible, that was not good at all . . .

I broke up with him, and on the next day . . . I was crossing the street, and a car hit me, and I went flying in the air in front of my twin sister, and

I lived . . . amazingly enough, I lived. I should have been dead, and I was incredibly lucky, and so of course I . . . and my sister said the same thing. My sister would say, "Dad's influence! Right? You survived because he helped."

After that, I felt that really strongly, he saved me. Like, why am I alive? I shouldn't have been alive. I shouldn't . . . I mean I went flying, and I just lived. My dad influenced me after he died! I said, "I'm getting married; I'm having a baby." It took me a while to get over everything . . . but I wanted to live! I kept saying, "Why, why, why did he save me? I'm meant to be here for some reason." I felt that it was because of him. Like he was trying to tell me something, right?

Sometimes the dad's presence is not quite so life-changing or dramatic but comes from the simple basics of life. We've written about foods and aromas bringing back memories and feelings, but tomatoes, in particular, seem to be essential to so much that is Italian. For some women tomatoes are almost a symbol of their relationships with their dads, one that reappears time and again. When asked what was helpful to her after her father's death, Christine P. responded:

Tomatoes . . . I remember it was about a year after my father died, and I had a community garden, and I smelled the tomatoes. And it was like all these sensations of him being, him holding me, skin against skin, hot summer days. He would be working in the garden without a shirt and maybe I didn't have a shirt on. I'd run, he'd pick me up. The touch of his skin and the touch of my skin, very sensual, all the senses going. The smell of dirt and tomatoes and sun and sweat made me really miss him and miss my happy, loving, affectionate father.

Her relationship with her father was complicated and it continues to be so. After his death, she describes him appearing in this way:

He came back and visited me after he died . . . Very frightening. He was very strong, he was very patriarchal, and he was not the loving father. It was like, you have to do this, this, and this, then you have to be this way and this way . . . [It was a] vision. I was alone in a room at a friend's house. It was like "boom" — a total body experience. Very intense. When I walked downstairs everyone said it looked like I'd seen a ghost. I had. My dad. Nowadays I don't dream.

At this point, she feels she has some say in what she experiences and remembers:

I'm surprised I'm saying all this about my dad in this moment because I don't usually go there, I go to the more pleasant memories . . . I think of him as a tall, blonde, happy Italian guy, drinking his wine or beer, singing, being where we used to go on picnics with the whole extended Italian family, sitting with his mother and his wife and his children and sisters . . .

Certain times he does [come into my mind]. Certainly approaching this interview he does. On the Day of the Dead I always think about him. All Saint's Day . . . I certainly think about him whenever I'm around a really luscious tomato and when I cook . . . When I hear a baseball game on the radio I think of him. Pittsburgh Pirates. Any time I eat polenta I think of him and *bacala* — his mother's food. When I make a salad and put things in it other than lettuce I think of him: "Ah, he wouldn't eat this," I say to myself.

Once he got a hole in one and I kept his golf ball. I have it in my kitchen drawer, and when I open the drawer, I see his lucky hole in one golf ball. I think about him. Then it's gone. It's not staying with me, but I know he's there. He lives with me — sights, sounds, smells, the golf ball, the radio sports, tomatoes — he's always there.

As time goes on for Anna D., she just keeps missing her dad:

I miss him, miss him, miss him. I miss my mother too, but my father, we had a different kind of relationship . . . I am struggling with exactly what to say, but . . . I feel he is with me all the time . . . He worked with us [at the bakery] after his retirement, and he was always around me and doing stuff and going places. I could send him out to different stores, different places, twenty times a day, and he would never say, "No."

When I go to the cemetery, I talk to him . . . I did that for his birthday, all the holidays. I go around the cemetery every Sunday anyway, but special trips on the special birthdays and holidays . . . I wish he was here.

C.N. emphasized:

He's still very much a presence in my life. It's not very many days that I don't think of him in some way, that something doesn't remind me of him, or I don't hear his voice in my head. I think, in many ways, he is still very much with me.

In summing up the interview, she commented,

I do obviously still miss him very much. It's good; talking about him keeps him alive.

The Questions Left Unanswered

Anne P. is left with longings:

As good a relationship as we had, I wish I could have known him better as a person. I think about that more now, because as my own kids get into their twenties I've gotten to think, I don't think they know me that well as a person, and I think, well, I had till I was almost fifty.

In some ways he was a very private person, and so I think I knew him very well as a daughter . . . him as a father, but I don't think I knew him all that well as a person, or as well as I would have wanted to . . . If he had been more of an outgoing person or maybe if I had asked more things or asked different things. As I got older I did ask more questions and I did put more pieces together, but I would have liked to have had more time.

Speaking about him with us was

bittersweet, one more case of evidence to me that his spirit is still alive and that our relationship is still alive.

Again we are reminded that "Italians tend to keep their dead with them" (Giordano et al. 2005), and we see here the comfort, for the most part, and the value of keeping our fathers near. We are living out the process of continuing our connections, through talking, dreaming, or cutting tomatoes. Sometimes we feel that soft presence; sometimes he comes unexpectedly and emphatically. We may grieve more, or more deeply, because of the connection, but it also sustains us.

CHAPTER TWELVE

How We Change
and Don't Change

*T*he fields of psychology and psychotherapy are devoted to understanding human change and growth. We see growth as always possible when someone has undergone such a major life event as the loss of a parent, but it can come in vastly different shapes and colors and may not even be detectable by those around the person.

The whole idea of change is provocative and engenders many questions: Do we change abruptly or gradually? Is it for the better or for the worse? Is it change if we are becoming more of ourselves, more of what we always were? Can we always see the changes that take place, or can others perhaps see them more clearly? Do we recognize a change when it happens or only in hindsight? How do we know that a change is related to one event and not another?

Profound losses can lead to profound changes. We do keep growing throughout our lives and through our grief — developing even as adults. For adult daughters who have lost their fathers, the period of time following their deaths can be one of change.

Evolving from her reactions to her father's death, journalist Clea Simon (2001) is one of the few writers who has examined a daughter's experience after her father dies. She describes the experience in this way:

> When I think of the changes that we all have gone through since losing our fathers, I find myself seeing the girls we were as well as the women we are now. I think of how we've grown, how we have learned to assert essential parts of ourselves that for so many reasons could not come to the fore while our fathers were alive . . . [His death] is an opportunity to recognize that the man who first held us did in fact shape us. And now that the mold of his strong influence is removed we can see what

we learned from him, and where our native structure, our basic form, reasserts itself. (p. 202)

In this chapter, the daughters describe the transformations they went through after losing their dads.

Creating a New Perspective

For Donna P. there was a great deal of change:

> It was at a time that I was going to be somebody's daughter and somebody's wife, so I did change. I did too because Dad took care of my mom. After he died, I became her social director and her nurse, taking her to doctors. So I had to grow up.

Verna L. felt she had changed:

> I've gotten maybe a little more confident. I feel better that I was there [when he died]. I feel really good about that. I feel good that we can talk about him; in the family we can joke about him now. It was hard at first, but now we can say, "Oh, who does that remind you of?" And then we'll say Vinnie. Like, my brother is an awful lot like him. He'll do the Jesus Christ [imitation] and everybody will look and stop and go, "Who's the Vinnie today?"

That really brings her father back.

For R.L., change came before his death:

> It was not at his death that I felt transformed. It really was a transformational process for me to be on the journey with him and my mother as his mind and body declined for three years. The transformation was through my witnessing the illness and how I view my parents. I felt privileged to be there to assist them.

Along with many others, C.Z. expressed the vulnerability of "moving up the chain to the older adult" and becoming an "orphan." In addition, she noted:

I feel like life is less interesting, less satisfying, duller. One thing I really wish for, and I just wish we could all have this, with all this virtual reality that we have. If we could just go back, and I could just be with my dad one day when he was vital, and have one of those conversations, maybe with all of this adult wisdom that I gathered, or could ask really the kinds of questions that I want to know now. I just wish I could have twenty-four hours, twelve, just with him. A deep longing is still within me.

Her father's death and then her own illness engendered change for P.B.:

I used to worry a lot, but I think losing my father and then getting sick myself, those are the two points in my life where I realized that life is short. I know it sounds cliché, but I think I just learned to let go and not dwell on bad things. Having one child, and a daughter, can I drive myself crazy thinking about what might happen to her when she drives back to school at night and parks her car and walks? Oh yeah, I could drive myself crazy. And I used to.

But since losing my dad, I realized that you have to celebrate their life. You cannot pull the covers over your head and revert to what could have been. I think things have happened in my life . . . since he's died, where I have learned to mourn . . . get upset and then move on.

Becoming stronger or more grown up was a theme for several women. Lisa saw this in herself:

I think I became stronger. I think I became more no nonsense. Part of me craves and misses what was there, but I wanted to create something for myself. I could have very easily gone into a path where I didn't . . . It got me moving. His death and then my accident, the combination . . . got me moving and I keep saying it was related to him saving me.

Andrianna's father died unexpectedly right before retirement, and she felt she changed:

At first you're bitter though. You know you do get bitter. That it's not fair that a man, he just said he was going to start having life easy, and he never got to get there, to enjoy life with us. Because here I had a brother with four years of college. [So it was] work, work, work seven days a week.

[The bitterness] does last a while . . . being that young and such a hardworking man and so good. I can't even give you an amount of years because it would be a long time. I can't say, because there's still times you think about how lucky some people are and how my brother, my kids, he'd be so proud of them. Never lived to see any of it, not even one of them. It would have been great. There's so much you miss out on.

C.N. expressed a sense of new possibilities:

In some ways, I feel a little bit more free to do things my own way that I might have felt more constrained when they were alive. Things like sort of a parting of the ways with the church and things that I have actually considered, seeking another church, which I probably never would have done while they were alive. Some things like that, but I wouldn't say I'm significantly changed.

Donna C.'s experience of herself after her father's death reflected a paradox that she eloquently described:

I won't say I feel changed as a person. I feel that I am more of who I should be. My father had certain expectations, and there are certain things that he was very proud of, such as when I got my doctorate. He had this expectation that once you are a professional, you do as much as you can. In that sense, I feel, yes, that part may be changed. You don't drop the ball; you have to keep moving forward in that regard.

CarolP shared what a friend had told her:

He said, "You're going to be surprised how much time you have on your hands," because caring for someone when they're having health conditions, it just totally absorbed me. Then I'm, "All right, what am I going to do? What am I going to do?" So I teach; I volunteer as a teacher. I take classes. I do that stuff to fill, initially it was like staring at the four walls. It's like, "Okay, you have to fill this time. How are you going to do it?"

Carrying On in Dad's Image

Some daughters, like Louise, felt continuity within themselves rather than change:

> I don't think I changed. Maybe a little bit. But I honestly feel like if I did I wouldn't honor him. My father was a nice, pleasant man, always smiling. If I changed because, if I all of a sudden turned into crabbiness, it wouldn't be honoring him.

She saw herself and her father as very happy people.

Anna D. felt similarly:

> I wouldn't say I've changed, but I tried to carry on all his beliefs and all his way of doing things . . . For example, he and my mother would take care of my children all the time. I do the same with my grandchildren. I am trying to do all the things he used to do.

Patricia R. saw something important that continued:

> I mean if there is [change], it's not conscious. The only other way I think [her father's death] may have a continuing impact, my brother's son is also a doctor and moved to Boston . . . I loved having them here. It was the creation of yet another family generation. Since I live alone, that was great . . . My house became the focal point for ten years of family activity . . . That's a connection to my dad because he would have liked that. My nephew was very fond of my father, so he has a lot of the traditions that he learned from my father. And his name is Patrick.

Our fathers are gone. The loss remains etched into the deepest parts of our psyches, reverberating and helping us grow, grow up, and, in most cases, grow stronger. Yet it also catches us at the most unexpected moments: when we turn a corner, open a drawer, pick a tomato, or hear his name.

If we can remain open to the loss *and* to living our lives fully in the here and now, weaving through both of these experiences sometimes simultaneously, sometimes separately, we will continue on this path.

PAUSE AND REFLECT

Take a moment to review the stories you have just read. Recall what those early weeks and months after your father's death were like for you. Reflect on the changes you saw in yourself and consider the questions below.

✦ *Grief is different for everyone. How did you experience the sound of your own "one heart breaking" after the death of your father?*

✦ *What do you remember feeling after you lost your father? What feeling did you have the most difficulty with? Can you think of that feeling now, without judging it?*

✦ *What are your stories about your father that bring comfort?*

✦ *Did relationships with other family members change after your father's death, either positively or negatively?*

✦ *Did you have dreams, images, voices, or "visitations" from your dad after his death? What were they telling you? How did you respond to them? Did they bring comfort, sadness, more connection, or more disconnection?*

PART SIX

LIVING WITH OUR FATHERS IN OUR HEARTS

*W*hile losing any loved one will leave us mourning, losing a parent propels us into the world of grief in a unique way, even when we are adults. No matter what our relationships have been, when our fathers die we become physically disconnected from one of the people who gave us life. We lose a genetic and lifelong connection that we don't have with anyone else — not with siblings, not with close friends, not with our own children, not with our spouse or partner.

The loss of a parent causes us to question our assumptions about who we are and who we will become as roles shift within the family and we forge a new identity. We have to ask ourselves, "Who am I as a fatherless daughter?"

In Part V we discussed the monumental changes in ourselves both of us experienced after the deaths of our fathers. How we thought about grief, how we related to our mothers and siblings, and how we approached the world shifted both unexpectedly and powerfully. Sometimes these shifts were born of the deep connection we had with our fathers; other times they seemed to arise because this connection had taken a different form — one without our fathers in our daily lives.

Over the years since our fathers' deaths, reconciling these changes has been embedded in a deep connection to our Italian culture, a culture that has given us a blueprint to continue the bonds and remember our fathers.

"A few years before he died, my father spoke to me words that could have well expressed the wishes of his generation and the generations that preceded him," relates oral historian Anthony Riccio, "'Anthony, if I die and you don't remember me, then I'm dead, but if I die and you remember me, then I'm alive — so don't forget me'" (2006, p. xx). There is a sort of immortality in our remembrance and talk of those who have gone.

Bona (2010) examines many Italian American authors' treatment of death and grieving and concludes that the writers "generally shift toward more open endings, rejecting not only the closure that death guarantees, but also suggesting their staying power as immigrant Italians to the new world, as Italian Americans" (p. 204). She feels that storytelling around death includes "lessons in survival and lessons for the future, reinforcing the fact that relationships change but do not end after death" (p. 208).

In this final part we look at the ways in which Italian American women experience and think about their dads after, in some cases long after, he has died. What has become of the intense missing and yearning? How have daughters "come to terms" with the loss? We explore what women have done to honor or remember their dads, how they have held their dads in memory. Finally, we consider how their deaths have changed us, changed our worlds, and what loss has given us, because that is key to the transformation that takes place inside of us.

Smelling the Roses (Donna)

Roses always had special meaning for my father. In the backyard of the house where I grew up, they grew in abundance along the fence that separated our yard from the neighbor's. They were the old-fashioned red climbing variety, and climb they did, softening the metal hardscape of the fence and maintaining some sense of privacy for us when we were out in the yard splashing in the pool or sunbathing.

I never knew if my parents planted the roses themselves or if they predated their living in the house, but my father especially loved those roses. He tended them with great care, carefully pruning them into manageable shape, stepping back frequently to admire his handiwork, consulting with my mother on whether this branch or that one needed to be removed. I also remember him cursing loudly if a thorn caught his finger and a Band-Aid was required, causing an interruption in his work. I loved the moments when I caught him in midmovement as he bent in closer, eyes closed, to take in their fragrance.

A photograph of my father, one that hangs in my office at home, says it all: he is standing in that backyard in a crisp white shirt, holding a bouquet of the roses over his heart, looking down at them, smiling. As I mentioned, my father loved those flowers.

We never had roses at our next house, though my mother grew peonies, his second favorite flower. Years later, when my spouse and I bought an antique home with lots of yard, my father and I discussed the possibility of planting a rose garden. His eyes lit up as we discussed the best spot for full sun, along the house or farther into the yard, tea roses or hybrids. This would be our joint venture, and I felt pleased that my father would be part of this house in this way. It was August when we moved in, so we thought that breaking ground the following spring would give us enough time to really plan it out and choose the right roses.

Spring did eventually come, but in grief I ushered it in without my dad — he had died that February, in the middle of a blizzard, the cold snowy landscape forestalling the rosy *primavera* the two of us had envisioned.

Bereft though I was, I knew that my father would have wanted me to continue with our plans for the rose garden. I chose the spot, put on my gardening gloves, and dug. Many tears watered that piece of land, but I planted roses whose names had special meaning for me: "Gemini" for my father's astrological sign, "Memorial Day" for his birthday, "Peace Rose" for his time in the military, "Altissimo" for our Italianness. Slowly that tiny oasis filled with color and fragrance, took shape with roses that represented the many facets of my father's life. The whole of him was there with me, in each vibrant flowering bud, in each greening leaf, in each waft of sweet-scented rose perfume.

Since it was first planted, ten years ago, the rose garden has grown in more ways than one. My mother, too, has since passed away so, for her, peonies now also burst open every June with their heady fragrance and over-the-top flowers. A rosebush has been planted in memory of my spouse's mother, as well. I planted a peony for my sister, who taught me most of what I know about gardening and who still advises me on caring for my roses.

It is a gentle intermingling, the roses with the peonies, as was my parents' working together in life and in the garden. As I write this, my father's birthday will come tomorrow, for yet another year, and I will sit by the rose garden and think of him. I glance up at the photograph of him holding the bouquet of roses against his heart, smiling, and remember fondly how much he loved those roses.

Thinking, Feeling, Feeding (Lorraine)

The centrality of family and feeding in my life, the legitimacy of strong emotion and connection present in my work as a psychologist, and what we call "critical thinking" in psychology come directly from my dad, who lived those every day. He remains in conversation with me over how to cut the garlic for garlic and oil, why olives need to be washed before they are dressed, and how essential it is to commemorate the big, sacramental moments of life — you must honor the baptisms *and* the funerals! In fact we had a grand "Joe Mangione Memorial Dinner" five years after his death, inviting friends, relatives, and those who had worked in his restaurant; the price of admission was cooking one of his signature dishes from the restaurant. He would have loved it. Every time we come together in celebration, his food is present, as is he.

I wish I had more of his resilience and optimism, and I work at that. I am constantly inspired by his integrity. I am motivated by his understanding of the need to really think things through and to do so from many different angles, and I try to do this in my teaching and writing as well as when trying to solve personal quandaries and questions about life. I hear his voice when I go to vote, and his independent spirit is reminding me, "Don't pull the party lever," for voting solely on the basis of party, any party, was, for him, the surest sign of not thinking.

I am surprised by how much I have taken on his love of history and his need to know and understand the larger world. This came together poignantly and profoundly when my daughter, at age fifteen and working on a history project, was reacquainted with her grandfather through a video he had made for Yale University's Fortunoff Video Archive for Holocaust Testimonies about his World War II experience of coming upon a Nazi concentration camp at Ebensee, Austria. Seeing this video was a hugely emotional experience for me, my husband, and my daughter.

We sat transfixed, sometimes weeping and sometimes just holding our breath, as we watched him carefully choose his words, wanting to tell exactly what he saw and felt, yet also not wanting to tell. His staccato breathing, his looking away and down, his holding a cigarette, and his subdued words conveyed his distress at telling the story that had to be told. Themes of integrity, connectedness, openness to emotion, and desire to understand spoke loudly as he described the horror he had witnessed and his responses to that experience.

His worldview and sensibility live on now in his granddaughter. Now that she has just graduated from high school, with honors, accolades, and a speech filled with both wisdom and exuberance, I see him beaming, traveling with her into her future.

Earlier in the book I wrote about walking with my dad as a child, as he sang and we talked. Years later we would dance at my wedding to the song he sang as we walked, "An Old Fashioned Walk." There was never hesitation in my mind about which song we would dance to. I.have kept walking; I have taken a walk almost every day of my life. It is my exercise, musing, connecting with friends, retreating into myself, loving the world, praying, being open to inspiration, moment of everything coming together. On the best days I walk with my daughter. Every day I still walk, in essence, with my dad.

CHAPTER THIRTEEN

FATHERS AS A PART
OF THEIR DAUGHTERS

*R*emember our discussions earlier in the book of the psychological processes of *internalization* — which explains that we take someone inside of us and that person becomes part of who we are — and *attachment* — which explains our early need to be in close relationships with other human beings, our caretakers? We see those concepts come alive in ourselves as we live with our fathers in our hearts. There is a crucial part of relationships that continues even when one person has died; we don't have to frantically search for some contrived "closure."

For Italians especially this continuity — this need "to keep their dead with them" (Giordano et al. 2005) — is true for us and for many of the women who speak through these pages. At times we may feel very alone, yet on some level we are connected to so much that is beyond us or in us, so much more than we are as individual entities. Being alone is an inevitable part of the human condition as is holding essential people inside our minds and hearts.

Just as the ongoing presence and influence of our fathers is alive for us, so for many of the women we interviewed are their fathers still an integral part of them, in small or major ways. There was sometimes a resurgence of influence after their dads died, and women spoke wholeheartedly about it, just as they talked about the influence in their childhood. They described mannerisms, ideas, personality traits, family life, politics, hobbies, and careers as carrying his stamp and being inspired by him.

Seeing Our Dads in Ourselves

Linda G. offers this political similarity between her father and herself:

I wouldn't call him a liberal; I wouldn't call him a conservative. He was just sort of living day-to-day as he thought it should be. He thought it was an absolute disgrace that the governor went in and blew up the Branch Davidians. He just said, "They weren't hurting anyone; why don't they just leave them alone?" That has stuck with me a lot: if people aren't hurting you, leave them alone.

Her sense of herself and her background of accomplishment come from him:

He had a good sense of personal potential; you make your own boat. I think that's an important message. Obviously there are external limitations, but he gave me a very strong sense that I have a good background, I have a strong background. Not an elitist background, but a very strong background, and I should be able to do whatever I want with that. He discouraged to a large degree, I hadn't really thought about this before, but he did discourage a traditional path of get married and be a housewife and have kids.

And what do I do? I talk about him a lot. I look at pictures. I had gone to the village in Italy where the family was from. I brought home all sorts of things . . .

She talks to

anyone who'll listen . . . actually my husband and my daughters and stepdaughter.

She inherited something else from him as well:

I have a lot of mechanical aptitude. I don't have much ability, but I have a lot of aptitude. My husband calls me "Little Tommy." He'll be doing something and need help trying to figure it out and I'll say, "Why don't you just do it like this?" And he'll reply, "Okay, Little Tommy."

P.B. still looks to her father for strength, and she shares a tendency with him:

I have a strong faith in God, but I also look for strength from my father . . .

He was a packrat, as am I, so when we cleaned out the house, it was just so — he had things. I do the same thing. You put something on the shelf and it's there until you die. His Bausch & Lomb science award from high school is there.

C.Z. feels her father's influence around spirituality and Catholicism:

I have such ambivalence about my Catholicism. I'm truly an American Catholic. I pick and choose. Given how angry I am at the church not cleaning house, it's one of the first places I fall back to because it is a place for contemplation and reflection, and it is where everybody goes. It feels really good when I need it. That piece of being Italian will never be expunged from me. It will always be there as my soul place, and I love that I meet my relatives there, and there's sort of an automatic ritual we can fall into that comforts. I know that that is huge for me.

I should say my father is the one I went to church with mostly; because my mother was always cooking the big Italian dinner, she'd give herself a pass. I'd go with my father down to this little tiny adorable church in Georgetown where they got married and knew everybody there. The incense would be going. I had a really close connection with my dad. He was my mentor there.

But my mom had an experience, because my older brother had very severe polio . . . When she went to church and was praying for him to live, she had this sort of angel touch her shoulder and get this information that he's going to be okay. When she told me that, it was for me like a green light that I could put all my other ways of looking at the world, like reincarnation, inside the Catholic ritual, and that was perfectly okay. From an early age I got that I don't have to go with the dogma necessarily, I can tweak it, I can do a "Catholic lite" if you will. That's how I made my peace with being there, being present to it.

When I travel to Italy, I love to go to the churches for the artwork, the quietness, the whole sense of tranquility that you can get there, that it is the center of the community. I guess that's what I was saying, it works for me still.

R.M. links her hard work and perseverance to the immigrant work ethic her father instilled in her.

Andrianna knows that you don't buy something that you can't afford, a legacy from her dad.

Pat M. is reminded of her dad when she goes to the doctor or takes her children for check-ups. He insisted on that, and now she does too. Our dads have become internalized as an important piece of our psyches.

CarolP's brothers see their father's influence in her:

> They do joke with me, "You're sounding like Dad." I'll do something and I'll look at my brother Bobby, and he'll get this look . . . I look at him and I say, "I turned into my father." "We're not surprised by that," he would say. But they just crack me up because when I say, "No you're not going to do it this way; this is how we need to do it and this is why," they're like, "Well you're right, but you're sounding like Dad."

It may be inevitable that many of us parent as our parents did. Joyce M. describes this connection with her father:

> I guess I was strict with my kids. I would do the same thing that my father did with me. If my kids weren't home, I was in the car tracking them down . . . My son would say to me, "Ma, how do you know what I'm going to do?" I'd say, "Danny, how did you think I got on this earth? It wasn't by osmosis I'll tell ya." I have picked up my father's traits of the kids being in at a decent time, respecting their parents, and being disciplined.

Patricia R. clearly sees her father living on in her:

> Italians, in some ways this comes from them. I have this optimism that he also had. While I am personally really skeptical of a lot of things, and I do analyze things, I'm much more optimistic than many of my friends. All I can think is that's the basis of it. Somehow he always thought we were going to be okay; we would make it . . . I do feel those things.
>
> One of the reasons I planted things, the Pasquale bushes, is that he had, the garden was a vegetable garden, but it was [also] a huge flower garden. Every year he made a new flower or a new rose; he would put them together. He would do the Patricia [named for her] rose . . . hybrids. I always have flowers in my house, because there were always flowers in our house.

GTest

Mom Med's

Areds 2 Eye Vitamin 2@daily

Tylenol 650 4@daily

Multivitamin 1@daily AM

Lexapro 5mg 1@daily AM

Amlodipine 2.5mg 1 M

Children Aspirin

Pravastatin

Aten

There is one other interesting quality that stays with me. I share a house with a good friend on the Cape on the water. I have these huge window boxes, and just like my father, I walk into the house and directly — he used to walk into the house and go directly out to the garden to check it out — and I do the same thing. I walk in and I go directly to those window boxes, because my father would say, "I'm going to see what sons-a-bitches is in the soil eating the plants."

He would pick the worms out. He'd call me at five o'clock in the morning, "I got the sons-a-bitches." There would be the worm dangling. I do that. After I take care of it, then I'll sit down and do my work.

Laura reports that on one of her last trips to see her dad,

he said to me, "If not for you," he "would have no real connection to family." I have that memory, that that was his connection, that he valued me.

She is grateful that he didn't suffer and was enjoying life, with great friends, playing cards every Friday night, especially since there had been some rough years earlier in his marriage when she wishes she had been there more. She still hears him in conversation

imagining what he would say, what advice he would give me.

C.N. demonstrated how her father remains part of her:

Sometimes I'll catch myself in a position, sitting and talking or doing something. Like this [she gestured with her hands], my father would be talking with his hands exactly that way. I know that I'm very much mimicking him all the time . . .

I will take particular pride in figuring out how to do something, maybe some home repair. Or, I'll come up with an idea for how to use something as a tool or to fix something. My husband will always say, "You are your father's daughter."

Her father also contributes to her worldview:

I definitely still see things through the lens of how he might perceive them or what he might have to say about it, my mother as well, but he always had an opinion about everything. He was not shy about expressing his opinion. He was a very strong personality.

Karen B. describes the phenomenon this way:

I have characteristics of my mom, but I was always very proud when people said I look like my father. I act like him. I have this terrible temper. He would blow up and then five minutes later get over it and apologize. Everyone around him would be like, "What the heck happened with this storm?" I'm exactly like that.

We have seen answers to the questions some might ask: How do you keep someone alive yet still live in the present? How do you build on your "staying power" as a daughter and a woman and an Italian American? That transformation is at the core of the way many of us have grieved and "resolved" our grief. The answer lies in internalization and attachment, again and again, which allows your loved one to stay with you, support you, and be part of you. And it just seems *so Italian* to keep the ones we love always in our hearts.

CHAPTER FOURTEEN

KEEPING OUR DADS NEAR

*M*any of us grew up in homes or visited grandparents who had homes with what seemed to be shrines or altars to deceased relatives, complete with candles and pictures and maybe a special bracelet or watch that a grandfather or aunt used to wear. The photos on these altars were objects of great respect and reverence.

We were struck by how well many of the women in our study preserved photographs and memorabilia of their fathers and other relatives. The photographs were living, daily reminders of their relationships. They sparked memory and all its meanderings as well as conversation in the here and now. We also saw memory and conversation arising from gardens, visits to cemeteries, food choices, children, and grandchildren. Through these we sometimes discover previously unknown aspects of our dads as years go by, and we grow in our understanding of him as a father and a man.

The Memories We Hold

One of the most moving examples of treasured memories was in Donna's interview with Helen Barolini. Years prior, Helen had interviewed many Italian Americans in upstate New York as part of an oral history project. Having wonderful foresight, during that time she also taped an interview with each of her parents. Though her father had died decades before, she said during the interview with Donna:

> Well, I'll tell you . . . I taped him . . . so every once in a while I'll play his tape, hear his voice . . .

What a testament to the enduring father-daughter bond, to have not only the internalized memory but also the possibility to hear her father present in the room, an active dialogue from long ago. In addition, she keeps the original copy of the poem she wrote for her father (presented in Chapter 1) on display:

> Well, I think of him every day because I see this — this is in my bedroom, you know.

C.N. had plenty of photos on display and was animated in talking about and showing them. She notes:

> I do keep photos around . . . that is their wedding. I've tried to, with some of these photos, keep the memory alive with my daughters . . . One time when my older daughter was home on vacation she scanned this photo, so that she could have it.

Karen B. holds a photograph in reverence as a reminder of family connection:

> We keep this photograph that was taken at my wedding of four generations. My dad, my brother, his son, and my grandmother. It's a beautiful picture.

A special picture of her golfing with her father is part of Lisa's remembrances, and sometimes:

> I just want to close my eyes and feel like what it was like on the Cape. I remember . . . there's a rake he used to use, or the lawnmower is going, that kind of thing. So I think there are still these connections. And the house is there. We redid the house because it needed work, but he would have been proud of what we did . . . Just the other day I was talking to my sister and said, "I just really miss Dad!" There are just these moments . . . and occasionally I find myself talking to him and saying, "That's what I did today, did you see? Do you know what he's [her son] doing?"

Diana F. keeps her father alive with a photograph and an endearing memory connected with it:

> My favorite photograph is one that everybody says, "Oh, your father was so handsome!" He was about twenty-one, and it's a real theatrical pose . . . and it's how I remember him, really, kind of theatrical. We joke sometimes, "Remember when Daddy used to wear those Bermuda shorts?" and he would only wear them around the house. I remember how white

his legs were. We used to say, "Daddy, don't go out with those shorts; people will see your legs." He would always say to us, "You don't think I have good legs?"

Verna's father liked to dress as certain historical characters throughout the year, and she described how her daughter now would

light a candle, put the picture out, and say, "This is Grandpa Vinnie." She said the kids just asked the other day, because they know he used to do Columbus, and with Columbus Day coming, they said, "Do we have a picture of Grandpa Vinnie?" I'm going to [show you] this [montage of newspaper clippings].

It was quite a collection of characters!

Right before her interview, Carol A. and her brother took a journey back to Long Island to revisit the family vacation home where they had spent many summers:

My brother and I are the only ones left [of our generation] . . . We decided to go to Long Beach to see our old house, and that was a lot of fun. In the summertime, some friends from the [Greenwich] Village who also had a house in Long Beach, they used to come over, drop in on the weekend, and we used to play this big game of twenty-one. We'd play it for pennies. Those were just very happy, silly kinds of games. I continue that with my grandchildren. It's a great source of remembered fun for me. We have our little cup of pennies.

It had been about thirty-five years . . . Oh! It was so different; I mean we wouldn't have recognized it . . . It was a summer community when we were growing up, and now it's a winter community. We were walking on the boardwalk. They have new benches now, with plaques with the name of the family that donated it. A number of those plaques were of people who had died and I would know them. Which made it so real to me . . . I actually knocked on the door — I was going to ask the people if we could see the house — the worst they could say was no. But my brother didn't want to go in; he just wanted to remember it as it was. Maybe he was right, because they changed the house, not in good ways . . . It wasn't a fancy place, but my mother really did decorate it very nicely.

Giovanna B.L.M. shared her memories of being understood by her father, of their deep psychological connection:

> I think I felt that I was understood by my father like no one else. We didn't have to talk a lot; we could anticipate each other's feelings and ideas. That I always felt, very strongly. When to talk . . . he knew when not to talk. He knew when I knew he understood, without saying anything. That would be the relationship that I so treasured.

The Objects We Keep

Margaret Gibson, a grief researcher from Australia, writes of the concept of "melancholy objects," things that once belonged to the deceased that become important objects in the lives of the bereaved (2004). These physical reminders to us of those we love can become important vehicles of our mourning.

Nightsticks, caponata recipes, and rings were just a few of the items the daughters mentioned as keepsakes of their fathers. Joann P. had her father's ring fitted for her, so

> whenever I need to feel him close, or I want to have him with me, I put the ring on my finger and we go!

LuLu kept her father's cane, which she still uses in her professional acting life:

> Near the end of his life, he used two canes. We buried him with one but we kept the other, and I kept his cane here. I did a play about a woman who fought in the Civil War disguised as a man, and I used this cane.

Adele still has her father's level, a reminder of his work as a laborer:

> It sits above the kitchen doorway, and he had carved his initials in it, F.A. I take it with me wherever I move. He used it on his daily job. I tell you, he was a craftsman; he was just great.

L. kept some of her father's clothing:

> Especially during the winter after he died, I had sweaters and jackets of his that I would wear. Every weekend I had on one of his sweaters, and

everybody knew it was one of his sweaters. It felt good, like he was enveloping me.

Diane G. felt it was important to pass on the legacy of an object of her father's to her son:

My father had only one ring. It was the profile of a horse, with horseshoes around it. He never wore it himself, and I know my son always loved it. I am giving it to my son when he turns forty. My son is going to fall on the floor when he sees that ring — and I am going to cry.

Sometimes this "stuff" gets attached to us and to others in very deep ways, as P.B. describes:

It's just hilarious because I'm very nostalgic and it's just so cool . . . what we ended up doing at my brother's office out in the hallway. It has a little curio cabinet, and we took a bunch of my father's, like his phone from the office, all kinds of quirky little desk things, his pen set, and we just made a little shrine of all his stuff . . . It's fun to keep him alive I guess . . .

I have a dispenser of dentotape from Serafino's Pharmacy from probably the 1950s that he never used . . . We found in his desk letters from an old high school sweetheart . . . For some reason he saved them. We got such a kick out of it. It was at that point where I said, "You don't know somebody until you know their stuff."

For Joyce, things of her father carry meaning for both her and the larger family:

I know the nephews wanted things of my father's. My one cousin wanted his hat that had the sign in it. I gave him that. The other nephew wanted another hat, and I gave him that. I just couldn't part with too much of his stuff.

With the last family reunion that my father went to, they would give what they called the elders a gift. My Uncle Joe was still alive. They gave him a pig because he worked for Tobin Packing Plant. They gave my father a train because he worked for the railroad, and my Uncle Dick a truck because he worked for the Highway Department. I have his train downstairs. It was only a plastic toy, but I've still got it.

Her final analysis:

> He's around me all the time. He might not be here, but he's here in spirit. And I handle it a lot better. I'm not saying I don't get teary eyed; I do, even though he's been gone thirteen years. I know he's in a good place now. Angry, eh, I probably still am. But I'm dealing with it.

Clocks are key for C.N.:

> I am sitting here looking at the clock that isn't working right now because my father had a hobby of collecting antique clocks and fixing them. There is one here, one in the other room . . . a bunch of them down in New Jersey. I've got all of these clocks that I just can't bring myself to get rid of because they were clocks that he had worked on.

While B. has held on to some of her father's beloved items, she also sees him in herself:

> I look at my hands. They're like my father's hands and like his bricklayer father's hands, my grandfather. I have his books, a couple with inscriptions from him to me. He gave me *Dr. Zhivago* when it was newly published in this country, and my first child, Larisa, was named from *Dr. Zhivago*. [He also passed on his] love of poetry. Francis Thompson was his favorite poet. I actually read "The Hound of Heaven," which he knew by heart, at his gravesite [during his funeral] . . . Some of my cousins remembered him reciting that poem to them.

Joyce remembers her father during reunions or holidays through items he treasured:

> Any time we have a family reunion, if it's around Christmas, Daddy's tree goes. We just had a family reunion Christmas party, and Daddy's tree went down there. Daddy was a part of the family reunion . . . If there's a family reunion not around Christmas, something of Daddy goes so that he's there. Because that was something that I was going to do for him, have a family reunion. So we've had one ever since that year.

Things her father collected are meaningful to R.L., and she wonders if they will ever find his little Fascist schoolboy outfit in the attic that he had to wear under Mussolini's rule in Italy.

The Interests We Shared

Jackie's father's presence in her life includes such diverse things as the stock market, gardening, artwork, and details of cooking:

> He liked the stock market, and he was very sharp about money . . . I think that was natural for me to be interested in that . . . It was just always there. After he came to this country, he was an artist for quite a while, then he wasn't able to make a decent living once he had kids. So he and my mother opened a small restaurant in an office building, and there was a stock exchange in that building. He would hang out in the stock exchange sometimes when he wasn't busy, so he had a pretty good knowledge of that whole thing.

Jackie's father always had a vegetable garden. Now she keeps on her refrigerator a picture of him and her mother in front of the garden:

> I have a small vegetable garden in my backyard, and I grow very specific vegetables that were part of my culture and essential to every Italian table. I'm growing tomatoes and basil, other herbs — there's some arugula in there, rosemary, tarragon — I think that's more French than Italian — and cucumbers. That's about it. Not a big variety of things, but I do think of my father and my family when I make a caprese salad, which is rather regularly.

Artwork done by her father, his brother in Italy, and other family members fills Jackie's home. She says:

> I guess I could say I feel his presence at times. I think about him a lot. I hear him telling me how to cut an onion. Tells me when I put the pasta in the water: "Stir it. Don't let it go; don't forget to tend to it like a baby." He would say, "You don't just throw the pasta in and set a timer." Things like that.

She imagines that he would be angry with the way she spends money and sometimes throws food out. She sees that in herself:

> Sometimes now, at this age in my life, when I get angry, I'm less tolerant of certain behaviors, and it does remind me of him.

To those of us with a dad devoted to food, whether growing, eating, or preparing it, Patricia R.'s words speak volumes:

> What my sense of Italian is, is that you always remember him at celebratory events. Holidays I make food from my dad's recipes . . . so he's always present . . . He had a way of making sauce, which I think I've learned well. I incorporate cleaning anchovies and frying the zucchini flower. I make a big feast of the things that he would make, and the things that he made that I loved, or his style of making chicken soup.
>
> The other thing he made when I didn't feel good, he always made Swiss chard. When I went to Calabria, that seemed to be a very traditional dish. It was never fancy cooking; it was rustic cooking . . . Those blue grapes [maturing at the time of our meeting] — I feel he's in the refrigerator. My friends are very funny; they say, "I see your father's been here."

For Pat M., the garden also looms large:

> I see a geranium or tomatoes in the garden. I think about his big garden and how every Sunday I would go and pick those tomatoes and say, "Why am I doing this? Because I don't really want this many tomatoes." He'd say, "Come and pick 'em." Then he would plant that big garden for us. We felt we had to help him and had to eat them. I kept saying, "Dad, don't plant so many."

Anna M. was affected by her father's gardening too:

> I was influenced by my father, so when I first moved to this house, I had a garden. I did that for about ten years. Then I realized the idea was great, but I was not one for weeding. It got to the point where the weeds were bigger than my tomato plants! It gradually got smaller and smaller. My father loved his garden and fruit trees. I liked to have flowers, and my father would say, "You can't eat a flower; put in a tomato plant!"

Food and family go hand in hand for Joyce:

> Even to this day, only Daddy and I liked turnips. For every holiday there's turnips on the table for Daddy and me.
>
> Another thing, *anginetti* cookies, Italian cookies. Every time I make *anginetti*, a cookie goes down and I bury it. My girlfriend, I didn't have

enough for her, and I had two cookies, and she said, "What are you doing with these cookies?"

I said, "Oh I'm going to take them down to my father."

She said, "I didn't get a cookie; don't tell me you're going to bury these cookies."

I said, "I most certainly am." So she took one of the cookies and ate it. I said, "You take that other cookie and I'm going to be very upset."

She said, "I can't believe you're going to bury that cookie."

I said, "I'm sorry, I'm burying that cookie. This is Daddy's cookie." So I am crazy.

Food has also become a memorial for Donna C.:

I mentioned before that he made a caponata. When I make a caponata I still make his recipe. Even though there may be a better recipe, that's my favorite and that's the one I make. There are certain things like that that you do.

C.N.'s family keeps her dad alive by doing

little things. My dad used to have a toast that he would say at a family get-together or holiday. He would always raise a toast and say, "*Sempre cosi*" [always that way]. I always liked that, so we do that as well when the family is together, and I always think of him when I do that. There are so many things that I do that make me think of him.

Golfing powerfully evokes Lisa's father for her:

The big thing is if you go on a golf course, we used to walk . . . it's quiet, and it's beautiful, and the air, and it's this golf course smell . . . pine needles and whatever. When you go, inevitably I close my eyes and I can just see him there with me. My sister and I keep saying when my son is big enough, we're going to start playing golf. We're going to do it . . . the two of us, because we both feel that. It was almost religious. They've written books on golf, kind of spiritual books on golf. For me it's more because of my father . . .

We had an outing for work the other day with . . . a driving range . . . for some reason I was like, "Whoo!" Maybe I was relaxed, but I was just hitting these balls a mile and having an internal conversation with my father saying, "Look at this! Dad, what is this? What's going on here. I don't understand! What am I doing right!" . . . I was really connected with him.

While B. has specific times when she purposefully thinks about her dad, he also is just with her in a more constant way:

One very specific thing is every birthday. I light a candle for each of my parents and I spend time meditating on them and thanking them for the life they gave me. I think about my father all the time, simply because of my approach to life. I could be listening to something on the radio and thinking, "Oh you know my father would be interested in that," or "That's something that my father might say." I'm studying something and he comes to my mind because of his constant life of study.

The Stories We Tell

In talking about them, we keep our fathers alive and with us. What we choose to tell and who we choose to tell it to speaks to how we feel about them.

Speaking of her father means so much to Lisa:

I crave the opportunity to speak about him, and I don't get a chance to do it because the world is very different than what I had, and . . . it was a world that was just beautiful. I had a beautiful world growing up and it's just gone. And I miss it. He was a big part of it . . .

My uncle would say . . . for the first few years after my father died, "Yeah, your father, he was the greatest." He'd tell me these stories; my uncle wanted to talk to us . . . It was so important to him to talk about my father. Then after he's gone, who's left to talk about it? Very few people . . . they don't talk about him anymore. It's very sad. But . . . my sister and I talk.

Karen B. also keeps her father alive through conversation, particularly with her daughter:

We talk about him: "Papa would have liked that about you; you have his photographic eye."

Rosanne B. talks about her father to keep him alive and this has changed . her life:

> My husband tells me he fell in love with me when I talked about my father . . . He says that you don't meet too many people who can speak so lovingly of their parents. I kept him alive inside myself. At our wedding we each read a little speech to one another . . . and I said, "I think my father picked you out for me." I kept him alive to myself. That's how I coped. I still think about him all the time.

Linda G. remembers how much her father used to talk about his grandparents, as she speaks about her similarities to her father:

> I might think something or I might phrase it or start it as my father would say. He talked a lot about his grandparents, the way the family came from Italy to this country. The grandparents came with one daughter, four . sons, and then two sons were born here. The family would go back to what would be my great-grandparents . . . I think some of my interest is a way of honoring him, the family, and the past. I've always known there were three baby girls who died and didn't come to this country. They're buried in the old cemetery in Orsara.

She hopes to go there soon.

The Faith We Hold

Faith plays a role in keeping some of the women's connection to their fathers. Maria T. described the painful road she traveled with her father as he succumbed to the ravages of Alzheimer's disease:

> There's the sadness and the tightness of going back to the time when he was ill and bringing all of that back.

Time has given her a new understanding, however, of what it means to be connected to her father:

> One thing I'd like to say, and this is a pretty dramatic thing, but I feel like as a Catholic if you really do believe that you're going to be reunited

at some point with your loved ones, it makes me feel that I really don't mind dying, ultimately, because I'll get to see my father again. I just had that thought in the past year.

Holidays are a major time to remember dad for many women. Pat M. notes:

On holidays, we always think of him. On Easter Sunday he would take a palm and dip it in water, holy water, and sprinkle the food. Another thing he taught me, that I never thought of either, that Easter is the most important holiday of the year, even bigger than Christmas . . . We go to the cemetery and take care of the flowers there and have Masses said.

Pat M.'s father's strong faith is described as she speaks about how important the washing of his feet was to her father. When he needed help with that

we just took a washcloth, and we just thought he wanted to feel comfortable. But, you know what? My sisters and I were talking; we believe that he was praying as he washed his feet, because Jesus washed the feet of his disciples.

For Pat M., missing her father is mixed with faith:

I still miss him every day and pray and talk to him every day. There is more to life, a life with God. He gave me the security to move forward and live life to the fullest . . . I feel his wisdom is being carried on in our family through my sharing of his life and beliefs with my grandchildren.

His memory will remain with us always. That is how I feel about it . . . I always thought, "Oh, he is floating on a cloud with all of his geraniums around him and his glass of wine in his hand" . . . I mean, you have to believe in something, and that is what I believed in.

The Guidance, Wisdom, and Support We Seek

Invoking their fathers, looking to them for guidance — particularly in difficult times — remains essential with some women, as Joyce describes:

If times are tough or if I have to go for an exam . . . I'd say my prayers and I'd say, "Oh, Daddy, please let it be all right; don't let anything go wrong." I say, "You're up there; talk to that man and let everything come out all right" . . . My daughter is another one. When she got married she had a miscarriage. We took a little angel and put it down there with my dad and I told my dad that this was his first great-grandchild.

Imma still remembers her father's advice to her:

"Always listen to your husband." I do! He would tell me, like, "Sometimes you and your husband have an argument, whatever, think about the good things that he does, that he did, that he is. He's not a smoker; he's not a person to go to clubs; he's a family man; he's a workingman." He would always tell me that.

The Interactions We've Had with Those He's Touched

Donna P.'s older brother reminds her of things about their dad, such as his teaching them to drive and "stepping on the gas pedal like there's eggs under there." When her younger brother turned fifty, her older brother wrote a card telling him how much he was like their dad and how proud their father would have been of him:

My younger brother, he's done well, businesswise and loves the horses, and my dad did too. My dad didn't have much extra money. He played cards when he could. My younger brother also loves to play cards. I found out things about my dad from my younger brother just recently, that when my mom was in the hospital, he was dedicated; he'd go and sit by her bed until eight o'clock. Sometimes then he'd go play cards afterwards, and he brought my younger brother.

The memories of others also helped Imma remember the man her father was:

When we went back to Italy three years ago — mind you, my father was gone forty years then — we went walking around the town [where she grew up]. Everybody, the elderly, I would say, "Hi, how are you?" They start asking me, "Who are you?" I say, "I'm the daughter of Maestro Carmelo," because my father was known in my town as Maestro Carmelo, and oh, right away their eyes opened up and everybody had a good thing to say about him.

Family connections bring our fathers back to us.

P.B. sees her father in her daughter's knowledge of players from the Giants from 1970.

Joyce's children have traits in common with her father and were close to him

because he was here all the time. He watched those two grow up.

B.'s children remember her father:

I think that he is a very strong influence on them. They will talk about him . . . They remember going fishing with him; they remembered him singing; my son remembers him singing "Sonny Boy" to him when they were cleaning fish together . . . He was always quoting Saint Thomas Aquinas to them too, speaking in Latin; it's the same thing! That's who he was . . . Luckily they knew my father for at least ten or fifteen years . . . It's how we pass on, and when I think about what I'd like to finish before I "pass on," it's the writing . . . it's through the words that I can pass on these stories.

C.N.'s daughters help her maintain the tie with her father:

The girls have mentioned that card game occasionally, in trying to teach it to somebody else. Italians call it *scopa*. We called it scoop . . . If they come across that, they'll say, "That's what we always did with Grandpa" . . . If a song comes up that he used to sing, we'll mention that, and jokes.

My father being this tool and die maker and a child of the Depression, he would save everything. He had all kinds of tools and stuff that he liked to collect because he always could find a use for it. He would figure out how to turn something into something else. We have this garage that we cleared most of the stuff out [of], but there is still an awful lot there.

My younger daughter is an artist, and she just made a poster for a play in Boston . . . that takes place in a junkyard. This was one of those things I thought my dad would get a kick out of. She said that when she did this illustration she was just picturing my father's junk in her mind . . . She came down to New Jersey on vacation while we were there.

She went in the garage and dug around and came out with a whole bunch of stuff and asked if she could have it to give to the people in the theater company to use as props . . .

She is very much like him in that way. I thought of it at the time . . . that my dad would have gotten such a kick out of the fact that she was using the stuff.

Her cousin brought back memories of Giovanna B.L.M.'s father:

A cousin recently came to visit with a movie, the home movies of the fifties, when we had no family here; so we had three friends, and we spent all our holidays with each other at each other's houses. She brought these films, and there's my father in the film and my mother. That was very exciting.

Her children have honored her father:

The greatest tribute was when our kids had their first baby: they named him Felice. Every day, I see Felice. I talk to Felice about his great-grandfather . . . [After her father died] I felt the closeness. I wish he had lived longer. I can't think of a single other person that would have enjoyed the grandchildren [as much as he would have].

I love to hear, well there aren't very many people left who knew my father, but I love to hear an aunt in Rome's descriptions of him. I mean everybody was in love with him because he was very kind and very proper. You know the life lessons, when you go to somebody's house for dinner you bring flowers. You can also bring chocolates if you want to, but you certainly bring flowers, the niceties. He was also very gentle . . . He cherished friendships. I have that. I think of things like that.

A deep transformation is taking place within us and within others around us and even within our homes and daily lives. While our fathers are gone, our attachments to them and to what they stood for remain, and we are working out ways to keep them "alive" while also allowing them to rest in peace. It is that same attachment from our early years, now both weathered and strengthened through years of living with our fathers. A song our children remember, an old home movie, an acquaintance in Italy, any of these can carry our fathers as we carry them in our hearts.

CHAPTER FIFTEEN

FORMAL MEMORIALIZING: OUR DADS LIVING ON IN THE WORLD

*F*or some women, finding a way to formally memorialize their dads was important, whether it was through a scholarship, a piece of art, a donation, an inscription on the Wall of Honor at Ellis Island, or an activity. Memorializing is another means to keep his memory alive and to contribute to the world in a way that would have meant something to him. Those activities can form something tangible to expand the bonds, keeping them deep and strong even in a world that does not always recognize the value of their continuing.

Locating the Lost Dad in the World

CarolP has lived all of her life down the hill from the major university she attended, so her memorial for her dad seemed almost a natural extension of her life with her father:

> I didn't need the money from the inheritance, so I used some of it to set up an endowment at the university in his memory. My brothers thought it was stupid. What they didn't understand is, education was so important to him. I set up an endowed scholarship, and it's not a full, but the interest will help the kid. It's something. It's a start. I did it for a female mechanical engineer, because he was so encouraging of women in the engineering society.

She also involves herself in cancer fundraisers:

> Donating to cancer [research and treatment] as well as the scholarship is the way I try to keep their memory alive.

R.M. memorialized her father with opera music:

I've always said that I credit my dad, my uncle, and my grandfather, because they would take me to the opera. They would always have great music. I inherited all their old records. I just gave them to a music department at a local college. They were thrilled because they have music faculty . . . really topnotch. I was very happy to give them those records.

C.N's artist daughter creates comic books and C.N's father is commemorated through her work:

She has actually incorporated my father in stories. My father is in a number of the comics that she has written. They are not comic strips, but more the autobiographical type of comics.

Food, gardens, and home weave together in C.N's memorializing as she speaks about the house on the Jersey Shore she still owns:

It's really a long haul for us still to go. I think about selling it all the time, but it's such a family tie. One thing that I continue to do and think of my father, down there we have three fig trees . . . my dad loved these fig trees. He was very proud of them because one of them was, we actually called it the family tree, because it was my grandmother's fig tree in Newark.

After she passed away, he moved it to our house. When we moved, we took the tree with us, and he eventually moved it down to the shore where it has just thrived . . . much bigger than it ever was anywhere else . . . He figured out how to make cuttings to make other fig trees, so that everybody in the family, all my aunts and uncles, each got a piece of the tree. Some of my cousins have fig trees.

He also made two other trees from the original one . . . and every year we have to harvest the figs . . . I'd bring them to some of my aunts, who don't have the trees anymore . . . We just brought a bunch back after Labor Day. That's really kind of a big deal, the whole thing about the fig trees and the fact that he loved them.

[The house is] . . . my tie to my family. It's the last place that the four of us lived all together [with her brother] . . . Our happiest times were really there. My parents had all our family photos with my brother and me growing up and the two of them when they were first married. We still have all of them on the wall. I can't bring myself to take them down. We have made some changes in the house, but . . . I just keep it as a memorial to them.

Creating from Grief and Love

For many of the women in this book, the creative process was critical to not only managing their grief but also memorializing and honoring their fathers. Writing is an important part of Patricia R.'s professional and personal life:

My first book I dedicated to my father. That's the other way I managed the grief stuff.

Christine P. found that her father and her art are intertwined:

Last year, while I was doing one particular piece of art, I realized I've always been attracted to war and war zones and thinking about war. I was doing a triptych — Vietnam, Afghanistan, and World War II — and became curious about my father's experience in World War II — what he experienced and what it must have been like — and I wondered why he never talked about it. I sent away for his Navy records to find out exactly where he was when, where he went. [I became] curious about that part of his life.

She continues, showing her view of life and time and how many phases of her father coexist with her now:

It [time] is a whole fabric of a person. I have a strong belief that time is not linear, that my father is here in all phases of his life with me, as are other people I know. Depending on where I drop my consciousness at a certain moment is where I find the father I have, even back then when I was alienated from him; and of course the loving affectionate father is there, too.

The conflict still exists; the love and affection still exist. At the end of the interview she commented that she felt soupy . . . he could be everywhere, where I drop down in this big bowl [of soup].

The food metaphor for consciousness and memory carries us as we imagine that big bowl of minestra and how it holds and nourishes us, swirling and steaming with bits and pieces to be discovered, some certainly tastier than others.

Maria T. managed her grief by honoring her father through the written word, particularly her poems. As she stated, her father lives on in them. She captured her sense of a void, which struck her the day after her father's passing, so beautifully in her aptly titled poem "The Day After" (first published in *Poet Lore*, 2012):

The Day After

I fold your shirts neatly into a pile
　　on what had been your bed.
　　　　Just below each collar, a white tape

with your name in black indelible
　　ink. I run my fingers over the soft
　　　　plaid flannel of your name,

white cotton undershirt of your name,
　　loose drawstring sweatpants
　　　　of your name, placing all into the black

plastic bag, along with the leather shoes
　　and slippers that rarely touched ground —
　　　　all meant for someone with nothing

to his name, who will wear these garments
　　you wore just days ago over flesh
　　　　that still sweated, shivered, rose and fell.

　　　　　　　　　© Maria Terrone
　　　　　　Reprinted by permission of the author.

B. is engaged in ongoing writing and artwork about her family and the Italian American experience:

[Her father was] a man of constant surprises, and since the Ellis Island show ten or eleven years ago, I've been doing a considerable amount of writing. Some is fictionalized writing about my family, and some is actual memoir. Asking these questions about my father's life is pretty constant, and it comes through in the writing that I do in a very organic way. It's not as if I sit down to start to write something. It's rather that the writing comes to me, visually, at four or five in the morning.

Things will come up around my father or my mother. But my father mostly. Because with my father, as I said, he was always rather enigmatic . . . You asked me about my father in the beginning, and I said he was an enigma. And I would say that even today . . . there's still plenty of enigma there.

She has two sculptures in her hometown of East Boston, where:

I always felt like a misfit. Part of me could fit as long as I didn't acknowledge all the rest of me . . . I went back as an artist and did a major public art piece there, which was very satisfying, because it was like coming home in a way that was my full self . . .

I often go to where my dad had one of the dry cleaning shops that he started, and . . . I remember going in there with my mother when I was little . . . my father was working . . . with one of those undershirts that has narrow straps . . . and he was very very tanned and sweating and I remember looking into his eyes and feeling so sad that my father was working so hard. It felt wrong. It felt really wrong. That was something that was in my life a huge amount . . . just feeling like my father's life didn't fit. It wasn't right. I'm driving in Boston fairly frequently these days, and how can I not remember those days? It's just there.

Daniela's poem was written several months after her father died; her commentary on it eloquently honors her father and his struggle:

American Sonnets for My Father

— for Donato Gioseffi (b.1906–d.1981) —
written in Edna St. Vincent Millay's
studio at Steepletop, NY, Nov., 1981

You died in spring, father, and now the autumn dies.
Bright with ripe youth, dulled by time,
plums of feeling leaked red juices from your eyes,

pools of blood hemorrhaged in your quivering mind.
At forty, I climb Point Pinnacle, today,
thinking of you gone forever from me.
In this russet November woods of Millay,
I wear your old hat, Dear Italian patriarch, to see
if I can think you out of your American grave
to sing your unwritten song with me.
Your poetry, love's value, I carry with your spirit.
I take off your old black hat and sniff at it
to smell the still living vapor of your sweat.

You worked too hard, an oldest child of too many,
a lame thin boy in ragged knickers, you limped
all through the 1920s up city steps, door to door
with your loads of night and daily newspapers, each worth
a cheap labored penny of your family's keep.
You wore your heart and soles sore. At forty,
not climbing autumn hills like me, you lay with lung disease
strapped down with pain and morphine, hearing your breath
rattle in your throat like keys at the gates of hell.
Your body was always a fiend, perplexing your masculine will.
You filled me with pride and immigrant tenacity. Slave
to filial duty, weaver of all our dreams, you couldn't be free
to sing. So be it. You are done, unfulfilled by song except in me.
If your dreams are mine, live again, breathe in me and be.

You never understood America's scheme.
Your wounded dream, father,
will never heal in me, your spirit mourns forever
from my breath, aches with childhood memory,
sighs for my own mortality in you,
which I, at last accept
more completely than ever when we
laughed together and seemed we'd go on forever —
even though we always knew
you would die much sooner than I
who am your spirit come from you.

Remember, "a father lost, lost his!" you told us,
preparing us with Shakespearean quotation
and operatic feeling for your inevitable death.

Good night, go gently, tired immigrant father
full of pride and propriety. We, your
three daughters, all grew
to be healthier, stronger, more American than you.
Sensitive father, I offer you this toast,
no empty boast, "I've never known a man more brave!"
The wound that will not heal in me
is the ache of dead beauty.
Once full of history, philosophy, poetry,
physics, astronomy, your bright, high flying psyche
is now dispersed, set free from your tormented body,
but the theme you offered, often forlorn,
sheer luminescent soul, glistened with enough light
to carry us all full grown.

© Daniela Gioseffi

First appeared in *Word Wounds and Water Flowers*,
VIA Folios, Bordighera Press, NY, 1995.
Reprinted by permission of the author.

After a very moving reading, Daniela commented:

I still can't read it without crying . . . To me, it's the quintessential
thing that you may be looking for: the effect of the father who was not a
Mafioso, who was not abusive, who worked like a dog as an immigrant to
raise his family and to inspire a daughter to her accomplishment.

I think that if you're interviewing women of accomplishment, you
might find many of them father-identified . . . You can see the emotion I
still have and it's over thirty years since his death. I still can't read that
poem without crying. I still have all this feeling for him and I still talk to
his picture on the wall the way he used to go to his parents' grave and talk
to them with ancestral feelings of worship.

As we sit with what our fathers have given us and how they have stayed
with us, Andrianna's response about "regrets" might ring true:

The only thing is, because I do it with my children, is always saying, "I love you." Back then it just didn't seem like you did it enough. That's a big regret. As far as saying, Dad, you were right, I think we did show that.

The interview for her was:

Phenomenal. Even after all these years, and I think you could tell just by seeing me talk, it still shows how much love you could have for a parent. I hope my children feel that way.

In a powerfully evocative poem published for the world to see, a tool Dad used that we keep in our house, a scholarship to benefit others as our fathers once benefited us, our fathers live on. We invest works, objects, and, most of all, our memories and feelings connected to them with parts of ourselves and parts of our fathers, and these in turn help to carry on the relationship. Italian culture with all of its art, architecture, literature, and poetry is rich with the capacity to endow symbols with great meaning, and we see that in our memorializing and carrying our fathers forward.

CHAPTER SIXTEEN

BEING ITALIAN AMERICAN: A LEGACY FROM OUR FATHERS

*O*ur fathers are gone. Nothing will ever bring them back although many of us have yearned for such a miracle. Yet a part of them that stays with us, and even grows over time for some, is that strong sense of being Italian American.

Some of those we interviewed had a sense of an Italian identity early, exploring it for much of their lives; for others it grew as they grew; and for others it became particularly strong after their fathers' deaths, becoming part of his legacy. While for most of the women this identity has been positive and life affirming, for some it involved painful aspects of society's response to Italian immigrants and stereotyping, something they had to overcome in their lives and thinking.

Cultural identity can take many forms, and any individual can integrate, ignore, reject, or embrace what her family and the larger ethnic culture has given her. However that process of cultural identity unfolds, it is always personal and meaningful. For several women, their Italian identity was intertwined with their family's involvement in an Italian club, or society, which is a mutual support society that encourages and promotes Italian culture and language. You will hear how some of the women have incorporated the club into their lives and identities.

Of the Essence: Italian Identity Runs Deep and Always

Rosa describes her Italian American heritage as being integral to the formation of her sense of self and credits her father with this:

> The way I have described who I am and what motivates me and what I do today is not a product of the twenty-one years I have spent in the

House of Representatives; who I am comes directly out of being raised in an Italian Catholic household.

It's hard to separate out my mother from my father, but in terms of what you are writing about — my father, the influence of his sense of right and wrong, his love, just reveling in being an Italian, an Italian American, the values of family, and the responsibility of hard work and giving back something — that's who I am now because of what that background, that legacy, gave me. It is the fabric of my life — what propels me forward. That's the grounding. It's who I am. This is the best way for me to say it, the best way for me to explain that relationship [with him].

Louise always had that sense of being Italian, but

it's gotten stronger. I've always had the interest because we grew up around the club, always were doing things like the Feast of Mount Carmel. My father was always very involved. He would bring home the newsletters and I would help him fold them. When the idea of the auxiliary was brought up to us, there were about forty of us who became founding members in 1989. I've been very, very active . . . I've been president for six years. We do try to do many Italian things, as many as we can.

Although C.Z.'s parents were integrated into American culture and business, they

were very proud Italians, and they wanted us to know about their backgrounds. We all knew our extended family. I always had this sense that you should find out more about your background. Being an academic, and then the field that I chose, it just came up for me that Italian dance history is really an underresearched area.

When it was suggested that we start doing study abroad programs, I thought [that was] perfect. I love Italy. I love being Italian. I'm really interested in dance history. I used to be a history major. I'm at that time in my career where I can contribute differently, not so much the technique but the more experiential general education. Well that felt like such an affirmation that my parents had said this is worth knowing about. Then I was able to pull all these pieces together for my own scholarship and for students to understand and have a window into this culture and dance history that is really underappreciated.

So it's all there . . . and I know it's hardest for that first generation, the ones that straddle. My grandparents actually too, but still I think we felt really protective of our parents because my mother would talk about the times when the Italians were discriminated against and how painful it was. We wanted to prove that we weren't wops; we were much more than that. We were great Americans. There's a way to bring all of that along. I think we have tried to do that, my brothers included. We live in the desire to hold on to and integrate all these aspects of growing up.

Andrianna was steeped in Italian life and traditions and commented:

It's just that you're raised with it [all things Italian], and it stays with you. Once you get married, it seemed like the cooking is right there. My husband always says the Irish food was very bland. It's just meat, potato, and a vegetable and that's it. I cooked seven days a week. My husband, even though he was Irish, he was more like an Italian as far as his ways go . . .

My grandfather was one of the original members of the Italian club in Troy, the founder in 1900 when the immigrants first came over. My dad belonged there too. West Albany, that's another club. I just got involved about eight years ago because I play bocce with three other girls. That club, you have to be of Italian descent with blood.

Here I am 100 percent Italian and was not able to join that club because my last name is Riley. It's horrible. My brother said that is, what would you say, discrimination? But then he said, no because it's a private club. That's why I was so upset. My brother came from Massachusetts and had to go to four meetings so that I could join because he was a blood.

But Troy I've been in all my life . . . I'm seventy-seven, so that's forty-something years.

R.L. had a strong Italian emphasis in her life from an early age:

I've always had that. I'm glad because when my father would call his mother, he'd be speaking a foreign language and I found that fascinating.

When his cousins would come over to our house, our house was so small so all of us [children] would be corralled down into the basement . . . and all the Italians looked so colorful and fun. We would spend every Sunday dinner at my maternal grandfather's house . . . with the Irish, Boston Irish, Catholic kind of culture . . .

And when my father's cousins would come over, it was always much more fascinating because the relatives had makeup on, they had perfume, they had gold, they were speaking another language. They were drinking angostura bitters; and they'd be having coffee, and my mother would put up the percolator for the Italian relatives; and things were more loud; and then we'd be called up one by one to be shown off and described in Italian, so it was always this fascinating part . . .

In seventh grade, I . . . took Italian and loved it. I remember my cousin with that book [he wrote] about having to hide out in the Tuscan hills when the Germans came through, also about the Buffalo soldiers, the black GIs that came through Italy and them getting to know the Italian cousins. At that point when he did his book signing at the Dante Alighieri Society of Massachusetts that's when I joined, but I've never continued.

I am a card-carrying member and I do have a life goal to become fluent in Italian, so that's always been there; I just haven't found time yet.

On an early trip to Italy she felt the connection:

From visiting Italy, we got to see my relatives; we got to see the house, the room my father was born in; we got to visit the graves of my *nonno* and *nonna* that I never met. And so back then I was very interested.

R.M.'s interest was always there too:

I published a book on Italian opera . . . That definitely came from my dad. I was thirteen when I was brought to the opera. When I was in graduate school I was working at the Metropolitan Opera. I fit in my schoolwork with my passion.

She has been to Italy thirty or forty times:

When I was younger, I used to just go visit my dad's brother. My dad had a younger brother and he was very highly educated, got his doctorate there, became a local parliamentarian. He was very influential, very highly respected, quite a character . . .

When I got older, I went to travel on my own. I used to teach students there and had faculty exchange with various colleagues at Italian universities . . . It was good . . .

My dad's sister was very dear to him and his brother. So when we went, we would always go to my dad's family. I was just there last year. There's a great twelfth-century Romanesque monastery there. Now that region is a national park. It's quite stunning. I only resent the fact that I don't have property there . . . That would have been nice.

CarolP says she has had the same level of interest in her Italian heritage her entire life:

I know it is a cornerstone to my life, like family is very important. You can, within a one-mile radius, find six Italian restaurants [in her neighborhood]. It's, like, "Which one am I going to choose tonight?" I cook for myself for breakfast and lunch, but I go out every night to eat. It's, like, "What did you have?" "Italian." "What did you have?" "Italian."

Joyce also spoke of the importance of the club and Italian identity:

It's funny because my mother's Irish. I never, if somebody says what are you, what nationality, I say Italian. I don't say Italian and Irish.

Of her Italianness, Patricia R. feels that

it's always been there. And I feel like I go to Italy as much as I can. My friend and I do lots of Italian things together. We're interested in the same things. The first time I went to Tuscany, we were in a cab going through the countryside and I looked out and I thought, "Oh my God, I look just like the countryside." I had all exactly the same colors on as the bricks and the soil. I thought I picked them, but it must have been genetic.

Becoming Italian over the Years

Families and individuals differ on how "Italian" they feel. While some of the women in the book felt their Italian roots from an early age, perhaps through the presence of relatives, special foods, language, or travel, others felt the connection grow later in life. Anne P.'s interest

> is certainly something that came in adulthood. In fact when I was a junior in college, that summer I went to Europe with two friends, and I had no interest in going to Italy whatsoever. I think there was a time in my life when I was embarrassed, or almost embarrassed, by being Italian, and I had to mature and come to appreciate being Italian.
>
> So I think as a kid, if I thought about it at all, I thought it was great. And then I had sort of an adolescent, young adult period of wanting to distance myself . . . and then coming back.

Donna P. was raised in a very Italian culture, moved away from it, and has since moved back toward it:

> The Italian Society opened up to women now twenty-two years ago, but I was working full time, raising a son, and caring for my mom, who sometimes would show up Saturday mornings because she was lonely, with her suitcase for the weekend. I just didn't take time . . . In fact my grandfather was one of the founders of the society . . . his name is on the plaque.
>
> When I retired, I decided I wanted to go back to those roots. Besides feeling my father's presence, my grandmother had lived right around the corner, so we would walk to the club . . . I needed to reconnect with that. Even though I'm older now, there are still women who were just a little bit older than me — you know ten years, maybe some of them twenty, God bless them — who remember me as a little girl. That's comforting.
>
> There's a woman whose husband and my dad were best friends. There's another sweet couple, the husband who I always knew, and he's so pleasant . . . he used to work with my dad. My dad was the elder and he was younger, and he would go out on the truck with my father. The friend tells me stories, that they would go to one of the Italian bakeries because my father loved the bread and the lunch they'd serve.

Carol A.'s interest in her Italian beginnings definitely changed with time:

> I think as I got older, and especially because I was divorced, I was looking for new roots, and that was a big impetus. Even now, I think of questions I never asked that I wish I had asked, so [I have] a lot of interest now.

I wrote a memoir for my grandchildren, which was published: *My Greenwich Village and the Italian American Community*. I wanted my grandchildren to know about that part of our family because none of them were old enough to know my mother in any meaningful way ... Or any of that kind of experience.

I was very pleased when my grandson had to do a report on immigrants for class, so he chose to do it on my grandmother. He interviewed me, and he did it on a computer and the voice-over with photos. I told all these heartfelt stories about my grandmother's life [but] it was like an academic study, drained of emotion ... but he didn't know them so why should he have the same emotion that I do? But it's a way of trying to keep it alive.

I took him to Italy. And now he's in high school, and he's studying Italian, so I'm very pleased about that. I took my son and his three boys to Italy, so they've had some exposure ... in some way we keep it going.

Others spoke of stigma around being or speaking Italian. Lisa has her job because of her Italian language ability that started when she was young:

I got to travel, and then I met all these Italians. Now I'm teaching my son and meeting all these Italians through work ... It was my mother, not my father who had not listened to people who said I was going to grow up with an accent ... At the time, it was looked down upon.

Sometimes we can be unaware of what it means to be Italian yet also take in the negative aspects or the stereotypes. G.D.F. had this experience in that she originally

didn't associate anything with being Italian as a child. I just knew that was what we were, and I knew that some neighbors were Jewish and some were Italian ... I unfortunately internalized all the things that a minority internalizes, accepted the negative characteristics that the dominant group will assign you. So you are dirty, you are ugly, your mother doesn't keep a clean home, you're stupid.

I internalized that for a long time, until I was in my early thirties, I think. My parents didn't; I didn't get any of that from them. Dad was who he was, and he never thought it was great to be Italian or not, or my mother either. I picked this up from my peers.

I was taking it in. When I was twenty-nine I was seriously involved with a man who in the end could not sully his Scotch Presbyterian family with marriage to an Italian Catholic from New York, which is good, because it would not have been a good match. But that got reinforced . . . I now think it's fine to be anything you are, and I am interested in my own heritage. I want to go to Polizzi Generosa and Vasto, where my mom's family is from.

Daniela speaks of how her Italian sensibility changed over the years, particularly with reference to her writing and publishing:

I want to give you my essay about forging my way into American literature with an Italian name. I feel that after he [her father] died I became aware that my name was Daniela Gioseffi. I have a poem about that. It's called "For Grandma Lucia La Rosa, 'Light the Rose.'" It has a lot to do with my Italian father and my Italian grandfather.

I feel that after he died I suddenly became more aware. I was always thinking of myself as an American kid. There were other Italian kids in my public school, and there were always plenty of other Italians around.

When I came to New York and I was trying to be a writer, I didn't see any Italian female names in American literature at all except Diane DiPrima on the West Coast. I'm in these early feminist anthologies in the sixties and seventies and I'm the only Italian female name, maybe Diane DiPrima and myself . . . I hadn't even met Helen Barolini yet.

In 1977 my first book of poems *Eggs in the Lake* came out . . . and I'm invited to the University of Buffalo to give a reading. Professor Ernesto Falbo, who founded *Italian-Americana* with Professor Richard Gambino, came up to me afterwards and says, "Do you realize you are one of only maybe two Italian female names in the history of American poetry that's ever published at all?" It was like an "aha" moment! Is that why it's been so hard? It's my Italian name . . . It's really been a cross to bear, but I kept it for my father . . .

I began to study the history of the Italian in America and the . . . tremendous prejudice against Italians. I began to realize that my father graduated Columbia University the same year that Sacco and Vanzetti were executed as anarchists by Judge Thayer, who called them "dirty dagos." That was a very prejudicial trial. Nowadays they never would have been killed, murdered, as it was, by the bigoted Judge Thayer, who would never get away with that today, with the defamation . . . They murdered an innocent guy, as an example of "You immigrants had better stay in your place and watch out" . . .

After that realization I became avid about writing articles and becoming part of the Italian American literary scene . . . When I published "Beyond Stereotyping: Breaking the Silence for Italian American Women" in *Ms.*, that was the first time they ever had a big article by an Italian woman, and they received many letters from Italian women saying, "Aha, somebody's finally stated our case and our cause and our problems."

The stories these women tell speak to how complicated the journeys were for Italian American daughters in the twentieth-century United States, a new homeland that simultaneously embraced, rejected, and was confused by the meaning and presence of Italians. Through those journeys, the women here, like so many Italian Americans, garnered strength and wisdom from their communities, their customs and traditions, their sense of the spiritual and the mystical, and, above all, the inviolable bonds of love and family.

Karen B. summed it up grandly:

Oh, Italians are the best in the world! They really are. They have a sense of history and pride, and there's substance there.

We have grown up with our fathers, lived with them, loved them, fought with them, renegotiated our relationships, watched them get older (for some of us, not quite old enough!), and now they are gone, truly gone, even if it has taken a while to accept that.

Yet we speak of them, plant gardens in their honor, hear their voices, write poetry of what we have lost and what we have gained, cook eggplant in their favorite way, talk to them in times of trouble or just to share some news, decorate their special tree at Christmas, see them in our cousin's hands or our son's ideals or our daughter's artwork, and even establish a scholarship in their names at a major university.

We have been with our fathers even as they have moved on from this world.

Pause and Reflect

There are many ways you can keep your father with you, remember him, continue the relationship, and memorialize him, as you saw through the stories in this part. Poems, gardens, stories, and artwork are just some of the ways you can say to your father, "Even after death, you remain important to me." Consider the questions below as you recall your father's gifts to you.

✦ *How do you live with your father in your heart now that he is gone?*

✦ *In your mind, take a walk back to your family home or the place your dad lived for many years, and see what parts of him you have held on to. Look for parts you might want to pick up now and parts that are better to not integrate. What gifts from your father could be kept alive within you? What gifts keep him alive?*

✦ *Ask your spouse, partner, children, brothers, sisters, aunts, uncles, cousins, and oldest friends these questions: Where is my dad in my life and personality now? How is he manifested? Sit with the answers a while until you are clear about what feels right and what does not.*

✦ *It is never too late to bring your dad back, for example, by offering a special toast on holidays, making a meal he loved, or watching an old favorite movie. You could also talk to the next generation about him in depth, allow yourself time to sit and feel who he is and how you are connected, or do a remembrance project you had promised to do, such as writing out his sayings, compiling a family history, or visiting older relatives.*

DAUGHTERS AND DADS: WHERE ARE WE NOW?

*W*e hope that you have breathed your way through this work slowly and with love, that you have met your father again in both new and old ways and feel better able to hold him and let him go at the same time.

We have listened to daughters speak of their Italian American fathers in life and in death, and we have found relationships that are not idealized, perfect, or cast in marble. These relationships, rather, are strong and resilient, needed work at times in life, and are sometimes still being reworked internally in death. These are relationships that encompassed the strains and stresses, the heartbreak and happiness of living as real people in the real world.

We see many daughters who felt truly known and deeply treasured by their fathers, who perhaps held a special (and, at times, complicated) place in their fathers' psyches, and who reciprocated the strength and complexity of their attachment to their dads. We see women forging their own ways to keep their fathers near, both in life and in death, and integrating these ways, or not, with their beliefs in what happens after we die.

A sense of the spiritual wafts around many of the stories, images, and connections, however it may be fleshed out with different practices or belief systems. Culture matters, and Italian American culture is often manifest through opera, art, music, gardening and growing, food and cooking, talking and gathering together, raising glasses of wine to mark the highlights as well as daily life — both the *quotidiano* and the sacramental moments — doing better, doing the right thing, and, most of all, honoring the family.

We see regrets and lingering sorrows: if only I had been there to care for him, if only we had talked more about our lives and ourselves, if only he had lived to see his grandchild marry, if only he hadn't worked so hard, if only I had told him I loved him. Death almost always comes too soon, and the deaths of some of our women's fathers came when they were tragically young, bringing a special heartache and regret.

We are reminded that the path through grief is long. It is really the path of growing, being, relating, loving, losing, and finding someone in a whole different way. It is the path of our lives.

There is something concrete and tangible, as well as elusive and ineffable, that stays with us, that lingers with us and in us, that taps us on the shoulder and reminds us of who we are and who our dads were and are. It is of a deeply textured fabric of dark and light, comprising the conflicts and disappointments woven through the joys and closeness. It is more fluid and encompassing than our daily lives, and it feels transcendent and universal. Yet it is encapsulated in the smallest of gestures, the look of a bricklayer's hand, the stirring of rotelle in a pot, the words that come to us when we need them, the vision that appears while we are driving, the harvesting of figs, a line from *La Traviata*.

We have cried and laughed with each other's stories, contemplated our own fathers and their many facets, joined together in this great living drama of life, death, and rebirth. Resurrection occurs in many forms, and the Italian sense of mystery and layers of reality underlie our experiences and invite us to keep our dead with us and carry on our conversation with them.

We are reminded of an old Italian saying, *A tavola non s'invecchia* (At table, one doesn't grow old). The table is longer and more bountiful than we can imagine; it stretches out to eternity, and we come back to the table over and over, as Italians always do.

ABSENCE AND PRESENCE: ELEGY FOR MY FATHER

Sometimes things become more apparent when they are gone: emptiness reflects clarity and veracity; absence reveals what was hidden or confusing, as if we are gazing directly into some awesome truth. Yet that sense of knowing and understanding can dissolve, and we are left with only our hopes and dreams, fragments of wishes and tears, yearnings and disappointments. Our world has gone askew again, and we reach for something to hold or search for someplace to stand.

We may go through this process time and again in our significant relationships as we come together and move apart and find ways to integrate or at least weather both absence and presence, both the void and the surge, that make up living and loving. In grief, where absence can dwarf all meager or grand attempts at coping, carrying on, and even putting one foot in front of the other, it is a formidable task to reconcile being and not-being. It is too stark; the empty plate is unarguably empty. This is what is asked of us repeatedly throughout grieving as we find a way to live with what no longer is.

We have a story, saved until the end, of absence transformed into presence through perseverance, serendipity, the grace of the universe, desire, and creativity. Sometimes in writing a book, living your life, or mourning your dad, kismet steps in and directs the process. This story came to us uncannily when, early in our writing process, Donna mentioned a poet friend who had lost her father very young and had written about his loss . . . Lorraine had previously found the exact poem, "The Light of Fallen Stars," on the *Italian Americana* website and used it in a presentation on Italian American women, poetry, and identity at the Calandra Institute; it is a stunning poem!

We asked the poet, Sylvia Forges Ryan, to be in this book because of her ways of living her history, understanding how absence can, and cannot, become something else.

Sylvia introduced her father in this way:

My experience has been living with the accents of my father, with the imagined sounds of my father's voice, making him present in my life, maybe more so because I didn't have him for very long in my life. He died when I was two years old. He came from Apulia and was an anti-Fascist leader and a labor organizer in Italy, trying to raise money all across the United States to send to Italy to oppose Mussolini, who personally wanted to see him killed.

I have records about him from the Fascist Museum in Rome, records of the surveillance he was under the whole time that he was living in New York and all the places he traveled, such as Canada and Cuba, trying to raise support against Mussolini's regime . . .

I really didn't know much about all of this when I was a child. My mother was from Germany. I was growing up in wartime, when it was not good to be German or Italian. After he [her father] died, my mother was offered a job in the United Garment Workers' Union in New Jersey. We moved there from New York. It was tremendously traumatic for her. I always liken it to being shipwrecked.

It was a real disaster because we moved to this very provincial town where there was a lot of prejudice against foreigners . . . you couldn't be Jewish . . . There were no blacks in the town. There was prejudice against Germans and Italians. We couldn't get a newspaper delivered or receive rations because my mother had a German accent.

Under these circumstances, my mother was not likely to talk a lot about my father, even though he was an anti-Fascist leader fighting for justice and liberty against a tyrant. Emotionally, it was extremely hard on her. She didn't really talk about him much; it was just too painful. I learned, therefore, not to ask questions because obviously I didn't want to put her in pain. She was my only protector, not having a father. Certainly she was all I had, so I didn't ask questions.

Consequently, the only time I really heard about my father was when we would have company. She would talk with her close friends about my father and his political activities. I remember how proud she was of him. I would sit quietly, taking in all I could.

She gleaned bits and pieces about him:

I grew up with a ghost presence, always wishing I had a real father. We didn't really grow up with a lot of Italian foods or customs, obviously. My mother made some things that she learned from him, because, like many Italian men, he was a good cook. We would have delicious Italian ices that she would make on hot summer days. We ate some foods that other people would not, like fennel, *finocchio* as we called it.

Over the years there were some things I learned about him — I knew that he was anti-Fascist. I knew he was a journalist. I knew he loved the opera . . . [and] he was a very passionate person.

Sylvia's father died in 1939, and it was only after her mother died in 1976 that she found pictures and her father's obituary and learned some very important facts:

Most of all, most shockingly, I saw that his name was not really the name that we ever used. His name was really Antonio DeSanguine. And my last name was always Forges. Through the Catholic Church he was allowed to come to the United States under an assumed name, and that name was Frank Forges, although he was not Catholic as an adult and I was not brought up Catholic.

Sylvia describes this as ushering in a new focus for her regarding her father:

So in '76 I almost, literally, fell off the chair when I saw, my God, my real name is DeSanguine, and I never even knew it. My mother never told me that. That was very shocking in itself. I was obsessed with that, whereas before I had been obsessed with not having a father and what he might have been like in my imagination.

Even as a child, I sometimes imagined that he really didn't die, because after all I never went to a cemetery. Actually he was cremated. I never could ask my mother, where are his remains, or was he buried, or even did he really die? I always had this feeling that, well, maybe he didn't die, which you know psychologically everybody can understand that yearning. When I saw these papers, my imagination then was, oh my God, I have this whole story, this whole background, and right here there are some of the answers, but of course there are never enough answers.

I started thinking more about him and trying to find out more information . . . This was all percolating, and I wrote a poem about what I did know about him, because I just knew little bits and pieces, little shards of information that came out now and then . . . Interestingly, when I wrote that poem and after it was published and well received, I felt, "Now at last I have found my father."

As a result of publishing "The Light of Fallen Stars," Sylvia was invited to join a traveling theater production about Sacco and Vanzetti and their fight against prejudice toward Italians. Her poem was the centerpiece of that production, and through it, she met people in the United States and Italy who knew of her father and his work. She worked with scholar Vincenza Scarpaci to include information about her father in Scarpaci's book *The Journey of the Italians in America*. She used to peruse books, looking for mentions of him and anti-Fascist activities; now there's satisfaction in seeing his name in a book. It tells her that he did exist.

She feels his influence in several ways:

Certainly politically. My mother, too, was very outspoken. As a child I was extremely shy. As I've gotten older, I have become much more politically outspoken myself. As I read my poem publicly I came to feel much more clearly that I am my father's daughter. I don't know that this is an influence; it may be more genetic that I feel very drawn to Italy and have been there numerous times, and I will go again.

I feel very comfortable in Italy. I can't explain it; it's where I really feel at home. My mother's family came from Germany and I've been there. I have a cousin there I love dearly — we're frequently in touch — but I'm still not drawn to Germany in the same way. I just feel an affinity for the people in Italy. I have very dear friends in Rome whom I met while searching for evidence of my father. They consider me part of their family . . . And I certainly love Italian food.

What feels most important and Italian about her father?

Passion. He was an extremely passionate person. Passion about the cause of democracy, liberty, love of art, love of music especially. His unwavering devotion to a cause worth fighting for. Appreciation of art and feeling a necessity of art in life. Love of food. Italians have a special thing about food. Love of life. I feel that in Italy. I feel that people have a much deeper feeling about life that I don't find with other groups so much. I don't know what you'd call that exactly, but I feel happier there. I feel positive energy and love of a good life. I don't mean materialistically, but love of beauty, love of conviviality, warmth.

Sylvia describes a shift that occurred after growing up without a father present or an Italian identity:

I didn't look Italian growing up . . . and I had a name which always was a mystery to me. I thought, what kind of name is Forges? That doesn't sound Italian. It doesn't sound American. It doesn't sound like anything. Where did that name even come from?

I had no Italian identity, which in a way protected me, because in school there was prejudice against Italians where I grew up. I didn't feel any of that because nobody could tell . . . I found that only as I discovered and then celebrated my father's life have I come to feel more and more Italian.

The loss is still with her but in a different way:

Naturally I still think about him. But I feel happier now that I've done what I needed to do. I think my father — and my mother as well — would be pleased. Through my poems and through establishing a proper place for him in the history of Italians in America, I've made peace with his absence. I feel fortunate that such odd circumstances made that possible, the things that I would never have dreamed, that I never imagined were possible. In a sense, I feel I have brought my father back to life.

Sylvia expressed her perspective on connecting with others and reclaiming her father:

All this happened, and how, why? I mean, it feels very much like it's happening through me. I don't feel like I was in charge. I'm so thrilled and happy that this all happened, but I feel like it fell to me somehow by just my being open and keeping my eyes open and talking about it a little.

She has come far from the little girl:

Wondering is he even alive or dead? Where is he? What's the truth, you know? Now I feel like I've uncovered much of the truth. There's always more I wish I knew.

She describes her role in this:

I'm almost an agent of having found my father. It was beyond my conscious active work. If I had tried aggressively on my own to do it, I never would have come to find out as much as I have by serendipitous, miraculous, wondrous ways.

Yet our conversation in the end came back to the loss, to his death, to her sad dreams, to an early poem she wrote of him by the seawall, with the silent ocean behind him.

Elegy for My Father

I'll tell you how I'd like to remember you:
You toss me in the air and always catch me;
You hold my hand along the darkening street;
Your smile says their words can never harm me.

But what memories could be left
Of you, who turned to ash
When I was just learning to name you?
Neither the key to a dusty forbidden trunk

Nor snapshots found scattered in the back
Of a drawer one autumn give much yield.
In one, the only photograph of us, you hold
My newness for a lifetime. Only in dreams

Are you real. You lean against a sea wall.
You look straight at me. I strain for a sign.
Behind you a whole ocean is silent.

© Sylvia Forges-Ryan
First published in the anthology *Essential Love:*
Mothers and Fathers, Daughters and Sons, edited by
Ginny Lowe Connors, Grayson Books, 2000.
Reprinted by permission of the author.

We see it all in Sylvia's story — great love, unassailable connection, disappointment, loss, hard work to reclaim something, openness to grief and to life, and keeping your dead with you. Daughters and dads hold each other, loss and grief are a force to be honored, and the Italian American influence is always abiding. Our capacity for attachment is fundamental, as is our capacity for meaning-making, and we see them both in Sylvia's story, in so many of the stories.

Conviviality, *with life,* the great Italian emphasis on being *with life* in its presence and absence, reminds us of the gorgeous practice from the late Renaissance of chiaroscuro, the dark and the light, calling to each other and setting each other off magnificently, or the pungent Sicilian taste of *agrodolce,* the bitter and the sweet together, tastes that sometimes fight, sometimes blend, but always enhance one another. We live with juxtaposition — and with our fathers in our hearts.

A FINAL REFLECTION

Where is the serendipity, the chance events, the grace of the universe in your story about having your dad and losing your dad? Has something important come to you because you happened to be open and accepting of it? Is this an attitude to cultivate going forth?

Biographies

ADELE (ARTURI) GRIFFITHS was born in New York City. She is retired and does volunteer work at her church, her local hospital, and Roma Lodge. Being Italian to her means family and faith. Her participation in this book is a tribute to her dad, who would be proud, not by words but a smile and a tear.

ANDRIANNA (ANN) RENNA RILEY is seventy-seven years old, retired, belongs to two Italian clubs in New York, one in Troy and one in Albany, and travels to play bocce. She and her identical twin sister (Class of 1951) excelled in sports and were inducted into theTroy High School Athletic Hall of Fame in 2012. Her dad would be very proud about what she has said about her childhood. She feels very lucky to have been his daughter.

ANNA CAROLINE MARUCA was born to parents who immigrated to the United States from Calabria, Italy. She graduated with a BS in business and spent her career in the insurance and investment field. She has often felt she had one foot in American culture, one in Italian. If her father was alive today he would be proud and happy that she is an American with strong ties to her Italian heritage.

ANNA DANIELE came to America from Salerno, Italy in 1970 as a teenager speaking only Italian and the local dialect. She and her husband own La Fiorentina, an Italian bakery and café in Springfield, Northampton, and East Longmeadow, Massachusetts. Family was most important to her dad, and it is to her too.

ANNE E. PIDANO, clinical psychologist and associate professor in the University of Hartford's Graduate Institute of Professional Psychology, is fortunate to be the granddaughter of four Italian immigrants and the daughter of an Italian American man of integrity, humor, and faith who treasured his family. Her father, a bit shy, might feel out of place in a book, but she appreciated the opportunity to bring him to life for others, as he still lives for her.

B. AMORE is an artist and writer. She studied at Boston University, University of Rome, and Accademia di Belle Arti di Carrara, and is the recipient of Massachusetts Cultural grants, a Fulbright Grant, Mellon Fellowship, and a Citation of Merit Award presented by the Vermont Arts Council. She is founder of the Carving Studio and Sculpture Center in Vermont and has won major sculpture commissions in the United States and Japan. Her multimedia exhibit *LIFE LINE — filo della vita* premiered at Ellis Island and is now a book, *An Italian American Odyssey*.

BARBARA DENICOLA is a University of Connecticut alumna and retired associate superintendent of schools. She also served as mayor of Hamden, Connecticut. She is immensely proud of her Italian heritage and the lifelong thread of continuity it has provided. Her dad would be pleased that his family has perpetuated his legacy of hard work, respect, kindness, honesty, and love of family and community.

BARBARA QUINN has written four novels, drawing greatly on her Italian American background. In her suspense novel, *Hard Head*, an Italian American woman journeys to Calabria and is caught in an ancient vendetta between two secret societies. Her late Calabrian father's tales of the 'Ndrangheta inspired the novel. He would be proud of the authors, and if he knew he was in this book he probably would play a "celebratory head tune" (her father's unique way of tapping out a song on his head).

CAROL BONOMO ALBRIGHT is a retired professor of Italian American studies from Harvard University Extension School and an editor of *Italian Americana*, a historical and cultural journal. She has a strong interest in things Italian and Italian American and in her grandchildren continuing their best traditions and values. Her father would be touched — moved to tears — to know what a force he was in her life and how much she loved him.

CHRISTINE PALAMIDESSI MOORE, a novelist and sculptor, said an Italian American heritage is an artist's blessing: providing an incredible understanding and appreciation of beauty, encouraging drama, and accepting a headstrong attitude. Her novels include *The Virgin Knows* (an Italian American novel) and *The Fiddle Case*. She is the web and senior editor at *Italian Americana*.

Her memoir *Grandmothers* is installed on a granite monolith at Boston's Jackson Square subway station.

CYNTHIA (CINDI) FUKAMI is professor of management at the Daniels College of Business, University of Denver. Cindi and her family continue to celebrate her Italian American heritage, primarily through cooking great food and drinking great wine. She is married with two daughters and spends her free time quilting and traveling.

DANIELA GIOSEFFI, American Book Award winning author of fourteen books, pioneered into literary accomplishment, keeping her father's surname. Her World Peace Prize book, *On Prejudice: A Global Perspective*, was inspired by his experiences. He'd be proud that *Blood Autumn/Autunno di sangue* won her the John Ciardi Award for Lifetime Achievement in Poetry. Her verse is etched in marble on a wall of Penn Station. She edits *www.ItalianAmericanWriters.com.*

DIANA FEMIA, a native of New Jersey, was a senior director at the New York Mercantile Exchange. Currently a resident of Washington, D.C., she is president of the Greater Washington, D.C., Region of the National Organization of Italian American Women and its national board treasurer. She says, "Since my dad instilled in me my love for all things Italian, I think he is smiling down on me now."

DIANE GUIDO currently works as an administrative assistant at a New York university.

DONNA CHIRICO is a professor of psychology and chair of behavioral sciences at York College/City University of New York. Italian American to her is not just an ethnic label; it is who she is to the core. Many times an argument with her dad ended, "So, that's what they taught in psychology!" Yet, his values took root and she is pleased to discuss his influence.

DONNA ZANELLA PARKER's parents, Mike and Betty, sacrificed to send her to Catholic school and sat through many tap dancing recitals! She worked for New York State from a secretary, Grade 4 to a health program administrator, Grade 23, a result of observing her parents' impeccable work ethic! She is proud of being Italian — the traditions, hugs, foods, sense of humor, playing cards — and hopes readers will understand the bonds Italians share.

GIOVANNA BELLIA LA MARCA, fiber artist, author, and chef instructor at the Institute of Culinary Education, New York City, published *Sicilian Feasts*, *Language and Travel Guide to Sicily*, and *The Cooking of Emilia-Romagna*. She takes pride in being Sicilian by birth, Italian by nationality, and American by citizenship. Her father encouraged her intellectual curiosity, and her story is a tribute to his values and progressive thinking.

GIOVANNA CAPONE is a poet, fiction writer, and mixed media artist. She lives in the San Francisco Bay Area and was raised in an immigrant neighborhood, a community that gave her an enduring sense of her Italian American roots. Giovanna's father had a huge influence on her understanding of people. He would have been proud of being included in this book but was so modest he probably wouldn't have said so.

HELEN BAROLINI, one of the most prolific Italian American writers, was born in Syracuse, New York and graduated from Syracuse University. After studying in England she went on to Italy to learn the language and claim her heritage. There she married Italian author Antonio Barolini. Awarded a National Endowment for the Arts grant, she wrote the novel *Umbertina* followed by twelve other books, including the famed anthology *The Dream Book*.

IMMA AIELLO was transplanted from Italy at age thirteen. She enjoys her return visits there but is proud of her accomplishments in America. Among her blessings are her children and twin grandchildren, her successful restaurant/ catering business, and her American citizenship. She believes her father would share her pride and applaud her participation in this book!

JACKIE KESHIAN's father emigrated from Sicily to New York in 1920. Growing up with non-Italian Americans in New Jersey, she felt connected to her Italian heritage but tried to blend into the community. Her parents emphasized self-sufficiency, education, and family bonds. She received an MS in nursing, and she combines practice with teaching. Her dad would be pleased that she shared about their relationship of love and mutual respect.

JEAN FARINELLI is founder of Edizioni Farinelli, a publisher of Italian language educational texts. The company is an outgrowth of her 9/11 experience, which prompted her to learn Italian and reconnect with her father's family in the small Abruzzo village from which he had emigrated to the United States in 1916. She formerly was chief executive officer of an international marketing communications company.

JOANN PANDOLFI was raised in abundant family traditions. She earned an MBA in food studies from New York University. Her passion for food and culture compels her to write about her family. Her dad would beam with pride reading from the stories of today's Italian American daughters.

JOYCE MICARE was raised in West Albany, "Little Italy," and was "Daddy's little girl." She has been married to a wonderful man for forty-nine years. She was a stay-at-home mom when her kids were young and now has two married children and two precious granddaughters. She returned to school for a public administration degree and retired after twenty-five years with the Research Foundation of the State University of New York.

KAREN DELUCA STEPHENS grew up in the Italian American neighborhood of East Boston and has an MA in philosophy. She recently completed her first screenplay, which weaves together baseball and the Italian immigrant experience during the Depression. If her father was alive today and knew about her contribution to this book and that events of his life inspired her movie script, she thinks he'd say, "That's my girl."

KAREN LUCAS BREDA is a third-generation Italian American born in Boston, Massachusetts. Karen became interested in Italy after college when she visited a cousin in Rome, where she has worked as a nurse consultant with the U.S. Consulate. As a doctoral student she conducted research on the Italian National Health Service. Karen currently teaches nursing at the University of Hartford in West Hartford, Connecticut.

LAURA MUSCATO MAGGIO is a licensed psychologist and the Director of Clinical Training for Springfield College's Doctoral Program in Counseling Psychology. Her father passed away unexpectedly in 2010, and her participation in this book was a way to pay tribute to him, the son of a Sicilian immigrant. Italian heritage is an important part of her identity. Her father would be proud that she participated in this book!

LINDA GRASSO, a sixty-four-year-old lawyer, specializes in business litigation. She is married, with a combined family of five children and eight grandchildren. She lives near Boston, which is rich in Italian culture, and enjoys it immensely. She lost her dad in 2009 suddenly. Not a day goes by that she doesn't grieve because they didn't get to say good-bye. Participating in this book has helped her keep memories of him alive and vibrant.

LOUISE DE PAOLO DONATO's grandfather and father were part of an organization that helped transition Italian immigrants into American society but allowed them to keep their heritage. The organization holds an annual Feast of Mt. Carmel, which includes a parade, the procession of the Blessed Mother, great food, and fabulous people. She is honoring her father by holding the position of women's auxiliary president of this organization.

LULU LOLO is a playwright/actor/international performance and multi-disciplinary artist. She has written and performed one-person plays Off Broadway highlighting her Italian immigrant family heritage and social justice. Her current work in progress is *Obits*, a play based on lives revealed in obituaries. LuLu is a lifelong resident of East Harlem/El Barrio on a street named for her father.

MADELINE ZONI grew up in Bristol, Connecticut, with a father who was born in southern Italy and brought with him a love of growing fruits and vegetables and making wine. She raised two sons and knows that her dad would be very proud of them. She worked as a teacher's aide when they were older.

MARIA TERESA GRIECO is a musician and music teacher. Her first piano teacher was her father, who studied at a Naples conservatory. As she matured she embraced her Italian American heritage through its culture, especially music, and even wrote poetry in Italian! Her father would be slightly stunned but very touched if he knew she participated in this book to honor their relationship and mutual heritage.

MARIA TERRONE, a lifelong communications professional, is also a poet with two collections: *A Secret Room in Fall*, co-winner of the McGovern Prize, and *The Bodies We Were Loaned*. She came to revere her heritage when she was an editor at an Italian American magazine. Her father, a gifted writer and teacher, would be proud of her participation in this project.

MARIANNA DE MARCO TORGOVNICK is a professor of English at Duke University and the director of the Duke in New York Arts & Media program. She has written *Gone Primitive, Primitive Passions*, and *The War Complex*. Her memoir *Crossing Ocean Parkway* began the story of her father told here. A new memoir called *Picnic in the Dark: Classic Books, Family Recipes* will complete it.

PATRICIA MORELLI is seventy-five years old, and fifty-four happy years of marriage have given her three children and seven grandchildren. She is a high school graduate, a retiree, and a volunteer at her church rectory. Her father would be honored by her participation in this book, her first writing experience. "That's Amore" is her family theme song. She is proud of her Italian descent.

PATRICIA PERRI RIEKER is an adjunct professor of sociology at Boston University and an associate professor of psychiatry at Harvard Medical School. She dedicated her first book, *The Gender Gap in Psychotherapy*, to her father, Pasquale, who taught her to see the world from the odd angles of being an Italian American. Her recent book *Gender and Health* extends that cherished legacy.

ROSA DE LAURO represents Connecticut's third district in Congress. Rosa grew up in New Haven's Wooster Square, where the spirit of Italy was strong. She learned about the world and formed her values in the local neighborhood and around her kitchen table. Her father's integrity and abiding commitment to people is her guide.

ROSANNE DE LUCA BRAUN is a documentary filmmaker. She treasures her heritage and participated in this book to bring to life the parents who gave life to her. Her documentary *Beyond Wiseguys: Italian Americans & the Movies* explores how the heritage of well-known Italian American filmmakers influences their creative work in Hollywood.

SABRINA RUSSO teaches high school Italian and takes pride in sharing her language and heritage with her students. Her parents are from Naples, and she was born and raised in Orange County, California. She knows that Pop is looking down at her now with his arms stretched back far, while saying to her, "I love you this much."

SYLVIA FORGES-RYAN was featured on the *Italian Americana* website, contributed historical information about her father for *The Journey of the Italians in America*, won first prize in the Italian American Historical Society of Connecticut Poetry Contest, and coauthored *Take a Deep Breath: The Haiku Way to Inner Peace*. Inspired by her father's courage and passion for justice and political freedom, she hopes her inclusion in this book furthers those ideals.

TIZIANA COTUMACCIO is the mother of two children and is married to Massimo Bagnasco, who was born and raised in Villabate, Sicilia. She is very proud of her Italian American heritage. Her father was her best friend and supporter. She knows that he is very excited to be part of this wonderful book. He would say, "I always told you we were the Number One Family."

VERNA LEDOUX was born in Cambridge, Massachusetts in 1947 and brought up in Watertown by second-generation Italian parents. She now lives in western Massachusetts. She has a daughter and a son and two grandchildren. She is divorced and is an administrative assistant to the dean of the School of Social Work at Springfield College.

Bibliography

Ainsworth, M.D. (1989). Attachments beyond infancy. *American Psychologist, 44*(4), 709–716.

Alba, R.D. (2000). The twilight of ethnicity among Americans of European ancestry: The case of Italians. In F.M. Sorrentino & J. Krase (Eds.). *The review of Italian American Studies* (pp. 41–74). Lanham, MD: Lexington Books.

Albright, C.B., & Moore, C.P. (Eds.). (2011). *American woman, Italian style: Italian Americana's best writings on women.* New York: Fordham University Press.

Archer, J. (1999). *The nature of grief: The evolution and psychology of reactions to loss.* Florence, KY: Routledge.

Arnett, J.J. (2006). *Emerging adulthood: The winding road from the late teens through the twenties.* New York: Oxford University Press.

Bona, M.J. (2010). *By the breath of their mouths: Narratives of resistance in Italian America.* Albany, NY: State University of New York Press.

Bonnano, G.A. (2009). *The other side of sadness: What the new science of bereavement tells us about life and loss.* New York: Basic Books.

Boscia-Mulè, P. (1999). *Authentic ethnicities: The interaction of ideology, gender power, and class in the Italian American experience.* Westport, CT: Greenwood Press.

Bowlby, J. (1973). *Attachment and loss: Separation, anxiety, and anger* (Vol. 2). London: Hogarth Press.

Carielli, D., & Grosso, J. (Eds.). (2013). *Benessere psicologico: Contemporary thought on Italian American mental health.* New York: John D. Calandra Italian American Institute, Queens College, City University of New York.

Ciongoli, A.K., & Parini J. (1997). *Beyond the godfather: Italian American writers on the real Italian American experience.* Hanover, NH: University Press of New England.

DiCello, D.H., & Coletta, C.N. (2009). *Contra genio*: The experience of the Italian American female psychologist. *Voices in Italian Americana, 20,* 12–41.

DiCello, Donna H. & Mangione, L. (2013). Italians tend to keep their dead with them: Navigating grief and loss in Italian American culture. In *Benessere psicologico: Contemporary thought on Italian American mental health*, Dominick Carielli & Joseph Grosso (Eds.), New York: John D. Calandra Italian American Institute, Queens College, City University of New York.

Drexler, P. (2011). *Our fathers, ourselves: Daughters, fathers, and the changing American family.* New York: Rodale.Erikson, E. (1950/1994). *Childhood and society.* New York: W.W. Norton.

Esposito, N.J. (1989). *Italian family structure.* New York: Peter Lang Publishing.

Field, N. (2008). Whether to relinquish or maintain a bond with the deceased. In M. Stroebe, R. Hansson, H. Schut, & W. Stroebe (Eds.), *Handbook of bereavement research and practice: Advances in theory and intervention* (pp. 113–132). Washington, DC: American Psychological Association.

Field, N.P., Gal-Oz, E., & Bonanno, G.A. (2003). Continuing bonds and adjustment at 5 years after the death of a spouse. *Journal of Consulting and Clinical Psychology, 71*(1), 110–117.

Freud, S. (1917/1957). Mourning and melancholia. In J. Stachey (Ed. & Trans.), *The standard edition of the complete psychological works of Sigmund Freud* (pp. 152–170). London: Hogarth Press.

Gambino, R. (1975). *Blood of my blood: The dilemma of the Italian Americans.* New York: Anchor Books.

Gambino, R. (1997). The crisis of Italian American identity. In A.K. Ciongoli & J. Parini (Eds.). *Beyond the godfather: Italian American writers on the real Italian American experience* (pp. 269–288). Hanover, NH: University Press of New England.

Gibson, M. (2004). Melancholy objects. *Mortality, 9*(4), 285–299.

Gilligan, C. (1982). *In her own voice: Psychological theory and women's development.* Cambridge, MA: Harvard University Press.

Giordano, J., McGoldrick, M., & Klages, J. (2005). Italian families. In M. McGoldrick, J. Giordano, & N. Garcia-Preto (Eds.), *Ethnicity and family therapy* (3rd ed.). New York: Guilford Press.

Granek, L. (2010). Grief as pathology: The evolution of grief theory in psychology from Freud to the present. *History of Psychology, 13*(1), 46–73.

Guglielmo, J. (2010). *Living the revolution: Italian women's resistance and radicalism in New York City, 1880–1945.* Chapel Hill: University of North Carolina Press.

Hardy-Bougere, M. (2008). Cultural manifestations of grief and bereavement: A clinical perspective. *Journal of Cultural Diversity, 15*(2), 66–69.

Klass, D., Silverman, P.R., & Nickman, S.L. (Eds.). (1996). *Continuing bonds: New understandings of grief.* Philadelphia: Taylor & Francis.

Konigsberg, R.D. (2011). *The truth about grief: The myth of its five stages and the new science of loss.* New York: Simon & Schuster.

Kübler-Ross, E. (1969/1997). *On death and dying.* New York: Scribner.

Lamb, M. (2010). *Role of the father in child development.* New York: Wiley.

Lippmann, P. (2000). *Nocturnes: On listening to dreams.* Hillsdale, NJ: Analytic Press.

Mangione, J., & Morreale, B. (1992). *La storia: Five centuries of the Italian American experience.* New York: Harper Perennial.

McWilliams, N. (1999). *Psychoanalytic case formulation*. New York: Guilford Press.

Messina, E. (1994). Life-span development and Italian American women. In J. Krase & J.N. DeSena (Eds.). *Italian Americans in a multicultural society* (pp. 74–87). Stony Brook, NY: FORUM ITALICUM.

Nielsen, L. (2012). *Father-daughter relationships: Contemporary research and issues*. New York: Routledge.

Parkes, C.M., Laungani, P., & Young, B. (Eds.). (1997). *Death and bereavement across cultures*. New York: Routledge.

Perls, F. (1969/1992). *Gestalt therapy verbatim*. Goldsboro, ME: The Gestalt Journal Press.

Riccio, A. (2006). *The Italian American experience in New Haven: Images and oral histories*. Albany: State University of New York Press.

Rosenblatt, P.C. (2008). Recovery following bereavement: Metaphor, phenomenology, and culture. *Death Studies, 32,* 6–16.

Rubin, S. (1985). The resolution of bereavement: A clinical focus on the relationship to the deceased. *Psychotherapy: Theory, Research, Training, and Practice, 22*(2), 231–235.

Rutan, J.S., Stone, W.N., & Shay, J.J. (2007). *Psychodynamic group psychotherapy* (4th ed.). New York: Guilford Press.

Scharff, J.S., & Scharff, D.E. (1998). *Object relations individual therapy*. New York: Jason Aronson.

Setterstein, R., & Ray, B. (2010). The parent-child lifeline. In *Not quite adults: Why 20-somethings are choosing a slower path to adulthood, and why it's good for everyone* (pp.118–143). New York: Bantam Books.

Simon, C. (2001). *Fatherless women: How we change after we lose our dads*. New York: John Wiley & Sons.

Slade, A. (2004). Two therapies: Attachment organization and the clinical process. In L. Atkinson & S. Goldberg (Eds.). *Attachment issues in psychopathology and intervention* (pp. 181–206).

Snyder, C.R. (1994). *The psychology of hope*. New York: Free Press.

Snyder, C.R. (2000). *Handbook of hope: Theory, measures, & applications*. San Diego, CA: Academic Press.

Tamburri, A.J., Giordano, P.A., & Gardaphe, F.L. (2000). *From the margins: Writings in Italian Americana*. West Lafayette, IN: Purdue University Press.

Index

Reviewer Comments on
Daughters, Dads, and the Path Through Grief:
Tales from Italian America

"DiCello and Mangione's compelling book feels like both a public honoring and a public mourning ritual where women gather together to talk about, reflect on, and contemplate the meaning of their dads influence in their lives both in their presence and in their absence.

"Weaving together the theoretical traditions of object relations, relational perspectives in psychodynamic theory, existentialism, attachment theory and the religious and cultural threads in Italian-American culture, the authors beautifully explore the multi-faceted, often-neglected, often complex, rich relationship between fathers and daughters in life and after their deaths.

"Written in an exceptionally accessible manner, this text is a warm and welcome addition to the scant literature on grief and loss among daughters and is a substantial contribution to the field of bereavement studies."

— **Dr. Leeat Granek**
Faculty of Health Sciences,
Department of Public Health,
Ben-Gurion University of the Negev

"Donna DiCello and Lorraine Mangione's wonderful book, *Daughters, Dads, and the Path Through Grief: Tales from Italian America*, is a gift for every woman who grew up in an Italian American household. Readers will undoubtedly come across a story — or several of them — and nod in agreement with the family circumstances described by the women interviewed.

"The authors tell us in the beginning of the book — 'each relationship tells a story.' Indeed, the variety of stories in this book illustrate the complex family relationships found in any home. A flood of unique memories — both difficult and joyful — race through your mind as you think about your own story.

"For the Italian American daughter, this book provides a new level of understanding of how our fathers tried in the best way they knew how to use their life's journey and experiences — against the background of a rich cultural heritage — to guide us in ours.

"I am particularly grateful to the authors for giving us the encouragement and tools to pause and reflect on our dads, and fully appreciate how they were people with dreams, hopes, and challenges of their own before they were our parents."

— **Anita Bevacqua McBride**
Executive-in-Residence,
Center for Congressional and Presidential Studies,
School of Public Affairs,
American University, Washington, D.C.

"These intriguing, amusing, inspiring and at times poignant stories about fathers and daughters add a much-needed personal dimension to the empirical data. A resource for college professors as well as for family members, *Daughters, Dads and the Path Through Grief* challenges the stereotypes of fathers as detached, distant and disinterested bystanders in their daughters' lives. By providing information about the impact of the father's death and the process of grief, the book addresses questions that have long been ignored by writers and by researchers. The richness, diversity, and complexity of father-daughter relationships throughout the life course is explored with depth, care and sensitivity — an exemplary book that will undoubtedly enhance the lives of its readers and deepen their understanding of this often overlooked relationship."

— **Dr. Linda Nielsen**
author of *Father-Daughter Relationships: Contemporary Research and Issues*,
Professor of Adolescent & Educational Psychology,
Wake Forest University

"*Daughters, Dads and the Path Through Grief: Tales from Italian America* contributes an important piece of the Italian American mosaic, exploring and revealing the true nature of Italian fatherhood through poignant voices of Italian American daughters."

— **Anthony Riccio**
author/photographer,
*The Italian American Experience in New Haven:
Images and Oral Histories*
and *Boston's North End: Images and Recollections
of an Italian-American Neighborhood*

"Brava!

"Drs. DiCello and Mangione have compiled a comprehensive and rare look at the complex relationship between fathers and daughters in Italian American families and the loss experienced when this important relationship ends. With exquisite sensitivity and with full, candid and in-depth psychological interviews, the authors explore the dynamics of growing up in an Italian family. This is one of very few psychological studies which enable the reader to leave behind the stereotypes that grow from the fantasies of authors and script-writers who write about our family dynamics. All ethnic groups will enjoy this very worthwhile and important work about Italian Americans."

— **Aileen Riotto Sirey, Ph.D.**
Founder,
National Organization of Italian American Women

"As I started reading this remarkable book by Drs. DiCello and Mangione, the smells, sights, and sounds that were part of my heritage as a Sicilian-American boy growing up in the Bronx came rushing over me. The moving stories of women who have grown up Italian in this country and who so loved their fathers reminded me of the kids on the streets, of my family, of the corner candy store, of the big mix of cultures in which my ideas of group dynamics and situational forces first begin to form. It's a beautiful book filled with love and loss, conflict and compassion, and the intensity of the father/daughter relationship. Ultimately, the act of keeping our lost ones near us, as Italians tend to do, can be a model for people from every culture facing the loss of a loved one. How the world and culture shape who we become and how we experience particular events in our lives has been a major theme in my research as a social psychologist, and I see it reflected so elegantly in this work. "

— **Philip Zimbardo, Ph.D.**
President and Director of Research,
Heroic Imagination Project